Willy Messerschmitt

Providence has given to the French the empire of the land, to the English that of the sea, to the Germans that of the air.

Thomas Carlyle

Patrick Stephens Limited, a member of the Haynes Publishing Group, has published authoritative, quality books for enthusiasts for more than a quarter of a century. During that time the company has established a reputation as one of the world's leading publishers of books on aviation, maritime, military, model-making, motor cycling, motoring, motor racing, railway and railway modelling subjects. Readers or authors with suggestions for books they would like to see published are invited to write to: The Editorial Director, Patrick Stephens Limited, Sparkford, Nr Yeovil, Somerset BA22 7JJ.

Willy Messerschmitt

FIRST FULL BIOGRAPHY OF AN AERONAUTICAL GENIUS

FRANK VANN

Patrick Stephens Limited

First published in 1993

British Library Cataloguing in Publication Data:
A catalogue record for this book
is available from the British Library

ISBN 1 85260 439 5

Library of Congress catalog card no 93-79169

Patrick Stephens Limited is part of the
Haynes Publishing Group PLC, Sparkford, Nr Yeovil,
Somerset BA22 7JJ.

Typeset by G&M, Raunds, Northamptonshire
Printed and bound in Great Britain by
Butler & Tanner Limited, London and Frome

Contents

	Acknowledgements	7
	Introduction	9
1.	Early years	11
2.	Further experiments with gliders	20
3.	The first Messerschmitt company	25
4.	First commercial orders	31
5.	The M 20 civil aircraft	39
6.	Further successes with light aircraft	46
7.	The fastest fighter in the world	55
8.	Problems with the Bf 109	64
9.	The Hess flight	74
10.	The Me 210 disaster	78
11.	The Me 262 jet fighter	87
12.	The America bomber	96
	The life and work of Willy Messerschmitt	97 – 128
13.	Military transports	133
14.	Differences of opinion	143
15.	Employment of prisoners-of-war and concentration camp inmates	151
16.	Messerschmitt as an employer	158
17.	Assessment of the opposition	166
18.	Messerschmitt's views on research	174
19.	Public relations	182
20.	Relations with Lippisch	190
21.	Messerschmitt the inventor	200
22.	Evacuation to Murnau	208
23.	Gathering clouds	217
24.	Twilight of the Gods	228
25.	Post-war years	234
26.	End of a mission	243
	Bibliography	249
	Index	251

Acknowledgements

This book would not have been possible without the assistance that I have enjoyed from many quarters. I am grateful to Philip Reed, the Deputy Keeper of the Department of Documents at the Imperial War Museum for readily allowing me access to information, and I thank the Trustees of the Imperial War Museum for kindly giving me permission to reproduce many extracts.

I would like to express my particular thanks to the custodian of the documents at Duxford, Dick Bright, who not only found all the files which I requested but also supplied me with cups of coffee, during the consumption of which he displayed an extensive knowledge of Messerschmitt and his aircraft. He provided documents the existence of which I was unaware, and constantly indicated to me paths which were worth further exploration. This book would be the poorer were it not for his contributions.

The library of the Royal Aeronautical Society contains copies of all the main European aeronautical journals from the mid-nineteenth century onwards. They comprise a valuable source of contemporary information on Willy Messerschmitt and his aircraft. I am particularly grateful to Arnold Nayler, the Society's librarian, for the efforts that he made to supply me with further references and photocopies of pages from early aeronautical magazines.

Professor Gero Madelung of the Technische Universität in Munich, the son of Messerschmitt's younger sister, allowed himself to be drawn into an extended exchange of correspondence. I am grateful to him for supplying information about his uncle which I could not have obtained from any other source. Herr Otto Pschorn, the proprietor of the Weinhaus Messerschmitt in Bamberg, also gave me some details about Messerschmitt's early life and cordially welcomed my wife and myself when we visited his restaurant in Messerschmitt's childhood home.

The Stadtarchiv of Bamberg replied in an astonishingly short time to my requests for information about the Messerschmitt family. I am grateful to them for their assistance. My thanks are also due to Captain Eric Brown for permission to reproduce an extract from the letter which he wrote to me regarding his participation in the interrogation of Messerschmitt after the war. Mike Ramsden kindly allowed me to reproduce a copy of the page of sketches made by Messerschmitt during his interrogation. I am grateful to Motorbuch Verlag in Stuttgart for permission to quote from Mano Ziegler's book relating his experiences when test flying the Me 163. Two documents relating to the Me 323 are to be found in the Public Record Office. (References WO232/24 and WO232/244). They are Crown copyright and are reproduced in this book with the permission of the Controller of Her Majesty's Stationery Office. Many of the illustrations in the book were supplied by Messerschmitt-Bölkow-Blohm. I would like to thank them for allowing me to use this material. In particular, I am grateful to Herr Hans J. Ebert for the assistance which he provided in making the photographs available. Other illustrations were provided by the Photographic Department of the Imperial War Museum, the library of the Royal Aeronautical Society, Herr Otto Pschorn and Philip Jarret. I owe them all a debt of gratitude. It goes without saying that any errors or misinterpretation of the facts are entirely my own responsibility and are not attributable to any of the many people who assisted me with information.

Lastly, I must thank my wife Janet for tolerating for so long what became my obsession with things Messerschmitt, and the hours that I spent in the archives at Duxford or tapping away on the word processor.

Introduction

In 1969 I was stationed in Munich as the representative of Hawker Siddeley Aviation with the task of co-ordinating activities with our German partners on the international Airbus project. I was fortunate enough to meet Willy Messerschmitt on a number of occasions to discuss matters of mutual interest, and during my conversations with him he recounted some anecdotes about his early career. It is very rarely that one has the opportunity to hear the reminiscences of aviation pioneers. It is not surprising, therefore, that they made a deep impression on me and gave me an interest in finding out more about his outstanding achievements in aircraft design.

When I started to look into what recorded facts were available about Messerschmitt's life, I discovered that although a large number of excellent books had been written about his aircraft, there was very little information available about the man himself.

Of the books and articles which did present a few items of personal information on the background to Messerschmitt's aeronautical achievements, some portrayed him as an unattractive personality, which was in sharp contrast to the impression that I had gained of him from our meetings. For example, an article published in the *Saturday Evening Post* on 8 April 1950 left the impression that he was a fervent Nazi, a warmonger, and what can only be described as the archetypal 'mad professor' who was just waiting for the next opportunity to design more death-dealing machines. David Irving's biography of Erhard Milch, *The Rise and Fall of the Luftwaffe*, missed very few opportunities to present Messerschmitt in a less than favourable light. This at least was understandable since it was in keeping with Milch's declared aversion to Messerschmitt, a feeling which was heartily reciprocated by the designer himself.

Other outstanding German aircraft designers had been better served. Ernst Heinkel had written his own memoirs, for example. In 1984, the Dornier company issued a special edition of their house magazine, *The Dornier Post*, to celebrate the centenary of their founder's birth.

I felt that Messerschmitt must have been a more attractive and interesting personality than that presented in any of the accounts of his life published to date, and my retirement gave me the opportunity to discover as much as possible about his life and working career.

The present book is the result of five years' research into the real Willy Messerschmitt. Not all of the facts that I have discovered were to my liking but, having unearthed them, I would be falsifying the picture if I re-interred them with the intention of presenting Messerschmitt as a more congenial personality than he actually was.

In this book I have as far as possible based my text on written evidence which is still in existence and the veracity of which can be authenticated. Most of this evidence is contained in the archives of The Imperial War Museum. A large part of the documentation of the Messerschmitt company was captured at the end of the Second World War and is still held in the Museum. Included in the 'Speer papers' is Messerschmitt's private correspondence with his family, other German aircraft designers, members of the Nazi hierarchy and his own business associates, together with the texts of lectures, day-to-day memoranda to his staff and drafts of ideas for new aircraft. These all serve to give a much clearer picture of Messerschmitt's personality and of his working methods. Almost all of the quotations in this book are taken directly from that source. The translations are my own.

To present all the information from the archives in chronological order would have produced a disjointed book, with items jumping about from one project to another, and would have caused a disconcerting interruption to the flow of the description of Messerschmitt's career. To avoid this, for the war years from 1939 to 1945, I have devoted individual chapters to one aircraft or one aspect of Messerschmitt's character so that all the evidence on one topic is gathered together. This inevitably leads to a time overlap between some chapters because the design of several aircraft was usually proceeding simultaneously. I hope that the end result presents a clearer picture than the alternative would have done.

Having been a youngster during the Second World War, I remember that at that time the names of Messerschmitt, Heinkel, Junkers and Focke-Wulf, with their incisive consonants and sinister vowels, were regarded as symbols of terror, quite different from the comforting sounds of Avro, De Havilland or Gloster. Today, in the more relaxed atmosphere of a united Europe, perhaps this biography will show a more personal and appealing aspect of the character of one of those famous German aircraft designers, and highlight the considerable difficulties under which he worked. Above all, I hope that this biography may contribute to a wider appreciation of the qualities of an undoubted genius in the field of aeronautical engineering.

Frank Vann
Hatfield, 1993

CHAPTER 1

Early years

The Messerschmitt family has been established for centuries in Bamberg in Northern Bavaria. Over a century ago they were granted a coat of arms, a copy of which can still be seen today in the Weinhaus Messerschmitt on the corner of the Langestrasse and the Schönleinsplatz in Bamberg.

The family were occupied in shipping goods into Bamberg along the river Main. In 1823 one of the more enterprising members of the family, Adam Messerschmitt, bought a cask of wine, shipped it to Bamberg and sold it glass by glass to his fellow townsmen. The Bambergers liked the wine and he was asked to repeat the operation on his next trip. So successful were the results of his enterprise that the shipper decided to set up in business as a wine merchant.

His son, Johann Baptist Messerschmitt, grandfather of the famous aircraft designer, had by then already been born in Bamberg on 7 June 1820. In the mid-1850s he married Margarethe Dütsch, who was 12 years younger, having been born on 20 August 1832 in the village of Zapfendorf not many miles north-east of Bamberg. Their son, Johann Baptist Ferdinand Messerschmitt was born in Bamberg on 19 September 1858. His first two names seem to have been discarded early in his life as, except in the most official documents, he was always referred to as Ferdinand Messerschmitt.

Ferdinand must at one time have been interested in engineering as a career since he studied the subject at the Technische Hochschule in Zürich. It was during this period that, at the age of 25, he married Emma Weil on 25 January 1883 in Zürich. A son, Heinrich, was born in 1884, but he died at the early age of seven years. After that the marriage remained childless.

Perhaps Ferdinand was disappointed by his wife's failure to produce another child, and this led to an estrangement. Whatever the reason, by the end of the century he had left his wife and was living in Frankfurt-am-Main with Anna Maria Schaller and their children. The famous aircraft designer was the second child of the liaison and was born in Frankfurt on 26 June 1898. A few days after his birth the child was baptised in the Catholic church and given the names Wilhelm Emil. His second name soon vanished into oblivion and, apart from some rare occasions when filling in official forms, he was to be known throughout his life as Willy Messerschmitt.

Anna Maria Schaller, Willy's mother, had been born in Zapfendorf on 23 May 1867. Her father was Johann Schaller, a master-tailor, born in Zapfendorf on 10 June 1836 where he died on 6 June 1919. Her mother was Anna Maria Kötzner, born also in Zapfendorf on 15 August 1843 where she died on 12 October 1916. Three of the aircraft designer's grandparents were, therefore, natives of Zapfendorf.

Willy Messerschmitt seems to have been confused about the date of his parents' marriage and the date of his father's death. When he was appointed to a professorship in the Technische Hochschule in Munich in 1937, he was required to fill out the standard form detailing his ancestry, in order to demonstrate that he had no immediate Jewish forebears, which would have debarred him from taking up such a post. Two pencilled drafts of the forms are still in existence, on one of which he states that his father was married in Bamberg at an undefined date, but the other equally clearly gives the place of the marriage as Frankfurt-am-Main and the date as 5 May 1905.

In fact, Ferdinand Messerschmitt was married twice. His first wife, Emma, died on 20 June 1903. His marriage to Willy Messerschmitt's mother, Anna Maria, took place in Bamberg on 1 March 1905 when the boy was almost seven years old. By then Willy had two brothers and a sister. Another girl was to follow two years later as the final offspring of Ferdinand's second marriage. What caused the delay in legalising the relationship is not clear. The reason is probably that, being Catholics, Willy's parents had to wait until Emma died before they could be married — divorce being out of the question for religious reasons.

At the time of Willy Messerschmitt's birth, Germany was already a powerful nation. It was less than 30 years since France had been decisively defeated in the Franco-Prussian War. The previous German minor states had been coerced by Bismarck into the greater German Reich, with the King of Prussia as the German Emperor. German engineers and scientists were at the forefront of technological development. Names like Daimler, Benz and Diesel were well known throughout Europe and the rest of the world. Graf Zeppelin was busy with the design and building of his first successful airship, but heavier-than-air powered flight was still a dream which would not become reality for another five years.

Willy proved from an early age to be a very intelligent child with a great interest in things mechanical. His pronounced domed forehead gave him the appearance of a highly intellectual deep thinker and, indeed, his mental capacity was out of the ordinary.

During the summer of 1909 the family were on holiday on Lake Constance when he first saw a Zeppelin airship at Friedrichshafen, the site of the Zeppelin works. The sight of these huge craft and the ease with which they rose into the air, inspired the young Willy with an enthusiasm for flight, although he saw its future in heavier-than-air aircraft rather than in the clumsy gas-filled leviathans produced by Zeppelin. At about that time, when he was only 11 years old, he must have decided to devote his life to the development of air transport.

Some accounts of Messerschmitt's life claim that he was also spurred on towards aviation after reading accounts of the Zeppelin crash at Echterdingen in 1908. If that is true, Germany owed two of its foremost aircraft designers to the Echterdingen disaster. In his autobiography, Ernst Heinkel gives a vivid description of witnessing the burning of the Zeppelin LZ 4 at Echterdingen. In typically graphic Heinkel prose he relates:

> Bathed in sweat, pressed ever more closely against the window, there entered into me as a gift from the Echterdingen disaster the realization of where, for me as an up-and-coming engineer, the great opportunity of the future lay and where in the general flood of technical discoveries and achievements which distinguished that period, something extraordinary could still be achieved: in the 'heavier-than-air' aircraft which was still little regarded in Germany.

As befitted his character, Messerschmitt's reaction was less dramatic but equally firmly based.

Also in 1909, Messerschmitt visited the International Aviation Exhibition in Frankfurt. The Frankfurt Aviation Society organized displays of gliding during the exhibition and these served to instil enthusiasm for gliding as a sport into many youngsters of the time. In particular, students from Darmstadt were inspired in the next few years to build a series of gliders, which advanced the science of gliding to a remarkable degree and laid the foundations for the outstanding achievements of German gliding enthusiasts immediately after the First World War. Messerschmitt was also captivated by the sight of actual heavier-than-air machines in flight — even though they were only gliders — and his resolve to become involved in aircraft design was reinforced by what he saw at Frankfurt.

His destiny took a decisive turn in 1910 when his parents moved back to Bamberg to take over the running of what remains today the Weinhaus Messerschmitt. The elegant hotel is still run by relatives of the aircraft designer. A commemorative tablet in the entrance hall serves to mark the fact that it once was the family home of Willy Messerschmitt and that, in fact, he founded his first aircraft company there. Willy must have felt immediately at home here in the large handsome house near to the heart of the beautiful city of Bamberg. In later life he had a great affection for his Bavarian homeland despite the fact that he had been born outside Bavaria in Frankfurt. He obviously considered himself to be a Bavarian by adoption.

As has already been mentioned, apart from being a wine merchant, Ferdinand Messerschmitt had himself been trained as an engineer. He, too, was interested in the developing science of aviation. It is possibly through his father's involvement with local aviation enthusiasts that Willy met Friedrich Harth who was an architect by profession but an aviation enthusiast by hobby. Harth had for some years been designing gliders and piloting them himself. He had gathered around him a small band of young enthusiasts which soon included Messerschmitt. Harth was quickly impressed by the enthusiasm that the 12-year-old Messerschmitt exhibited for all things concerned with flying. Harth was at that time experimenting with his gliders on a hill, named the Ludwager Kulm, close to Bamberg from which he made frequent flights. It was not long before he had agreed to allow the youngster to enjoy a flight in one of his gliders.

Perhaps the best summary of the early events in Messerschmitt's life is that which he himself provided during a talk which he gave for overseas listeners on the radio on 8 December 1942:

> In my very earliest youth I followed with enthusiasm the development of airships and aircraft in the newspapers. Long before the First World War I started to build model aircraft, and in this way, in 1910, I got to know State Architect Harth who was carrying out tests with sailplanes in the neighbourhood of my home town, Bamberg. At that time there was no more welcome occurrence for me than to be asked by Harth to help him with his experiments. From then on I was a youngster with an enthusiasm for gliding. As a result I had the opportunity when I was still a schoolboy in 1913 of making my first flights in a glider. Every free minute which school allowed me, I devoted to the further development of sailplanes and, as a result, I gained ever greater influence over the design and building of sailplanes and gliders. If, as a youngster, I had taken up gliding in order to fly, later on I became more and more interested by the technical aspects, that is the design of aircraft.

From then on, the pattern of Willy Messerschmitt's life was decided. His only interest was to be aircraft, and his ambition was to design the best and fastest heavier-than-air aircraft in the world.

Before long, he was acting as principal unpaid assistant to Harth, helping him to construct his aircraft and, as he says, picking up any number of useful tips about the design of gliders. In 1913, when Messerschmitt was 15, he and Harth completed Harth's fourth glider and prepared it for flight trials. Unfortunately, the area around Bamberg was not ideal for flying, and it became obvious that they would have to find a more suitable location.

Harth decided that it would be an advantage to them to transfer their activities to the area known as the Rhön, situated north of Bad Kissingen and about 100 kilometres north-west of Bamberg. After the First World War this area was to become the centre for German gliding. The hill, named the Wasserkuppe, formed an admirable site for launching gliders and is still used for that purpose almost 80 years later. An extensive museum of German gliding with an interesting selection of historical gliders can still be visited there today.

In the summer of 1914, Harth started to move his aircraft and facilities to the long ridge known as the Heidelstein in the Rhön. A suitable hangar was built there, and in it he and his team of young volunteers constructed Harth's latest design for a sailplane, the S 4. The flight tests had hardly been started when the First World War broke out and put an end to further efforts. Harth and other members of the team were called up for service in the German forces. At the time Messerschmitt was too young to be enlisted and returned to his lessons at the Realschule in Bamberg.

In May 1915 Messerschmitt decided to return to the Rhön and continue work on the S 4. When he arrived there he discovered that the hangar had been broken into by vandals. The aircraft was in pieces and all the tools and equipment left there had been stolen. Messerschmitt had kept in contact with Harth and knew that he would be enjoying a period of leave later in the year. If the flight tests were to be continued, the aircraft would have to be rebuilt quickly. The few remaining serviceable pieces of the aircraft were retrieved from the hangar and transferred to the 'Alten Hofhaltung' at the rear of the family home in Bamberg. Harth kept up a continual stream of letters to Messerschmitt with advice and drawings to enable the glider to be rebuilt. Modifications were introduced into the original design of the S 4 so that the new aircraft included several improvements to alleviate problems encountered during the abbreviated flight tests.

The importance of Messerschmitt's contribution to the design of the new aircraft was recognized in the machine being named 'Harth-Messerschmitt S 5'. The wing area was 20 square metres (215 sq ft) and the empty weight was only 65 kg (143 lb). Flight control was by wing warping. There were no conventional ailerons, but a series of cables twisted the structure of the outer wings to alter the local angle of attack in order to increase or decrease the lift generated. The Wright brothers had used a similar system on their early aircraft.

Harth's long-awaited leave finally arrived in the August of 1915, and arrangements were made to transport the completed aircraft to the Heidelstein. Assisted by Messerschmitt and an enthusiastic French prisoner of war, Harth moved the S 5 by road to the Rhön and started flight tests at the beginning of September. The aircraft proved to be very successful. In a period of less than two weeks a number of flights had been made by Harth, covering distances of up to 300 metres (328 yds) and attaining an altitude of 20 metres (66 ft). The landings were smooth and the controls showed themselves to be perfectly reliable.

Ferdinand Messerschmitt, Willy's father, died in April 1916. On the forms for the Munich Technische Hochschule, mentioned earlier, Willy seems to have been unsure of the exact date of his father's death, since he quoted two different dates — both of them wrong. The records of the Stadtarchiv in Bamberg give the correct date of 28 April 1916.

Despite Willy's obvious enthusiasm for aircraft, it is unlikely that Ferdinand Messerschmitt senior, at the time that he died, had the remotest idea of the fame which his second son would earn. He could have had no suspicion that his family name would within 50 years be as widely recognized internationally as those of other famous Germans including Beethoven, Schiller or Goethe — if for somewhat different reasons.

Willy was too young to take over the wine business, even if he had been interested in doing so. In fact, although a taste for fine wines remained with him throughout his life, Willy had no interest in the wine trade. Instead, when Ferdinand died, his eldest son, who had earlier emigrated to America, returned to Bamberg to take control of the family fortunes.

Willy continued to devote his attention to designing aircraft. Encouraged by his success with the S 5, Messerschmitt, again with the help of Harth, started on the design of an improved version of the aircraft — the Harth-Messerschmitt S 6. Messerschmitt's later career was distinguished by his desire to achieve the minimum weight for the structure of an aircraft. This was a virtue which he sometimes pushed beyond acceptable limits with unfortunate results, as will appear later.

His efforts at weight reduction on the S 6 were successful. The new aircraft had a greater wing area than the S 5 — 22 square metres (237 sq ft) but weighed less, only 52 kg (115 lb). The aircraft was a high-wing monoplane with a fuselage of welded steel tube which was left uncovered in an effort to save weight. Again, control was effected by wing warping. Flight tests took place, again on the Heidelstein, in August 1916 with Harth at the controls. On one occasion, Harth managed to keep the aircraft in the air for $3^1/_2$ minutes and achieve an altitude of 10 metres (33 ft) after taking off from the top of an incline. In 1917 it was Messerschmitt's turn to be called up for military service. Despite his desire to be involved in some form of flying activities, he was inevitably allocated to a mortar unit of the German army. According to his entry in *The Yearbook of the German Academy for Aeronautical Research of 1941/1942* he was later discharged from the army for health reasons. According to other, less reliable, reports he was transferred to the 'cradle of Bavarian aviation' at Schleissheim near to Munich before being demobilized at the end of the war. What is certain is his enrolment in 1918 as a student in the Technische Hochschule of Munich, an institution whose successor still has an enviably high reputation today as an engineering university. He remained there for five years studying mechanical engineering, and graduated in 1923 as a Diplom Ingenieur.

Even while he was studying at Munich, Messerschmitt was continuing to collaborate with Harth on the design of new gliders. Further tests with the S 6 were carried out in May 1918 in the Rhön. Based on the results of these, a start was made on the design of the next aircraft — the S 7 — the building of which occupied their time until February 1919.

In a lecture which he gave after his appointment to the post of Professor in the Technische Hochschule in Munich just before the Second World War, Messerschmitt explained why he and other young pioneers were compelled to confine the use of their talents to the design of gliders.

He explained the situation as follows:

Owing to the Treaty of Versailles, Germany was forbidden for years to build powered aircraft. A group of brave young men did not allow themselves to be frightened off and thought: 'If we can't fly with engines, then we will do it without engines.' The aviation departments of the Technische Hochschule produced most of the pioneers in the development of aviation after the war. Necessity produced a virtue; without the experience gained in flying sailplanes it would have been impossible to bring modern aircraft so quickly up to the present standard of development. I am proud of the fact that I was able to set up my own factory, which can operate so successfully, by way of glider and sailplane construction — without ever having to work in an outside aircraft firm.

A leading personality in the gliding field after the First World War was Oskar Ursinus, who served as a figurehead for all German aspirations in the aeronautical field and particularly in the design of gliders. In an attempt to co-ordinate the efforts being made in the post-war years in aircraft design, Ursinus proposed that the Rhön should become the centre for all future activity in building and flying gliders.

Messerschmitt and Harth were some of the earliest to respond to Ursinus's call. As Messerschmitt put it in the radio talk referred to earlier:

It is understandable that, on the basis of the experience I had gained before and during the war, I was one of the first of those who, after the war had been lost, took a lively interest in the establishment of the sport of gliding. Up to 1922 I worked on perfecting sailplanes more and more, until I decided to transfer my experience in the field of gliders to the construction of powered aircraft.

In 1919 and 1920, an extensive series of tests with the S 7 was carried out in the Rhön. Among other improvements investigated, spoilers were tried at the wing tips to replace the conventional rudder. These were intended to create drag at one wing tip so as to pull the aircraft round in a turn, at the same time reducing the lift on the inner wing and causing the aircraft to bank correctly. The flight trials were successful and led to yet another developed version, known as the S 8. It had a fairly high wing-loading for the time and needed a head wind of about 15 metres (50 ft) a second to get into the air. As the designers expressed it: 'They wanted to fly like seabirds.'

On 13 September 1921 the S 8, with its wing-warping controls, set up a new world record for gliding flight by staying in the air for 21 minutes. Messerschmitt went into print for the first time in an article which appeared in the two leading German aviation magazines, *Flugsport* and the *Zeitschrift für Flugtechnik und Motorluftschiffahrt* at the beginning of October 1921. It is worth reproducing the article in full as an example of Messerschmitt's own style of presentation:

The 21 Minute Long Flight on the Heidelstein on 13th September 1921
On the 13th September a wind of about 10 to 12 metres per second was blowing from a south-westerly direction. It was characterized by extreme gustiness and marked changes of direction. The wind often slackened for

a moment to be followed straight afterwards by hurricane-like gusts of up to 20 metres per second. The flights took place from the ridge of the Heidelstein on the west side. There is a slope of about 2 to 3 degrees towards the south and west. The adjacent slopes have a gradient of about 4 to 6 degrees over a distance of 100 to 200 metres; from there for several kilometres they extend level or have a slope of 2 to 3 degrees.

In the first place some flights were carried out of over 6 minutes duration with no loss of altitude. In the meantime, the wind had increased and it was decided to extend the flight over a longer time and to look for more altitude. At the same time, there seemed to be the possibility of achieving take-off without any assistance.

At about half-past-eight in the morning, the aircraft took off. Harth let the aircraft take off from the ground on its own, making use of strong gusts. By the skilful use of other gusts, greater altitudes were gradually attained.

The aircraft soon reached an altitude of 50 to 60 metres and flew into the wind in a south-westerly direction climbing steadily in stages. Under the control of the pilot, the aircraft was then turned into a more westerly direction as far as the Bischofsheim to Wüstensachsen road which was about 1200 metres away. The aircraft lay there at a height of over 100 metres with its altitude continually varying.

Harth then described a curve and flew back to the starting point, circling around there in wide circles at a height of about 150 metres.

The flight was then extended in a south-easterly direction as far as the Weisbacher Jungviehweide about 1.5 kilometres away. Here a turn was executed again and the aircraft turned back once more to the take-off point, which again was flown round in a wide curve over long distances with the wind.

In doing so, the machine was far behind the take-off point and, for part of the time, over the wooded slopes on the opposite side of the Heidelstein which run down towards Wüstensachsen.

The aircraft was again piloted slowly into the wind to a landing. The aircraft touched the ground after 21 minutes and 37 seconds. The landing place was about 150 metres in front of the take-off position and only 12 metres lower down.

The flight took place almost the whole time over nearly level ground so that the exploitation of rising currents of air seems to be excluded and, hence, the energy was gained only from the varying speed of the wind. It seems worthy of note that the speed of the aircraft was subjected to greater variations into wind. It was also obvious that the machine always gained height when a turn was initiated. When flying down wind, no loss of height could be noticed.

During the whole flight, the aircraft lay steady in the air and responded exactly to the control movements. The great success, which was achieved with the utmost ease, and during which the aircraft was definitely in the control of the pilot at all times, can only be attributed to the use of a warped wing. From the ground it could clearly be seen how the wing surfaces were always moving and to a certain degree automatically adapted themselves into the most favourable position relative to the wind, whilst the fuselage stayed in an undisturbed position.

The objective of continuous flight without an engine now seems to have been achieved. For about ten years, systematic tests with warping wings have been carried out by Harth and Messerschmitt. The recently achieved successes have demonstrated that a glider has now been produced which can be flown with ease for long periods in even the most gusty conditions without physical effort from the pilot.

Messerschmitt

The quiet confidence in his own abilities and the faith in his designs, which were to characterize Messerschmitt throughout his life, are already evident in the last paragraph of this report written at the age of 23. A footnote appended to the original article says: 'The editorial board of the magazine has accepted this article because it has great confidence in the impartial work of Messrs Harth and Messerschmitt. It must be recommended to Messrs Harth and Messerschmitt, however, that they make their future flights in front of independent observers.'

CHAPTER 2

Further experiments with gliders

As a result of the success of the S 8 sailplane, Messerschmitt had established a reputation for himself as the foremost designer of gliders in Germany. His aircraft now held the world record for duration of flight in a glider. However, the German gliding world was limited in extent, and Messerschmitt's name was far from receiving acclaim in the aeronautical world in general.

Emboldened by his success, late in 1921 Messerschmitt decided to attempt a more unconventional design of aircraft. So sure was he of his own ability to design an aircraft unassisted that he did not even seek the advice of Harth in achieving his goal. As a result, the new aircraft — the S 9 glider — was to be the first aircraft solely designed by Messerschmitt. Once again he relied on wing-warping for the rolling control, but this time the aircraft took the form of a flying wing with no real tail surfaces. (The next time that Messerschmitt would be involved with a tail-less aircraft was over 20 years later, and the aircraft would be the famous Me 163 'Komet' rocket-propelled fighter.)

The wings were swept forward in an attempt to arrange for the centre of the wing lift to coincide with the centre of gravity of the aircraft. The pilot had two levers side by side which operated the warping control of the corresponding wings. Pushing both levers forward twisted both wings nose down, reducing the lift symmetrically and causing the aircraft to descend. Pulling both levers back increased the angle of attack of both wings and caused the aircraft to rise. Operating the levers differentially, that is, pushing one forward and the other back, reduced the lift on one wing and increased it on the other so that the aircraft banked in a turn. Movable spoiler surfaces at the wing tips were opened on the appropriate side to produce drag and assist the aircraft to turn.

For the early 1920s it was an extremely unconventional design. Like many of Messerschmitt's later aircraft, the S 9 demonstrated his preparedness to take risks in the search for more efficient designs by introducing innovations in the overall layout of an aircraft or its structure.

The S 9 was an inventive effort but it was not successful. The stability of the aircraft left much to be desired and the flight tests were soon abandoned. For the time being Messerschmitt had to return to more conventional designs. It was probably his experience with this aircraft that prejudiced Messerschmitt so strongly against tail-less aircraft and helped to make him less receptive to Lippisch's proposals for similar aircraft in the 1940s.

Despite his continuing studies in Munich, Messerschmitt still found time to design and build more aircraft. By 1922 he had been co-operating with Harth for nine years on design, and Harth had piloted all of their joint ventures. However, Harth had suffered serious injuries, including a cracked pelvis and severe concussion, in a crash in a Pilotus glider at the end of 1921. He never completely recovered from those injuries. As a result, Messerschmitt was compelled to look for a new pilot.

At that time, among other activities, Messerschmitt had set up a gliding school on the Wasserkuppe and had, in his turn like Harth before him, assembled around himself a band of young flying enthusiasts. He fitted up a bowling alley in Bischofsheim as a workshop, and engaged paid helpers to assemble his new design — the S 10 sailplane. By the spring of 1922 a number of these youngsters had qualified for the glider pilot's licence in Messerschmitt's new aircraft. Among them was Wolf Hirth, later to be the most famous of all German glider pilots and who was to be honoured by having a gliding trophy named after him.

The S 10 was Messerschmitt's most highly developed glider to make use of wing-warping as a means of flying control. All his earlier aircraft had had a pylon projecting vertically above the wing centre-section from the top of which radiated the control cables used to warp the wing. In order to reduce the drag, the S 10 replaced the cables by two struts running up from the keel of the aircraft to operate the warping mechanism.

Probably because of the advantages in allowing the wing to twist, Messerschmitt designed the wings of his gliders with only one spar instead of the more conventional two-spar layout. On the S 10 the single tubular spar was braced to the fuselage by a strut. The ribs, and with them the wing structure, rotated about the spar under the influence of the warping mechanism. Messerschmitt was so impressed by what he saw as the advantages of the single spar wing that he later patented the idea and adopted its use on many of his later powered aircraft, including the Me 109. Once again the flying controls of the S 10 consisted of two joysticks side by side, each stick twisting the wing on that side.

Four aircraft of the S 10 type were entered for the Rhön Gliding Competition of 1922. They won a number of events, with Hirth and Baron von Freyburg distinguishing themselves by their handling of the machines.

A contemporary report in a German aviation magazine stated that 'in conversation with the constructors, one gained the impression that the aircraft was carefully thought out aerodynamically as well as being well designed structurally.' However, the wing of the S 10 was of a high aspect ratio and this led to some problems. The four aircraft which were entered in the competition did not all have the same geometry for the warping mechanism and the report already quoted above commented: 'With some of the aircraft demonstrated, on which the bracing struts were closer to the fuselage, one often had the impression that they were not responding to the intended control movements and, as a result, serious accidents were caused. This behaviour could be explained by the fact that the free end of the wing extending beyond the last supported point was so big that, when the wing was twisted, it did not follow the motion correctly because of lack of adequate stiffness. As a result, the whole of the wing was not twisted in the required direction but only a part of it. On aircraft with smaller aspect ratios, the wing-warping has worked better apparently.'

It should not be forgotten that at the time of all these activities, Messerschmitt was still a full-time student working towards his degree in Munich. He can have had little opportunity for the traditional student spare-time pursuits. What little free time he had from his studies must all have been devoted to aircraft design. Indeed, already in 1922, spurred on by his successes to date, Messerschmitt was soon busy refining the design of the S 10 into a new type — the S 11.

The S 11 was intended as an improvement of the S 10 from an aerodynamic point of view. For the first time, Messerschmitt succeeded in accommodating the whole of the wing-warping mechanism inside the wing. Getting rid of the network of warping cables and the struts which had replaced them produced an even greater reduction in the drag. The fuselage, which on his earlier designs had been an open-work welded steel tubular structure, was constructed of plywood, completely boxed in, again with a marked reduction in the overall drag of the aircraft.

Unfortunately, the tests with the S 11 were unsuccessful apart from some short flights. Repeated structural failures occurred which were attributed to faulty manufacture of control hinge components by outside contractors. Harth had still not recovered completely from his crash injuries sustained in the previous year, and the pilots who attempted to master the tricky characteristics of the wing-warping control system of the S 11 could not emulate Harth's earlier successes.

One cannot fail to admire the tenacity of Messerschmitt in pursuing his aims. Undeterred by past failures, the young man embarked on a new design — the S 12. The new machine was built from the components intended for the S 11 (plywood fuselage, new wing profile) and the cable controls saved from the S 10. This machine was doomed because of the combination of a new wing section with the old cable control. It was only after five crashes, in which luckily no one was seriously injured, that Messerschmitt discovered the true reason for these unpleasant events. The report in an issue of *Flugsport* of 1922 explains the problem, which today would be attributed to aeroelastic effects:

The wing section of the S 11 and the S 12 was developed from that of the S 10, but the design was significantly better and was later used by other aircraft builders (Konsul, Darmstadt). Since, however, time was pressing during the construction of the S 12 — because the machine had to be ready for the Rhön Competition of 1922 — the properties of the section could not be checked in a wind tunnel. As a result, whereas the centre of pressure on the S 10 was close behind the point of rotation of the wing, the centre of pressure of the new section was about 100 mm [4 in] behind it. Hence, as soon as the wing had a negative angle of attack of more than -3 degrees, the centre of pressure wandered even further back along the chord. At the instant when it passed the point of attachment of the warping strut, the wing rotated about this fixed point and the spar, until then bent upwards, was suddenly bent downwards. This rapid displacement of the wing produced an instantaneous loss of lift which could not be recovered by any control movement because pulling on the vertical lift control cable only produced further bending of the spar as a result. All of the crashes of this type can be attributed to this cause.

On the basis of the accumulated experience and as a result of a series of discussions and detailed calculations, the significantly modified S 13 was built in the spring of 1923. Using the same layout as had previously been tried on the S 9 and the S 11, Messerschmitt succeeded in installing all the warping control cables entirely inside the fuselage and the wing. Moreover, this machine exhibited for the first time a new design of single stick control.

As the machine was well thought out in other details too, it gave the impression of being at last a useful glider controlled by wing-warping. After a few successful flights, however, the machine was found to be uncontrollable in the air, and was unfortunately destroyed in a crash because of the buckling of a steel control tube which had been delivered in a weakened condition by a subcontractor. The wall thickness of the tube could not be checked on installation.

Once again, the structural failure was attributed to faulty workmanship by an outside supplier. It must have been obvious to Messerschmitt, however, that his designs were too close to the bone structurally. His strength margins on the design of the structural components were not adequate to cater for the inadequacies introduced in the manufacture of the actual parts.

Messerschmitt's solution to the problem was to look for an airfoil section the centre of pressure of which did not change its chordwise position as its incidence was changed. Using the knowledge of aerodynamics which he had acquired during his studies, he succeeded in designing a new airfoil section with a fixed centre of pressure. This is still recognized as one of the most successful airfoil sections for glider wings under the designation, Göttingen 535.

Using this wing section and a new control system with only one control column, Messerschmitt designed the S 14 glider, two of which were built for the Rhön Competition of 1923. The proof of the success of the young designer's innovations was provided by the performance of the S 14 in a field of highly professional competitors. On 30 August 1923 Hackmack in the S 14 attained the highest altitude of the competition in a wind of 20 metres per second. No other aircraft was able to equal the height of 303 metres (994 ft) attained by the S 14.

The truth was that, in the hands of an experienced pilot, an aircraft controlled by wing-warping was capable of surprising feats of performance. Messerschmitt was forced to recognize, however, that for the average pilot, wing-warping had no advantages over the standard ailerons mounted on the trailing edge of the outer part of the wing. He did use wing-warping once more in the design of his first powered aircraft, but from then on it was abandoned for all time. The twin control columns required for the operation of the controls were much more difficult to master than the single stick required in the conventional arrangement. It was found that only specialists with hours of experience could successfully handle the wing-warping aircraft. As a result they rapidly lost favour and were soon to be superseded by the conventional layout used ever since.

Although aeronautics was not a recognized subject for a university degree, Messerschmitt in 1923 succeeded in getting the design of the S 14 accepted by the university authorities as his thesis for his degree in mechanical engineering. He graduated in the summer of 1923 as a Diplom Ingenieur and was at last ready to launch himself full time into serious commercial aircraft design and manufacture.

His experience with gliders had served to familiarize him with both aerodynamic and structural design problems. He was now determined to extend his activities to the field of powered flight.

Harth did not want to abandon his gliding activities and had no desire to accompany Messerschmitt into the design of powered aircraft. As a result, a difference of opinion arose between the two men who had for so long collaborated in producing a memorable line of sailplanes. By mutual agreement, they resolved to go their separate ways. Harth was still hampered by the injuries he had suffered in the crash, and appears to have given up gliding shortly after his break with Messerschmitt. He was soon in further difficulties, losing his job as an architect because of his membership of the Nazi Party, which at that time was not a recipe for advancement. His fortunes only revived after the rise to power of Hitler in 1933, when he was appointed Chief Planning Officer for Bamberg.

The next glider that Messerschmitt was to design would be the Me 321 some 20 years later. For the moment, his creative abilities were to be devoted to the development of powered aircraft.

CHAPTER 3

The first Messerschmitt company

As soon as he had graduated, Messerschmitt decided to found his own aircraft design and construction company — 'Flugzeugbau Messerschmitt Bamberg'. This was an astounding step for one so young, and it serves to demonstrate that unwavering faith in his own innate capabilities which he had throughout his long life.

In 1924, for the first time, the Rhön Competition invited entries from powered gliders. This presented Messerschmitt with the opportunity for which he had been waiting to establish a reputation for himself in the design of motorized aircraft. He set to work immediately and had soon designed the S 15, an experimental aircraft with a 500 cc Douglas motor-cycle engine giving 3 1/2 horse power.

An enthusiastic and colourful description of the machine appeared in the German aeronautical magazine *Flugsport*:

> The construction of light aircraft in Germany is based on experience with gliders in the Rhön. Without the intensive research into gliders, the development of the light aircraft would not have been possible. At present different light aircraft are being built, tested and prepared for the Rhön competition from the 1st to the 30th of August.
>
> The well-known glider constructor, Messerschmitt, has produced a light aircraft with a 500 cc twin-cylinder engine with which a flight of 43 minutes has been achieved. The altitude attained was 600 metres [1970 ft].
>
> This machine has a span of more than 14 metres [46 ft] and a length overall of 5 metres [16 ft] and is equipped with a motor-cycle engine of only 3 1/2 horse power. On the 16th June 1924 it had already achieved a flight lasting 23 minutes at an altitude of 450 metres [nearly 1500 ft] when piloted by Seywald.
>
> On the morning of the 19th June at 8.30 a.m. it took off for a successful flight lasting 19 minutes and reaching about 300 metres [984 ft] altitude. The weather was very unsuitable for test flying. Strong thermals tossed the aircraft about from one wing to the other, but the pilot methodically described circles. It was a wonderful sight as the elegant machine, with its engine running like clockwork, circled over the parade ground at Bamberg.

A sporting crowd had assembled on the aerodrome in the afternoon, patiently waiting for calmer weather. Towards four o'clock the sky had clouded over and storms were gathering over the river valley. A patch of blue sky finally reappeared towards six o'clock. The engine did a perfect short test run. The propeller was changed and the engine was restarted. The machine rolls out, rocks and, after about 200 metres [656 ft], lifts from the ground. After about 500 metres [1640 ft], the pilot closes the throttle and lands.

Excitement at the take-off point. But the machine is already turning as it taxis and takes off near to the take-off point. At a height of about a metre, the machine returns and lands smoothly by the tent. So back to the first take-off point. Change of propeller. The newly mounted propeller does not appear to give enough thrust. The incidence of the blades is too high and the low-powered engine cannot reach its best performance. The first propeller is put back on again.

As a result of good design, changing the propeller takes only a few minutes, then — throttle open and a smooth take-off. The machine lifts off after 200 metres [656 ft] and climbs; climbs and makes wide turns over the woods in the background; turns to the left and flies along the edge of the flying field towards the town. After five minutes, the take-off point is crossed at a height of about 150 metres [492 ft]. More banking to the left and towards the woods again.

After 13 minutes, the machine crosses the take-off point again at a height of 300 metres [984 ft]. A marvellous sight. Buffeted by gusts, surrounded by black storm-clouds, the machine describes curves in a small blue patch in the sky illuminated by the evening sun.

And then, 500 metres [1640 ft] up, a turn to the right, a turn to the left, a figure of eight and loops over the aerodrome. The light aircraft seems to behave perfectly in a bank, and to respond to the controls easily and effortlessly. The public is entranced. Already 30 minutes have gone by. The sky is closing up again, the patch of blue is getting smaller. The black storm-clouds are always getting nearer, but the pilot passes over undeterred. The town is crossed at a height of 600 metres [1968 ft], then suddenly the song of the engine stops and the machine glides silently. In a wide curve the pilot turns towards the east and puts the nose down. With a rushing sound the machine approaches the ground near to the take-off point. The aircraft hovers at a height of 4 to 5 metres [13-16 ft] over the ground; hovers and hovers and comes ever closer. Then a railway embankment. The spectators' hearts stop beating, but the pilot quietly controls his aircraft, an imperceptible movement of the controls, the machine neatly soars over the embankment, banks and touches down, 30 metres [98 ft] roll and the machine comes to rest. A 43 minute flight!

Enthusiastic onlookers hurry to the machine which has landed about 200 metres [656 ft] away. Pilot and designer, closely surrounded, are in animated conversation. The mechanics and onlookers push the machine into the tent. The flaps close and the flying field sinks into a deep silence.

The machine is an unbraced monoplane with the wing lying above the fuselage. The wing is in three parts with the break-points between the centre-section and the outer wings covered with strips of celluloid of about a handsbreadth. When the machine is in the air, it is possible to see through the gap at the joint so that it looks as if the wings are following the centre-section without any attachment. The leading edge of the wing is skinned with plywood, as is the fuselage. The engine and airscrew are improbably small. The 500 cc Douglas runs marvellously and starts at the first turn even when the machine is cold. The propeller is a toy. Without the pilot the S 15 weighs only 180 kg [397 lb].

The test pilot, Seywald, commended the excellent flying qualities of the S 15. Particularly praiseworthy is the ease of control and the agility of the machine. The wing warping, which is a design of rolling control used and manufactured only by Messerschmitt until now, has completely vindicated itself. The glide slope is very flat.

The Messerschmitt Company, which until now has built only gliders, has achieved a complete success with the design of the S 15. It is now possible to proceed with the series production of the machine. As we hear, there are already orders placed for the S 15.

The Arbeitsgemeinschaft für Luftverkehr und Flugtechnik in Würzburg, which already has three gliders of the Messerschmitt Company, immediately ordered an S 15 after the successful flights. The aviator, Seywald, will enter the Rhön Competition this year with the test aircraft.

One can only hope that the Messerschmitt Company, the head of which has pursued his objectives with such great determination and at great financial sacrifice, will, as a result of the unique success of last Thursday, finally receive the financial support to which it can lay claim rightfully on the basis of its achievements.

Encouraged by the performance of the S 15 and its enthusiastic reception by the public, Messerschmitt proceeded to design two entrants for the 1924 Rhön Competition. These were designated the S 16a 'Bubi' and the S 16b 'Betti', the names being the nicknames of his brother and sister. The aircraft were similar, but differed in that the S 16a 'Bubi' was a single-seater with a 14 hp Douglas Sprite engine, whilst the S 16b 'Betti' had a 21 hp 500 cc engine and was a two-seater.

Messerschmitt's concern for obtaining the best aerodynamic performance is evinced by the fact that both aircraft had an aspect ratio of 15. This represented an amazingly high ratio of wingspan to wing mean chord for its day. The wing could be dismantled into three sections by means of two hinged joints and could then be rotated lengthways for transport by road. Again, the wing featured a single spar and, despite its span of 14.4 metres (47.2 ft), it was mainly a cantilever with bracing struts very close to the root.

The 'Betti' could attain a speed of 115 kph (71 mph) on its 21 hp engine whilst consuming only one litre of petrol for every 3.2 kilometres (2 miles) flown.

The propeller was situated above the engine and was driven by a chain drive to the propeller shaft. The two aircraft were approved by the competition authorities as entrants. Unfortunately, to Messerschmitt's great disappointment, despite some early successes and their outstanding ability to climb and glide, they did not fare well in the actual competition.

The S 16a suffered a propeller failure in flight at a considerable altitude. Because of the vibration, the propeller block was torn out of the fuselage together with the propeller. The pilot, Seywald, was forced to make a steep gliding descent and managed to achieve a pancake landing without injury to himself. The aircraft was a total write-off. On the S 16b the propeller drive chain failed in flight and the aircraft had to be withdrawn from the competition.

Messerschmitt was obviously deeply disheartened by the failure of his two designs. His experience with gliders had not prepared him for the additional problems associated with powered aircraft. He had at least now learnt in no uncertain way that as much attention had to be devoted to the engine installation as to the aerodynamics and the structure, and the knowledge that he needed could only be acquired by experience.

In the years ahead, Messerschmitt would experience many further problems with powerplants, although these would mainly be because of the unavailability of suitable engines to power his aircraft at the time required.

Having extracted all the knowledge that he could from the shortcomings of his first powered machines, Messerschmitt set about designing his next aircraft. He also considered that the time had come to change the system he was using to designate his creations. All the earlier aircraft had been designated by the letter 'S' standing for Segelflugzeug, or sailplane. From now on they were to have the designation 'M' so that their authorship would be made quite clear. This method of identifying Messerschmitt aircraft persisted until the RLM (the German Air Ministry) introduced its new system of numbering aircraft after 1933.

About this time Messerschmitt met a man who was to play a large part in his later career. This was Theo Croneiss, an ex-fighter pilot who had scored five victories during the First World War. Croneiss had founded a private flying school and he was looking for a light aircraft to use as his basic trainer. He was very impressed by Messerschmitt's ability as a designer, and was probably the first to appreciate what the young man was capable of in the aircraft design field. He prevailed upon Messerschmitt, presumably without too much effort, to design for him an aircraft derived from the successful S 16 designs.   Messerschmitt set to work immediately on the design of his next aircraft, the M 17, which appeared in 1925. This was a two-seater light aircraft intended for training or sporting flights. It attracted considerable attention because of its docile flying characteristics and its remarkably low weight. For the first time an aircraft had been produced, the empty weight of which was less than its payload. In fact, its empty weight was only 94 per cent of the payload.

A contemporary report describes the aircraft fully:

Dipl. Ing. Messerschmitt has displayed his light aircraft, type M 17.
The aircraft is a monoplane with the wing arranged above the fuselage. The fuselage is made of longerons which are connected by a series of frames, and skinned with plywood.
The wing is in three parts. The centre-section is attached to the fuselage by four bolts. The outer sections are connected to the centre-section by another four bolts and are easily detachable. The bending loads are car-

ried by the main spar. The part of the wing forward of the front spar is made of plywood to form a torsion box. The part of the wing aft of the spar consists of profiled ribs and is covered with fabric.

The construction of all the control surfaces and the tail surfaces is similar to that of the wing itself. Beneath the wing in the fuselage are the compartments for the pilot and the passenger. Large openings in the sides afford good visibility in all directions.

The undercarriage is housed in the fuselage and only the ends of the wheel axles project from the fuselage. The stub axles are supported and sprung by rubber bungees. The whole undercarriage can be removed from the fuselage by undoing a few bolts.

The engine which is used is either the A.B.C. 'Scorpion' or the Bristol 'Cherub' of about 25 hp. However, a different engine with the same weight and output can be installed instead. The sheet steel bulkhead carrying the engine is attached to the fuselage with four bolts. Any danger of fire is eliminated by a fireproof bulkhead.

In its construction the aircraft is extremely simple and all the components are designed in accordance with present day experience in aerodynamics.

Span	11.6 m
Length	5.8 m
Height	1.5 m
Wing area	10.4 sq m
Empty weight	180 kg
Payload	190 kg
Maximum speed	c. 159 kph

The numerous references in this report to 'four bolts' are interesting in view of Messerschmitt's opinion of the Airbus wing design referred to later in this book. His basic principle in structural design throughout his life was to keep the structure as light and as simple as possible. This policy had obvious advantages in the design and strength analysis of structures, and even greater benefits when carrying out maintenance work on aircraft in service.

At least five examples of the M 17 aircraft were built. The excellence of its flying characteristics was exhibited by its successes in many competitions. These included a number of the most prestigious events in the German aviation programme. The Oberfrankenflug (Upper Franconia Flight) from 2 to 4 May 1925 brought the M 17: First Prize in the altitude competition; First Prize in the speed competition; and Second Prize in the overland flight.

During the International Flight Competition in Munich from 12 to 14 September 1925, Theo Croneiss obtained in the M 17: First Prize in the altitude class; First Prize in the speed class; and Fifth Prize in the relay flight.

These prizes could not fail to attract public attention to the new aircraft. Its greatest success, however, which attracted world-wide attention, was the crossing of the central range of the Alps during a flight from Bamberg to Rome in September 1926. The total flying time for the journey of 1620 km (1004 miles) was 14 hours 20 minutes. It was not only the distance flown which was remarkable. Continued flight at the altitudes required to cross the mountain range was by no means commonplace in those days.

Messerschmitt had now made his mark as an outstanding aircraft designer. He was beginning to attract the attention of leading figures in the established aircraft industry. Hugo Junkers wrote at the time: 'To fly over the Alps at 4500 metres in a Messerschmitt 29 hp two-seater is a fantastic achievement which I heartily congratulate.'

The Deutsche Versuchsanstalt für Luftfahrt (German Aeronautical Research Institute) described the M 17 as 'the best airframe design since 1917'.

CHAPTER 4

First commercial orders

By 1926, Messerschmitt was enjoying an increasing number of successes with his powered aircraft at German flying meetings and competitions. As a result he was beginning to see ever more clearly the day when he would be able to compete on equal commercial terms with aircraft manufacturers like Heinkel and Dornier, who had been established long before he had entered the field. The next step forward was to establish his company on a firmer basis and to demonstrate that he was a force to be reckoned with in the design and manufacture of commercial aircraft. With this objective in mind, he converted the Flugzeugbau Messerschmitt Bamberg into a limited company — the Messerschmitt Flugzeugbau GmbH Bamberg.

By this time, Theo Croneiss had founded his own air transport company, the Nordbayrische Verkehrsflug (North Bavarian Airline) and was looking for a suitable aircraft to use on its routes. He had been so impressed with the performance and flying qualities of the M 17 that he gave Messerschmitt a contract to design and build a small passenger aircraft of the type that today would be described as a 'feeder' aircraft, carrying small numbers of passengers into large airports where they transferred to larger aircraft with a greater range.

Messerschmitt set to work immediately, basing his new design on the experience he had gained with the S 16 and M 17; but this time the aircraft was to have an all-metal structure. Once again the 'four bolt' philosophy for the main structural joints was in evidence.

In a lecture which he gave in 1941, Messerschmitt provided some interesting details of the process that he went through in designing and building this successful aircraft, the M 18:

About 14 years ago, I was given a contract to develop a small passenger aircraft from the head at that time of the North Bavarian Airline. The experience with the small two-seater M 17, which was developed directly from sailplanes, and which achieved a number of successes in competitions, was to be made use of for larger aircraft. I had prepared the new design in plywood construction, as it was familiar to me from sailplanes. The design schemes were already well advanced when Herr Croneiss, the head man responsible for the airline mentioned, asked me to see him and explained in a long statement that a wooden fuselage was not acceptable for a passenger aircraft because of the danger from splintering in a crash. He proposed welding the fuselage from steel tubes in the conventional frame construction. However, as I had very little experience of welded designs, and as a sheet metal design using a high-strength aluminium alloy (Dural) seemed easier, we agreed to build the fuselage of the aircraft out of sheet metal. The wings and tail unit were to be made as before out of wood.

Only in the course of the design did I first decide, contrary to the wishes of the customer, to build the other parts of the aircraft out of sheet metal. Apart from a considerable delay to the programme, this attempt went well. I was able to gather useful experience for the future. The aircraft, the M 18 was a complete success.

I had absolutely no experience of metal construction and I had first to form a picture of the strength characteristics of sheet metal construction by an enormous number of detail tests. The time spent on the design of this type of aircraft was decisive for the development of my metal aircraft in general. I took great care to ensure that adequate strength was obtained with the smallest expenditure of material. The requirements of the specification were well suited to that end as can be imagined. In order to make the operation reasonably profitable, five people with baggage were to be carried at about 140 kph (87 mph), as was then usual, with only 120 hp. I was also successful in using the external skin of the aircraft to carry loads to a great extent. Even then, as today on all my aircraft, the wing comprised one spar which carried the shear and bending loads, a few ribs to stiffen the skin, and the sheet metal covering which held it all together and, in particular, made the wing torsionally stiff. Put in basic terms, the wing was a tube, the walls of which were stiffened. The parts of the wing behind the spar were designed in the usual way as an assembly of ribs with fabric covering.

The advantages of stressed skin construction explained here at the outset were not, therefore, the actual reason for going over to metal construction, but the safety requirements of my customer led me to this line of development. Only later experiences showed that metal construction, when used properly in many branches of transport engineering, produces many advantages relative to all other forms of construction.

The assembly was carried out in a similar way to shipbuilding. A succession of frames were joined together by longitudinal stiffeners, and the sheet metal covering was laid over this relatively light framework and attached to the framework with a large number of rivets.

On my first aircraft I had no confidence in riveted joints. With thin metal sheets — mostly only 0.4 to 0.6 mm thick — it was a question of rivets with a diameter of 3 mm on average. As a result, during the assembly, I had one extra rivet put in between each pair. That was lucky for me because, through lack of experience, I had forgotten that the rivets provided by the rivet supplier had to be heat-treated before being driven.

When the aircraft was being inspected by the certificating authority it was proved that the un-heat-treated rivets would not be adequate. As far as they were concerned, I would have to drill the thousands of rivets out again and replace them by heat-treated ones. But tests showed that, by spacing the rivets more closely, adequate strength had been achieved. In later production, I went back to the wider rivet pitch by using properly heat-treated rivets.

One can sense from that description the pleasure that Messerschmitt experienced in being 'one up' on the certifying authorities.

The original version of the M 18 was designed for one pilot and three passengers, yet its all-up weight was only 1030 kg (2270 lb). The prototype was powered by an air-cooled 7-cylinder Sh 11 Siemens-Halske engine giving a nominal 80 hp. It flew for the first time on 15 June 1926 with Croneiss in the pilot's seat, and only six weeks later it was ready to enter service with Croneiss's airline at Fürth, near to Nuremberg.

By the next year an improved version, the M 18b, was being built which carried four passengers in addition to the pilot. The all-up weight had increased to 1200 kg (2645 lb). The engine was now a 9-cylinder Sh 12 with a power of 100 hp. Over the next two years the type was further developed into another 12 versions. One of these was to give Messerschmitt great satisfaction when it was ordered as an aerial photographic aircraft by a Romanian company. That was the first time that he obtained an export order for an aircraft of his design. Other orders followed for versions with bigger engines of up to 300 hp. Most of these were bought by German (including Bavarian) companies, but others were the subject of foreign orders.

With this aircraft Messerschmitt had finally broken into the commercial market. His planes were distinguished by their excellent performance and flying characteristics. They stood up well to the operating conditions in a commercial airline, and the extreme simplicity of Messerschmitt's structural design made them easy and cheap to maintain.

The M 18 was a high-wing monoplane. The details of the wing and fuselage construction have already been given in Messerschmitt's own account of the design and building of the aircraft. The tail surfaces were all made of light alloy with fabric covered control surfaces. Access to the passenger cabin was facilitated by sweeping down the underside of the fuselage close to the ground and thus dispensing with the need for a ladder at the door. The undercarriage was sprung by rubber bungee cords, and only the wheels protruded from the fuselage so that there was no drag from the undercarriage structure itself.

The aircraft were remarkably cheap to operate. The North Bavarian Airline had a fleet consisting exclusively of the M 18. With it they were able to operate profitably by charging only 60 to 70 pfennigs a kilometre, while their competitors were having to demand 2 marks a kilometre, or three times as much, for similar journeys. Later versions of the M 18 had engines of up to 325 hp and could carry eight passengers.

The 'Sachsenflug 1927' (Saxony Flight) was the next major event in the aviation calendar. Messerschmitt determined to design a plane with the object of taking the prize at this event. It was to be the M 19. The 'Sachsenflug' was intended to encourage the construction of small aircraft with a particular emphasis on light structure. Messerschmitt rose brilliantly to this challenge by producing a plane with an empty weight of 140 kg (308 lb) and a payload of 200 kg (440 lb), a ratio of empty weight to payload of only 0.7, a figure which was rarely to be equalled by any designer in the future.

The rules for the competition had been drawn up by the Deutsche Versuchsanstalt für Luftfahrt (German Aeronautical Research Institute). They had laid down what they believed to be extremely stringent conditions for the difference between the empty weight and payload of competing aircraft. Because of the unbelievable achievement in this respect by the M 19, the formula for the technical assessment of the aircraft produced a result of 'infinity' in the case of Messerschmitt's plane, and it had, therefore, already taken the prize of 60,000 marks before the final flight trials had taken place.

In the M 19, Messerschmitt for the first time designed a low-wing monoplane. Instead of following up the success of the M 18 with metal construction, he reverted to an all-wood structure. The wing again had a single spar, by now a Messerschmitt trademark, and a very high aspect ratio betraying the former designer of gliders. The engine was a 2-cylinder Bristol Cherub of 28 hp. Theo Croneiss piloted the aircraft in the flight trials — a mere formality, of course, as the M 19 had already been acknowledged as the clear winner of the competition.

The M 19 was one of Messerschmitt's unadulterated triumphs. It had further enhanced his reputation as an aircraft designer. Moreover, it had gained a considerable amount of prize money for its creator. The whole of the 60,000 marks was to be invested in his aircraft company.

The professional publications of the time gave freely of their praise for the young aeronautical genius. One aviation magazine stated: 'With this aircraft an advance has been achieved which had not been anticipated by anyone.'

All that now hampered Messerschmitt's further development as a leading light in the aviation field was a lack of capital to develop more aircraft. In the mid-1920s, following the lifting of some of the restrictions imposed by the Allies at the end of the Great War, the German government was doing all that it could to promote the regrowth of the aviation industry. Accordingly, Messerschmitt applied to the Bavarian government for a subsidy to finance his future work.

That government's willingness to provide capital for a new aircraft company was somewhat tempered by the unsettled financial climate prevailing at the time. There already was an active aircraft company in Bavaria, the Bayerische Flugzeugwerke (Bavarian Aircraft Works) — more usually referred to as BFW — situated in Augsburg. BFW had for some time been receiving a state subsidy. In the light of the budgetary problems existing at that time, the Bavarian government could not see its way to subsidizing two aircraft companies simultaneously. Accordingly, the proposal was made that Messerschmitt and the BFW should join forces and receive a subsidy for the joint enterprise.

Although Messerschmitt throughout his life preferred to handle his own affairs without being dependent on others, he realized that this proposal offered him the production facilities of a much larger company than his own. He would become the Chief Designer of the new company and a member of the Board of Directors. If he turned the offer down, his future was by no means secure. After careful consideration he put all his misgivings on one side and agreed to enter into negotiations with Bayerische Flugzeugwerke.

The arrangement took place in two separate stages which were covered by two separate agreements between Messerschmitt and BFW. The first of these agreements was signed on 3 June 1927, and it dealt with the conditions under which Messerschmitt would grant a licence to BFW to build the M 18 aircraft. The second agreement, dated 8 September 1927, fixed the conditions for Messerschmitt's future employment as Chief Designer of BFW.

The text of the first agreement, which is preserved in the Imperial War Museum, reveals the profitable bargaining position which Messerschmitt had already established for himself relative to BFW:

Agreement between Bayerische Flugzeugwerke AG, Augsburg (BFW) and Messerschmitt Flugzeugbau GmbH, Bamberg (M)

A. Licensing Agreement

1. BFW will receive and M will make over, whilst refraining from his own building or selling, a licence for the designs produced by M with all rights of construction and sales; M will hand over the working drawings for series production and will undertake to himself support the series production in BFW.

2. BFW will pay to M for each item sold after delivery a licence fee of 3% of the selling price of the airframe. The selling price is understood as excluding any commission paid to retailers and agents. The account will be made up monthly.

3. M will leave it to BFW to handle all the existing contracts and any which come up in the future. The detail parts already manufactured for the former will be taken over by BFW, as will the orders already placed by M for materials for these contracts. The applications already received by M from interested parties for the M 18 and other types will be given to BFW for further handling.

4. All improvements of the individual types designed and manufactured after the conclusion of the agreement will be at the disposal of BFW after compensation of the cost price.

5. Modifications to the design of the individual types may only be undertaken without the approval of M if the German Aeronautical Research

Institute (i.e. the airworthiness authority) expressly demands it.

6. The type designation will be: BFW-M No.... The products will carry on the name plate the designation 'Lizenz Messerschmitt'.

B. Design Agreement

7. M undertakes to take over and carry out the design responsibilities of BFW; BFW undertakes to determine the design parameters with the customers together with M.

8. M is entitled to carry out design activities on his own account or for third parties, but BFW retains in all such cases the right of licensing within the meaning and in accordance with the conditions of the present agreement. If BFW does not wish to make any use of a design which it is offered, M is entitled to make use of it elsewhere; the precondition for this is, however, that these types are essentially different from those built by BFW.

9. The payment for these tasks will be made by reimbursement of authenticated design man-hours and a 100% supplement for expenses. In particular cases a fixed payment can be agreed.

10. For the period of the agreement, BFW possesses the sole rights to the use of patents for the types being built under licence. M undertakes not to release these patents for their outside use by others.

11. BFW accepts a monthly guarantee for design work to the extent of 1000 design man-hours.

C. Experimental Shop and First Prototype

12. BFW will transfer to Herr M personally the independent management of the Experimental and First Prototype Shop for the types of aircraft designed by him for BFW in accordance with Para. 7. This department will be responsible in a commercial respect directly to the management of BFW; the wage scale and engineering organization will be in accordance with that for the whole company. The work to be done in the Experimental Shop will be defined by agreement between BFW and Herr M.

D. General Conditions

13. For the first adoption of the licence for the M 18, BFW will pay to M the difference in the balance of the Messerschmitt GmbH company determined on the day of the adoption, but not exceeding the total of 66,000 Reichsmarks. Instead of the full or partial cash payment, BFW reserves the possibility of taking over the liabilities of M to a corresponding amount.

14. BFW will lease to M the rooms situated on the first floor of the design

building at a price of 325 marks a month and will allow M the shared use of the printroom against payment of the prime costs.

15. The available jigs of any sort for the series production of the M 18 and the existing workshop fixtures of M will be taken over by BFW up to a total value of 10,000 marks.

16. The stocks of material and partly finished components will be taken over by BFW at the value determined on the day of acceptance and paid for in cash.

17. The period of the agreement is set at five years; the agreement will run tacitly for a further three years if notice is not given by a registered letter three months before the expiry by one of the parties.

18. Any differences arising from this agreement will be decided by a court of arbitration without the right of appeal, to which each of the parties will send a representative who in turn will select a chairman. If the arbiters cannot agree about that person, the President of the Chamber of Industry and Commerce of Augsburg will be consulted about the nomination.

Augsburg, 3 June 1927.

The final contract which Messerschmitt and BFW ultimately signed on 8 September of the same year runs to no less than 11 pages. In the main it recapitulates the terms already contained in the earlier agreement.

In brief, Messerschmitt undertakes to act as designer for BFW. He agrees to support BFW as an adviser and to put all his acquired experience at the disposal of BFW. He agrees to move to Augsburg and to set up his design office in the BFW factory in rooms for which he will pay a monthly rent of 325 Reichsmarks, including heating and lighting. In similar terms to those used in the licensing agreement, he is also allowed to use the printroom on payment of the cost price of materials.

BFW, on its part, guarantees to provide Messerschmitt with a minimum of 3000 Reichsmarks' worth of design work a month. Where it is necessary for agreeing the technical specification of design work and 'where this is possible without undue expenditure of time and money', Messerschmitt has the right to take part in laying down the technical requirements with the customer. Messerschmitt himself will be paid 1000 Reichsmarks per month. BFW also undertakes to pay Messerschmitt a premium for every aircraft of his design which is sold. The amount depends on the number sold.

A table in the contract lays down the scale of payments involved. For each type of aircraft that he designs, Messerschmitt gets 4% of the first 100,000 Rm of sales. This amount reduces by 0.25% for each succeeding 100,000 Rm, bottoming out at only 2% for the ninth to fifteenth amounts of 100,000 Rm. After that, Messerschmitt receives no further premiums from BFW.

If a design should fail to sell or could only be sold at a price which did not cover the design and construction costs, the losses are to be shared between BFW and Messerschmitt. An insurance fund is to be set up to cover Messerschmitt's costs from any eventual failures of this sort.

A clause in the agreement which was to cause ill-feeling much later was the one concerning payment for the use of Messerschmitt's patent rights and licensing agreements. Messerschmitt was still unhappy about the way in which his rights had been treated when the Second World War was drawing to a close. At that later date he found it necessary to employ a lawyer to establish his rights in the matter.

A formal declaration of common interest was finally signed on 8 September 1927. Messerschmitt signed twice, once as a private individual and once on behalf of Messerschmitt Flugzeugbau GmbH. It must have appeared to Messerschmitt as if everything was now moving steadily in the direction that he most desired. He had a well-paid position of considerable prestige in an established company. Moreover, he was free to design whatever he thought fit within reason to meet the requirements of the market. He was as yet still very young and filled with enthusiasm for aviation and everything connected with it. He had now no shortage of opportunities to demonstrate his talents to a wider audience, at home in Germany and abroad. He must have felt as though the future was beckoning him to higher things in more senses than one.

CHAPTER 5

The M 20 civil aircraft

Following the signing of the agreement with BFW, Messerschmitt was able to assume the reins of power in a substantial aircraft company. At the age of 29, only four years after graduating from the Technische Hochschule in Munich, and with only four years of experience as an aircraft manufacturer, he had become Chief Designer and director of an established, if somewhat minor, aircraft company.

Messerschmitt had by this time attracted the attention of the German Ministry of Transport. Deutsche Lufthansa had now been established as the national airline, and there was a need for a civil aircraft capable of carrying eight to ten passengers, or a payload of 1000 kg (2205 lb). It is indicative of Messerschmitt's growing prestige in the civil aircraft world that he was given the contract to design an aircraft to fit the new role.

Work on the design of what was to be the M 20 started during the second half of 1927. Messerschmitt took the basic layout of the M 18d as the starting point for his new design and fitted a BMW engine of 500 hp. Unfortunately, despite the fact that the aircraft was eventually successful in service, the M 20 was to prove one of the worst experiences of Willy Messerschmitt's life as a designer; and its after-effects were to follow him down the years, as will be revealed later.

The first flight took place on 26 February 1928. The attachment of the covering to the wing cannot have been up to standard because, during the flight, some fabric tore off the trailing edge of the mainplane. Alarmed by the sound of tearing fabric, and fearing a major structural failure, the pilot reacted precipitately and abandoned the aircraft. He made use of his parachute, but the aircraft crashed and was completely destroyed.

Considerably disturbed by this apparent demonstration of a lack of structural integrity, Lufthansa cancelled the order which they had already placed for two aircraft of the type.

The second aircraft, the M 20, made a completely uneventful first flight on 3 August 1928 and, as a result, successfully passed its certification tests and was cleared for airline operation. Lufthansa then reinstated the order for two aircraft which were delivered in 1929. Further orders from Lufthansa followed.

In the early part of 1928, the Bavarian government, and indeed the German Ministry of Transport, was being subjected to criticism because of the size of its investment in the aircraft industry. So it decided to sell its shareholding in BFW. Messerschmitt could not afford to purchase all of the shares himself and was compelled to look around for financial assistance. Luckily, since his early days in Bamberg he had been acquainted with the wealthy Michel-Raulino family who had made a great deal of money from newspapers and tobacco. One of the daughters of the family, Baroness Lilly von Michel-Raulino, had taken an interest in Messerschmitt's activities from the beginning of his career.

Just after World War I, Lilly had married Otto Stromeyer, a member of a family of entrepreneurs in Konstanz. Together they invested in promising commercial enterprises, and are sometimes referred to in books about Messerschmitt's aircraft as the 'Stromeyer-Raulino financial group'. Messerschmitt succeeded in convincing them that his company was a good investment. He himself purchased 12.5% of the BFW shares, whilst a group made up of Lilly, her relations and Herr Stromeyer bought the remaining 87.5%.

From then on, Lilly, who showed every evidence of possessing a keen business brain and who later became a member of the board of management of his company, acted as an adviser to Messerschmitt until the end of her life.

In the late 1920s the Stromeyers were divorced and Lilly later reverted to her maiden name. She became Messerschmitt's close companion for the remainder of their lives. Messerschmitt never had any children of his own, but his nephews and nieces always referred to Baroness von Michel-Raulino as 'Aunt Lilly'. He clearly felt bound to her by a debt of gratitude for the help which she had given to him at some of the most critical stages of his career.

Messerschmitt's indebtedness to the Baroness von Michel-Raulino is clearly shown in the minutes of a Board meeting held in 1937 to discuss the sharing of the profits deriving from licensing agreements among the shareholders in the company. Although Messerschmitt by that time owned 70% of the shares and Baroness von Michel-Raulino only 30%, Messerschmitt had insisted that he should receive only 60% of the profits and she 40%. This was queried at the meeting, and the minutes record that:

> As regards Frau Stromeyer, Herr Messerschmitt wanted to make it clear that, in recognition of the many years of co-operation and support which she had given him in times of the deepest crisis, he wanted her to share to the same degree in the better results which were expected, the more so because she had received no interest whatever on a sum of about one million Reichsmarks.

Messerschmitt and Lilly eventually married in 1952 when he was 54 and she was 61. Why they delayed so long before entering into a marriage which they had both obviously long desired is one of the mysteries of Messerschmitt's life. But that was still in the future.

The new Board of Directors of BFW took over the running of the company on 1 July 1928. Otto Stromeyer was made Chairman of the Board, whilst the management of the day-to-day affairs of the company was shared by Messerschmitt and Fritz Hille.

After trials with the second surviving prototype, Lufthansa were eventually so satisfied with the performance of the M 20 in service, that in 1929 they placed an order for ten more aircraft of a developed type — the M 20b — which were all to be delivered over the next three years.

It appeared that BFW were well on the way to success. Orders for other light aircraft had been received and the Design Office was fully loaded with work on a number of aircraft simultaneously. In fact, it was soon to become obvious that the company had taken on more work than it could handle. The outgoings on materials for the new aircraft were more than the company could finance successfully. This state of affairs could not continue for long before severe financial problems were bound to appear. The company was suffering from what would today be called a cash-flow problem.

The final blow was the loss of two of Lufthansa's M 20b aircraft in unexplained crashes. At the time the managing director of Lufthansa was Erhard Milch, and these failures did little to improve Milch's opinion of Messerschmitt. He was convinced that Messerschmitt habitually designed his aircraft with little regard for structural integrity in the hope of saving the last ounce of weight. Whether Milch's opinion was correct or not is a matter for some debate. There is evidence that Messerschmitt always cut the structural weight of his aircraft down to the very minimum acceptable for the maintenance of adequate structural strength, but so does every other designer of efficient aircraft.

The science of calculating the loads in an aircraft structure was not so advanced in the 1920s as it has since become. As a result the load in any single item of the structure was not known with any great accuracy. There was, of course, an overall factor of safety to allow for discrepancies between the actual state of affairs and the calculations, but any designer was likely to find himself very close to the acceptable limits if he tried to cut the weight of the structure down to the absolute minimum as Messerschmitt always did.

If a serious error was made, the result might be the failure of the main wing spar, with catastrophic results for the aircraft and its occupants. In the case of the M 20 the initial structural failure had been minor, involving only the attachment of the fabric to the wing structure. The results of the two subsequent failures, however, were to have a dramatic effect on the career of Willy Messerschmitt. Henceforth, Milch was to have little regard for Messerschmitt's talents as a designer, and before long he would be able to exert a great and malign influence on Messerschmitt's fortunes.

BFW's financial difficulties were soon apparent for all to see, including the directors of Lufthansa. The final blow fell when the airline cancelled its order for the M 20b and demanded the return of the deposits which it had paid — money which the company did not have available.

The company results for 1930 showed a loss of 600,000 Reichsmarks, and there was no alternative but to declare the company bankrupt. The terms of Messerschmitt's memorandum of understanding with BFW allowed him to extricate his design team intact from the ruins of the larger company, whilst retaining his rights to the designs and patents on his inventions. Messerschmitt was compelled to sell his car to pay off the more pressing creditors, and he determined to satisfy the remainder rather than go into bankruptcy himself. In this he was eventually successful.

A legal battle ensued in which Messerschmitt was supported by Baroness von Michel-Raulino. They, in conjunction with the official receiver, were able to compel Lufthansa to reinstate the order for the M 20b. Work had also been progressing on the design and construction of the M 28, ordered by Lufthansa for use as a high-speed postal aircraft, and the airline was forced to honour its order for the prototype of that aircraft also.

As a result of all this legal manoeuvring, the official receiver reached an agreement with the creditors of BFW. The bankruptcy was not finally discharged until April 1933 when the company was free to resume operations. A secondary effect of this enforced settlement with Lufthansa was the increased animosity of Erhard Milch, which was to have such an adverse influence on Messerschmitt's career during the war years.

In the end, Lufthansa were very satisfied with the service provided by the M 20. The fleet of aircraft were all given the names of regions of Germany, and they formed the backbone of Lufthansa's internal routes for many years. So successful were these machines that six M 20s were still in service with Lufthansa in 1942. The last of them was destroyed in an Allied air attack in 1943.

Once again the success of the machine was due to the Messerschmitt design philosophy of 'light and simple'. The payload to empty weight ratio was not as startling as that for the M 19 but was still a highly respectable 1.18, a figure which was unrivalled by any commercial aircraft of the same size at the time. With a maximum speed of 220 kph (136 mph) and a cruising speed of 180 kph (112 mph) from a 500 hp BMW engine, the M 20 outperformed all its competitors at the time that it entered service.

While the arguments with Lufthansa regarding the fate of the M 20 were still going on, the Aviation Department of the German Ministry of Defence approached Messerschmitt to see whether he would be interested in designing for them a military aircraft. They were having a certain amount of difficulty in getting co-operation from some of the longer-established German aircraft constructors and were hoping for a more compliant attitude from a relatively new and inexperienced designer. The Ministry were hoping to order two aircraft, the first a two-seat trainer and the other a bomber. Messerschmitt, ever ready for a new challenge, agreed to design both aircraft.

It is extremely surprising that both the two-seat trainer, designated the M 21, and the bomber, known as the M 22, were biplanes — the only biplanes that Messerschmitt ever designed. Neither was successful. It is something of a puzzle as to why Messerschmitt at that stage of his career should have abandoned all his principles in favour of a layout which he had completely rejected until then. All of his early experience in gliders had led him to believe in the superiority of high aspect ratio mono-planes. Possibly the pundits in the Air Ministry insisted that the aircraft had to be biplanes in common with most of the aircraft in service with the German Air Force at that time. Although prototypes of both aircraft were built, no orders for them were forthcoming.

Even before the near disaster with the M 20, Messerschmitt had turned his attention again to a sporting aircraft capable of winning the top prizes in a major flying competition. The new aircraft was the M 23, a classic design of exceptionally clean lines with outstanding performance. The first version of the M 23 was displayed at the Paris salon in July 1928, where it created a great impression.

Messerschmitt was soon at work developing the aircraft for more powerful engines. The M 23a with an ABC Scorpion II engine of 34 hp was ready in time for the Berlin International Air Show in October 1928, where it attracted great interest because of its compact shape and gener-ally eye-catching appearance. A third version fitted with an Armstrong Siddeley 'Genet' 5-cylinder radial engine of 90 hp was delivered to the DVL (German Aeronautical Research Institute) for testing to assess its capabilities for the 'East Prussia Flight 1928/29'.

With Theo Croneiss again at the controls, the M 23a was the winner of that competition, including a three-day long distance flight which lasted from 3 to 5 March 1929. The aircraft attracted so much attention by its success in that competition and by its excellent aerobatic capabilities that limited production was started which lasted until the middle of 1929.

By then, Messerschmitt had come up with an improved model which was to become the definitive version of the aircraft, namely the M 23b. This was fitted with a German engine, the Siemens 5-cylinder radial with an output of 80 hp. Five aircraft of this type were entered for the 'International European Flight of 1929'. The overall winner was Fritz Morzik in the M 23b with registration D-1673.

Also in 1929, Willi Stoer bought an M 23b which he entered for the German Aerobatic Championship of that year. He came second in the contest, and went on to appearances with his aircraft at other leading air displays.

All of this favourable publicity was attracting more attention to Messerschmitt's abilities as a designer, and more orders for the M 23b were not long in coming. Nor was he slow in improving the design of his aircraft. In later years he was known as an adept in designing aircraft which were capable of continual development as better engines became available to power them. The Bf 109 fighter was the prime example of this, but early signs of the same philosophy were already obvious in the M 23 series.

For the 1930 competition season Messerschmitt produced the M 23c. It differed from the M 23b in having an enclosed cockpit and a more powerful engine, either the 110 hp Argus As 8 4-cylinder in-line engine or the 150 hp Siemens Sh 14a 7-cylinder radial. The demand for these aircraft for the 'Round Europe Flight' of 1930 was so large that BFW in Augsburg had to lay down ten aircraft at the same time.

Messerschmitt decided on some basic modifications. Because of the requirement to install the new Argus As 8 engine of 110 hp, and the emphasis placed in the competition rules on an 'enclosed pilot and passenger station', he designed the front part of the fuselage as a riveted dural structure and provided both seats with a glazed cabin roof. In addition, the vertical and horizontal stabilizers were rounded-off to a more aesthetic shape than the severe rectangular shapes that he had used earlier.

The previous year's winner, Fritz Morzik, again took the overall prize by a brilliant performance which combined the best of piloting with the best aircraft. As a result the sporting aviation world was further reinforced in its opinion that Messerschmitt was the best constructor of sporting aircraft in Europe. His M 23 was operated as a training and aerobatic aircraft not only in Germany, but also, for example, in Brazil, Austria, Romania, Switzerland and Spain.

There were some design problems on the way to this success. It was found that at high angles of attack there was unpleasant buffeting of the tailplane. The vibration of the tail unit was sometimes so violent that it gave cause for concern regarding the strength of the tail structure and the rear fuselage. A series of extended flight tests carried out by the German Institute for Aeronautical Research showed that this was the result of the tailplane being in a vortex caused by separation of the air flow on the upper surface of the wing at high wing incidences. The problem was finally cured by fitting a fairing at the wing to fuselage junction which delayed the separation of the flow.

The first fairing which was fitted eliminated the tail unit buffet, but it was very difficult to manufacture. Indeed, its manufacture proved so expensive that it was unlikely to find wide acceptance among owners of the aircraft. An improved design of fairing was produced by Professor Madelung of Stuttgart — the husband of Messerschmitt's younger sister. This family co-operative venture constituted the final solution to the problem. The test reports stated that the influence of the fairing on the flight performance of the test aircraft was small and, indeed, fell within the limits of accuracy of the measurements.

As a result of its excellent design and outstanding performance, the M 23 proved to be Messerschmitt's most successful design to date. Among the satisfied customers who purchased the aircraft was Rudolf Hess, a close friend of Messerschmitt and one who would be of great help to him in the years ahead.

Messerschmitt's achievements in the design of such successful aircraft over those few years are made the more remarkable by the fact that the threat of bankruptcy was hanging over the BFW company for the whole of the time involved.

CHAPTER 6

Further successes with light aircraft

As was noted earlier, there had been no official course in aircraft design in the Technische Hochschule of Munich at the time when Messerschmitt graduated. All of the professional knowledge was held by the few engineers actually engaged in aircraft construction.

By the end of the 1920s, universities were coming to the view that aeronautics was a legitimate branch of engineering. They would need to offer courses to train the designers and technicians required by the coming expansion of the aircraft industry. Suitably experienced staff could only be found among the ranks of the most gifted exponents of the art of aeronautics. Among these was Messerschmitt.

In 1930 he was offered a lectureship in aeronautics by his *alma mater*, the Technische Hochschule of Munich. He accepted with gratitude this recognition of his experience and knowledge of aeronautics. It was only seven years since he had graduated from the same institution, which at that time did not even offer a course in aircraft design. The offer of a lectureship by the university is an indication of the standing which he had managed to achieve in a remarkably short time as a practical aircraft designer. The class lists for Messerschmitt's lectures are preserved in the Imperial War Museum. It is interesting to note that the name of Claudius Dornier, the son of the founder of the famous German firm of aircraft builders, appears in one of them, as do many other future prominent figures in the German aircraft industry.

The teaching post was only a part-time occupation, and work on designing further new aircraft continued as Messerschmitt's main interest in life. During the bankruptcy proceedings which would decide the future of BFW, Messerschmitt continued to design light aircraft with the intention of gaining more prestigious prizes in international air competitions. The M 27 monoplane was a developed version of the M 23b and it was again characterized by its extremely light structure combined with rugged design. Despite the fact that it won the Deutschland Competition and obtained second place in the race around the

Zugspitze, it only went into limited production.

A more successful design was the M 29, a two-seater sporting machine. This was an aircraft whose elegant appearance is still outstanding today. It was designed for the Round Europe Flight of 1932. As soon as the aircraft appeared it was acknowledged as the favourite for the competition. Its technical refinement was widely admired, and the standard of workmanship employed in its construction was considered to be beyond comparison. The M 29 flew for the first time on 13 April 1932. Six aircraft were ready for entry in the competition by August.

One notable innovation which distinguished it from earlier aircraft was the cantilever streamlined undercarriage. Messerschmitt had always been concerned by the drag produced by the undercarriage structure needed to support the wheels. The cantilever design eliminated the need for a network of struts for that purpose. But it involved some new problems in the design of the structure of the aircraft, since all the undercarriage loads entered the wing at one point instead of being distributed over a number of attachments.

The enclosed cockpits were covered by perspex-type panels, and because of the careful design to reduce drag to a minimum and the excellent finish incorporated during the construction, the M 29 achieved a top speed of 260 kph (161 mph) with its 150 hp engine. Its outstanding aerodynamic design, including the use of large flaps and slots, gave it a landing speed of only 65 kph (40 mph). The result was a ratio of maximum speed to landing speed of four to one, which at that time had never before been achieved.

Messerschmitt himself always regarded the M 29 as a significant milestone in his advancement as an aircraft designer. It was to the experience gained in its design and construction that he attributed a large part of his success with the Me 109 fighter. In the lecture which he gave to the German Academy of Aeronautical Research on 26 November 1937 he made clear his indebtedness to the knowledge that he gained from his work on the M 29:

> I attempted in 1932 to produce an aircraft which was as fast as possible: a two-seater light aircraft with an engine power of only 150 hp and a landing speed of only 65 kph [40 mph], which, however, by careful forming of its shape and surface finish, by using wings with slotted flaps and, for the first time, a cantilever-leg undercarriage, attained a speed in horizontal flight of 260 kph [161 mph] despite its low landing speed. I learned a great deal from this aircraft that I could use very profitably later for the design of fighter aircraft.

In the event, the M 29 was not able to take part in the Round Europe Flight because two of the aircraft were involved in unexplained accidents, and the aircraft is mainly interesting because it was a direct ancestor of the future Bf 108 Taifun and the Bf 109 fighter.

The Nazi party finally came to power in Germany in 1933. This was not entirely an advantage for Messerschmitt. Erhard Milch who had been Managing Director of Lufthansa during the preceding negotiations regarding the bankruptcy of BFW, and who was far from being a friend of Messerschmitt, now came into a position of great power as Secretary of State for Air in the Nazi government. Goering had a very high regard for Milch's abilities as an organizer and as a judge of aircraft. In his new appointment Milch had the responsibility for allocating design and manufacturing contracts to industrial organizations. From the experience which he had gained from his earlier encounters with Messerschmitt, Milch was determined that the young designer would never design aircraft for the Luftwaffe. He made every endeavour to limit BFW to the manufacture of other designers' aircraft in a sub-contracting role.

But not all of the new circumstances were disadvantageous to Messerschmitt. One of his closest personal friends, the World War I fighter ace, Ernst Udet, had also reached a position of great authority. By 1936 he would advance to the position of head of the Technical Office of the Air Ministry, a body which had a decisive influence in determining the aircraft to be ordered for quantity production. His influence on such decisions was to be exceeded only by that of Goering and Milch. Unfortunately, although he had himself designed and built a number of successful sporting aircraft, Udet's judgement was badly flawed. Because of his limited experience during the war — which was confined to fighters — he was mainly interested in fighter aircraft; neglecting completely to provide the Luftwaffe with heavy bombers. This was to prove a costly error of judgement for the future operations of the Luftwaffe.

By the time that the Nazi party had taken over power in Germany, BFW had been salvaged from bankruptcy. Messerschmitt had established himself as its manager in co-operation with a very capable engineer, Rakan Kokothaki, who was to be associated closely with Messerschmitt until the debacle of 1945 when the German aircraft industry ceased to exist. The total number of employees of the reformed Bayerische Flugzeugwerke AG was only 82, but it was a start.

Looking back some years later, Messerschmitt regarded the rise to power of the National Socialist Party as the foundation of his success as an aircraft designer and manufacturer. During a lecture which he gave in 1941 he summarized his view of events as follows:

> Until 1933 it was a very miserable life working in aviation. Much experience could not be evaluated. It stayed in the heads of a few people and remained as unrealized projects. This impossibility of developing ideas was more oppressive than the lack of commercial success. There is probably no branch of engineering which must be as thankful to our leader Adolf Hitler and our Generalfeldmarschall Goering, as we aircraft engineers. It is to them that we owe the great expansion of aviation in Germany. Only through their methodical support was it possible in a few years not only to catch up on the advances abroad but to bring Germany, in almost all branches of aeronautics, to the head of all countries.

In view of the rapid intended build-up of the Luftwaffe, it was not in Milch's interest, in spite of his aversion to Messerschmitt, to neglect the manufacturing capabilities of BFW. As a result, contracts were allotted for the manufacture under licence of Dornier Do 11s and Heinkel He 45s. These orders at least provided useful profits for BFW and enabled it to re-establish itself as a sound financial enterprise. Milch had no power to prevent Messerschmitt from designing aircraft at his own risk for sale on the private market. He was only able to impede him from obtaining government contracts for the design of military aircraft. Whether Milch's baleful regard affected Messerschmitt's design abilities is doubtful. However, in the next year or two no outstanding aircraft of his design issued from the Augsburg factory.

The Ministry of Transport then offered Messerschmitt a contract to design a two-seater biplane training aircraft. The project was given the official designation of M 32, but Messerschmitt could never take any interest in designing biplanes. After some initial sketching of ideas, the project was abandoned. This was followed by what was probably the most bizarre design ever to emanate from Messerchmitt's brain. Dr Porsche had just developed the 'People's Car' the descendants of which, the Volkswagens, are still a common sight on our roads today. Possibly inspired by this venture, Messerschmitt was soon working on the design of a 'People's Aeroplane' which was given the type designation M 33.

The M 33 was an aircraft reduced to its simplest possible form. The high wing supported what can only be described as a gondola which housed the pilot and the engine of only 15 hp. The airscrew was mounted above the wing, and this arrangement necessitated a drive mechanism using gears. The tail unit was attached to the wing by a steel tube projecting from the trailing edge. A flying prototype was never completed. The design proceeded only as far as a mock-up, which presumably was scrapped at the latter end of 1933.

It was in 1933 that Messerschmitt became a member of the NSDAP, the National Socialist German Workers' Party. In the information which he was compelled to provide on his appointment as a professor at Munich University in 1937, he had to quote all details of his membership of political parties. Membership of communist organizations or other parties unacceptable to the Nazi government would have debarred him from holding a post in a teaching establishment. The form which he completed to satisfy the political requirements and to establish his non-Jewish ancestry also included the information on his parentage which was quoted in Chapter 1 of this book.

Under the heading of 'Summary of membership of the NSDAP, its branches, associated groups, etc.' Messerschmitt quoted:

NSDAP: 1 May 1933
        Membership No. 342354
SS: Corresponding member ('fördendes Mitglied') since 2 March 1932
DAF (German Labour Front): Yes, since 30 December 1933
NS-Bund Deutscher Technik (National Socialist Association of German Engineers): Since 1 July 1937

Reichsluftschutzbund (State Air Defence Association): Yes, Membership No. 117 717
NSV (National Socialist People's Welfare Organization): Yes.
Sports clubs: German/Austrian Alpine Association since 1 January 1937

One party organization which Messerschmitt does not mention in the above list is the NSFK, the Nationalsozialistisches Fliegerkorps, a branch of the NSDAP for those involved in aviation matters. He must have joined the NSFK after he had provided the information quoted earlier, because in April 1945 he received a letter from a man named Braun in NSFK Gruppe 14 (Hochland), who signed himself as 'NSFK Obergruppenführer'. The letter, which congratulates Messerschmitt on the award of the Knight's Cross with Swords, is addressed to 'NSFK-Brigadeführer Prof. Messerschmitt'.

Messerschmitt was probably enrolled into the NSDAP by his close acquaintances, Theo Croneiss and Rudolf Hess. Croneiss had a high position in the Party as a Brigade Leader in the SA. Hess had almost the highest status of all, being officially recognized as Hitler's deputy.

Anyone who hoped to attain to high position in Hitler's Germany found it an advantage to belong to the National Socialist Party. Such members may or may not have supported all of the less desirable activities of the party. In this respect, it is remarkable that Messerschmitt joined the party at such an early date as 1933. What is even more surprising is his statement that he had supported the SS since March 1932. This militates somewhat against the idea that he only joined the party as a form of protection for his position in the then existing form of German society. It suggests rather that he had at least a limited sympathy with Hitler's wider aims.

There is no doubt that Messerschmitt was a nationalist. Like many Germans of his generation, he deeply resented what he saw as the injustice imposed on his country by the Treaty of Versailles. It is obvious from his writings that he had a life-long ambition to restore Germany to its rightful place in the world. He was also a socialist. His praise of Theo Croneiss in the funeral oration which he gave for his dead colleague, paid more attention to the work done by Croneiss in providing his workers with decent living conditions than with any of the less attractive Nazi activities. Messerschmitt was also proud of the welfare services provided for workers in the Messerschmitt factories. He attributed their efficiency to the system inaugurated by the Nazi government.

Whether the combination of nationalism and socialism in Messerschmitt's make-up adds up to national-socialism with all its evil connotations is doubtful to say the least. Messerschmitt's attitude to life and his fellow men was far removed from the brutalities perpetrated by the staunch supporters of Hitler's plans for the supremacy of the Aryan master race.

All in all, Messerschmitt must have regarded the rise to power of Hitler as a benefit to his own ambitions. There was now no doubt that extensive rearmament of Germany was going to take place. That must provide opportunities for the aircraft industry. Sooner or later he would be sure to obtain a profitable contract for some military aircraft, and he was ready for the challenge.

Meanwhile, Messerschmitt's next venture was another fully aerobatic sporting aircraft — the M 35. It was regarded as one of the most successful aerobatic aircraft ever produced. Based on developments of the M 27, it incorporated the cantilever undercarriage leg first used on the M 29. Its handling characteristics were exemplary, and it soon became a favourite with pilots who wanted an agile but easily controllable machine.

As might be expected, the low monoplane wing was of single spar construction. The fuselage was made of welded steel tube with a wooden tailplane covered in plywood. The powerplant was a 150 hp Siemens SH 14a engine which gave a top speed of 230 kph (143 mph). In all, 15 M 35s were completed, and they were soon winning prizes at aviation meetings all over Europe.

The M 35 was to prove another link between Messerschmitt and his friend Rudolf Hess. In 1934 Hess won the Zugspitz Trophy in the M 35. In the following year Messerschmitt's own works pilot, Willi Stör, won the German aerobatic championships in an M 35, and repeated the achievement in 1936. The experience that Messerschmitt acquired on the M 35 was a further contributing factor to the success of the Bf 109.

Despite his many achievements in the field of sporting aircraft design, Messerschmitt was still regarded with some suspicion by government circles in Germany. There was still a long way to go before he was accepted as a member of the aeronautical establishment.

He was presented with an opportunity to change the course of his career in 1934. The University of Danzig offered him the post of Professor of Aeronautics. Acceptance would release him from all the problems associated with his efforts to establish himself as a leading figure in the German aircraft industry. His first instinct was to accept the offer. It was flattering to be considered as capable of heading a university department teaching aircraft design to the next generation of aeronautical engineers.

Messerschmitt contacted officials in the Air Ministry to ascertain whether he had a future in the German aircraft industry. The reply must have hurt him since it indicated that he was not highly regarded as a designer and would do better to accept the teaching post being offered to him. Luckily for the future Luftwaffe and, no doubt, to the chagrin of Milch, Messerschmitt's friends convinced him that he had a future as an aircraft designer. He turned down the offer from Danzig.

Messerschmitt's differences of opinion with Erhard Milch were soon to have more positive results for the designer's future career. Because of his inability to obtain any significant contracts from the Air Ministry or the state airline, Lufthansa, Messerschmitt was compelled to look for orders from abroad. In June 1933, his fellow director, Rakan Kokothaki, was sent to Bucharest to enter into negotiations regarding a civil airliner for use by the Romanian state airline. Kokothaki was successful in his dealings because he returned with a contract to build a small transport aircraft powered by a Gnome-Rhone Jupiter radial engine of French manufacture.

The project was allotted the number M 36, and design of the new aircraft proceeded very rapidly. One aircraft was built in Germany and operated by the Romanian state airline. So successful did the performance of the aircraft appear to the Romanians that they decided to buy the design from Messerschmitt there and then.

This success in obtaining a foreign contract produced a sour reaction from German officialdom. The Technical Office of the Air Ministry complained in no uncertain terms that Messerschmitt should be designing aircraft for the Luftwaffe instead of wasting his undoubted abilities in providing aircraft for foreign governments. This was the opportunity for which Messerschmitt had been waiting to enable him to counter the adverse influence of Milch. He pointed out forcibly that, as he was unable to obtain contracts from his own government, he had no alternative but to seek contracts abroad to avoid having to put his design department out of business.

It was probably this state of affairs which led to Messerschmitt being invited to submit a design for the projected new single-seat fighter for the Luftwaffe, despite the misgivings of Milch. In the meantime, however, Messerschmitt was to produce another outstandingly successful design, examples of which are still flying today. This was the M 37, later to be renamed the Bf 108 Taifun.

At about the same time, Messerschmitt was to take into his employ an outstanding aircraft designer whose name is almost unknown today, even in professional aeronautical circles. He was Robert Lusser, who had started his design career with the Klemm company. Later he moved on to Heinkel where he was involved in fighter design. Design at Heinkel's was almost entirely in the hands of the Günter brothers, and Lusser's talents posed too much of a threat to their domination. As a result Lusser moved on to Messerschmitt in 1933, arriving just in time to become involved in the design of the M 37.

In a field like aircraft design, which depends so much on teamwork by a collection of experts, it is difficult to allot responsibilities for individual aspects of any aircraft to a particular designer. No doubt Lusser made a significant contribution to the design of the M 37, but it is hard to find any evidence to justify the statement made by Rudiger Kosin in his book, *The German Fighter Since 1915*, that Lusser arrived at BFW 'just in time to design the Bf 108 (M 37) for the round-Europe flight of 1934'. There are too many features of the M 37 which bear the hallmark of Messerschmitt design for there to be any doubt about who was the prime progenitor of the overall concept.

After leaving Messerschmitt, Lusser went on to Fieseler where he designed the V 1 flying bomb. He will appear again later in Chapter 16 on the occasion when Messerschmitt sought to intervene in Lusser's activities on that project.

The immediate incentive which led to the design of the M 37 was the Challenge de Tourisme Internationale race of 1934. Messerschmitt had now behind him all the experience that he had gained in the design of the M 19, M 23, M 27, M 31 and M 35. The expertise in aerodynamic design which he had accumulated was now to be combined with a new venture in structural design. For the first time in a Messerschmitt design, the whole of the structure of the aircraft was to be made of metal sheet, with no recourse to wood or steel tube.

Another innovation was to be the introduction of a retractable under-carriage as a means of reducing the drag. The wing was once again of single-spar construction. A short centre-section was made integral with the fuselage, and the wings were cantilevered out from that. Leading-edge slats were again used to improve the stalling characteristics. The fuselage offered accommodation for a crew of four, a pilot and co-pilot sharing dual controls, with two passengers behind. At the rear of the passenger compartment was an ample luggage stowage space. The cabin was completely enclosed, a novel feature for the time.

The new aircraft flew for the first time in June 1934. On its first appear-ance it was accepted by all observers as a remarkable step forward in air-craft design. Its elegant lines and sleek appearance left no doubt as to the advance that Messerschmitt had made. Its handling characteristics appealed to pilots who found it extremely responsive to the controls. The slotted wing produced a low landing speed whilst the 225 hp Hirth engine with its three-bladed propeller gave a top speed of 300 kph (186 mph).

In order to clear up any confusion regarding the correct designation of the M 37, now is the time to report that the German Air Ministry at about this juncture was in the process of introducing a completely new system of identifying aircraft. Aircraft designed by BFW would in future be allo-cated the letters Bf. The M 37 was, therefore, renamed the Bf 108. (Further confusion would arise later when Messerschmitt aircraft were given the designation Me before their type number. That is the reason why the famous fighter had, at different times, the designations Bf 109 and Me 109.)

In 1935 a well-known German lady pilot, Elly Beinhorn, made the round trip to Istanbul and back in one day in a Bf 108 which she had named 'Taifun' — Typhoon. So attractive did this name appear for the fast new aircraft that it was subsequently adopted for all aircraft of the type.

Messerschmitt, never satisfied with his aircraft, was soon at work introducing modifications to improve the type. A more powerful Siemens Sh 14A engine was fitted and the tail skid was replaced by a tailwheel. By then Messerschmitt's applications for patents on variable pitch propellers show his interest in extracting more performance from an aircraft by this means. An Argus type of variable pitch airscrew was soon available as a standard fit on the Bf 108.

During the late 1930s the Bf 108 scored a number of successes in international competitions within Europe and further afield. The Luftwaffe made use of the aircraft in a variety of roles ranging from target towing to communication duties. Production of the Bf 108 continued for some years after the war ended. In France they were renamed the Nord 1000 and put into production for the French Air Force.

The Bf 108 was without doubt Messerschmitt's most successful civil aircraft, and can with justification be regarded as the forerunner of all modern light aircraft. It had pioneered all-metal construction, the retractable undercarriage, the enclosed cockpit and a standard of handling which placed it far in advance of any of its rivals at the time of its first appearance.

In order to correct one false statement which is sometimes advanced: the success of the Bf 108 could not have been the reason why Messerschmitt was entrusted with the design of the Luftwaffe's new high-speed fighter, the Bf 109. At the time that he was first involved in developing the 109, the Bf 108 had not yet flown.

CHAPTER 7

The fastest fighter in the world

There can be no doubt that the Bf 109 fighter was Messerschmitt's most successful aircraft. It was certainly the aircraft which made his name a household word, not only in Germany but all over the world. However, the circumstances under which Messerschmitt secured the contract to build the Bf 109 are not clear even today, and probably never will be fully explained.

In 1934 the Nazi government of Germany no longer made any secret of the fact that they intended to build up a new Luftwaffe which would at least deter other European powers from interfering with Hitler's plans for expansion. The standard German fighters of the time were still old-fashioned biplanes, and a new generation of aircraft was needed to establish German superiority in the air. In particular, there was a need for a fast fighter aircraft which could protect the German homeland from attack by enemy bombers.

The specification for the new single-seat high-speed fighter with which the new Luftwaffe was to be equipped was issued in 1934. German fighters had traditionally been supplied by the Heinkel, Arado and Focke-Wulf companies, and it was to them that the development contract was given. The final choice of the aircraft to be ordered in quantity was to be made by a gradual process of elimination as the designs progressed. If more than one contender then remained, flight trials would decide the winner.

There was at that stage no thought of asking Messerschmitt to participate in the competition. Messerschmitt's very few attempts at designing military aircraft had been complete failures. In addition, his reputation with the German Air Ministry had not been enhanced by the structural failures of the M 29 light aircraft which had never been fully explained.

One of those with decisive influence on the final decision was the Secretary of State for Air, Erhard Milch, who — as we know — was a bitter enemy of Messerschmitt following the affair with the structural failure of the M 20 and the cancellation and forcible reinstatement of the Lufthansa order.

Undeterred by the lack of official confidence in his abilities, Messerschmitt started the design of his own high-speed light fighter without government support. All of the knowledge and experience that he had gained on his early gliders and small powered aircraft was used to produce what he regarded as the best possible fighter aircraft. The fact that it did not coincide with the official specification issued by the Air Ministry served only to encourage him to prove that he was right and that the other designers and the compilers of the specification were wrong.

The thinking which went into the design of the Bf 109 was expounded by Messerschmitt in a lecture which he gave in 1941:

Simple as a modern aircraft may appear from the outside, it is nevertheless a device which, fully equipped, is more comparable in its engineering with a pocket battleship than an automobile. If we look at an aircraft from 1918 and compare it with an aircraft of today, the clean simple lines of the modern aircraft make a pleasant impression. But it looks quite different if we look inside the aircraft. At the end of the war, the aircraft was still quite simple in its equipment, with a few bits of controls for operating the engine, a simple compass, an altimeter and an airspeed indicator, and armament mostly consisting of a small number of weapons which were mechanically operated.

The development of improved flight performance, higher speeds, and greater altitudes demanded modern complicated engines with superchargers and variable pitch airscrews, which are necessary to obtain adequate efficiency for high-speed flight and for take-off. The demand for good communications with the home base, the necessity of flying in bad weather, blind flying and indeed landing at night and in fog, required the installation of radio apparatus, long and short wave transmitters and receivers, direction finding equipment and the rest. In addition, modern aircraft, in so far as they are military aircraft, have to have much more powerful armament than at the end of the World War. Whereas earlier the defensive armament consisted of machine guns, the cannon has become indispensable along with the machine gun. The offensive weapon, too, the aircraft's own bomb, has been considerably further developed with all the associated equipment. Mechanical operation of all these items of equipment was no longer possible in the long term, so that, for example, the variable pitch propeller had to be automated to relieve the load on the pilot.

The trend of this development demanded the employment of help from specialized companies. Without an electrical installation of quite a large size, without a hydraulic system and without a compressed air system, a modern aircraft is no longer imaginable. But it is not the purpose of a lecture to inform you about the development of all the parts of the aircraft. I will restrict myself, therefore, in the first place to the development of the metal construction of the airframe, i.e. of the aircraft without any equipment and without the engine.

I have told you something about the large number of items of equipment so that you can see how important it was to further develop the design of the airframe of the aircraft so that the load-carrying structure of the aircraft could as far as possible be accommodated within the external skin and close to it, in order to obtain the necessary space for the multitude of items of equipment to be installed without enlarging the aircraft for a particular application.

The next slide shows you an aircraft's fuselage of the old type. You can see a welded frame fuselage. The parts in the picture are, however, only the load-carrying framework. The skin giving the outside shape is added by stringers, so that the usable space is only a fraction of the space enclosed by the outer skin. The structural components take up a large part of the total space. The necessity of providing space in the cheapest way compelled the development of stressed-skin construction. But stressed-skin construction brought strength advantages relative to the framework type of structure. The load-carrying parts of the structure — we are talking about elements which are loaded in bending and torsion — must for strength and stiffness reasons be arranged in or on the outside skin. In this way the outside skin which is required for aerodynamic reasons was usefully incorporated into the load-carrying structure. Better utilization of space, better utilization of material and increased stiffness are the main characteristics of stressed-skin construction relative to the old fabric-covered braced frame structure. Stressed-skin structural design does not necessarily impose pure metal construction. Improved timber, plywood, and moulded parts can be manufactured for aircraft. Wood is a very good structural material; it can easily be worked and joined reliably with glue. On the other hand, wood is not suitable for mass-production. Moreover, it is not so uniform in its strength as metals.

In a radio talk of 8 December 1942, in which he described his early beginnings as an aircraft designer, Messerschmitt also said:

If at the time it surprised others that such a young designer was successful in that competition with his aircraft, for me it was only the assured result of the application of the experience which I had gained in aerodynamics during my long practice of sailplane design. It is widely known that, as a result of the restrictions which the Versailles Treaty placed on us Germans, very few means were available for the development of aircraft. Until the political changes of 1933 it was a hard life for the existing aircraft industry, if indeed it is possible to speak of an industry. With extremely limited resources I designed and built a series of sporting and transport aircraft which were suitable, because of their high performance, to serve as the preliminary steps towards a high-performance fighter.

When, soon afterwards, I got the contract to develop a fighter, it was obvious to me that in its aerodynamic form it should be based on a high-performance aircraft like the M 23 and M 29. At the time I made an attempt to equip the smallest possible light aircraft with a powerful engine in order to produce a fighter which exceeded in its performance anything that had been seen before.

Messerschmitt had always been more capable as an aerodynamicist than as a structural designer. As we have seen already, a number of his aircraft had suffered structural failures in flight, particularly in the tail area. His search for improved aerodynamic performance led him to investigate the use of high-lift devices. Ever since his meeting with Frederick Handley Page in the mid-1920s, Messerschmitt had been enamoured of the Handley Page slot which he incorporated into most of his later aircraft, including the Me 262 jet fighter.

Messerschmitt knew very well that the speed of an aircraft fitted with a given engine can best be increased by reducing the size of the wings. In fact, having smaller wings compels the aircraft to fly faster to generate the same amount of lift from the reduced area. But, providing the new fighter with a small wing would lead to difficulties when the aircraft came into land because a smaller wing means a higher landing speed, which must, for safety reasons, be fixed at some acceptable level above the stalling speed. Fitting the Handley Page slot allowed more lift to be extracted from the smaller wing before it stalled. This reduced the stalling speed and permitted the aircraft to land at a lower speed than would be possible with an unslotted wing. The Bf 109 was also equipped with flaps which again reduced the stalling speed in the landing configuration.

It is reasonable to assume that Milch had no part in inviting Messerschmitt to join in the competition for the new fighter. The secret of how Messerschmitt managed to enter the competition must surely be sought in his relations with prominent members of the Nazi Party. One of his particular friends, Ernst Udet, is known to have promoted Messerschmitt's ambitions. The influence of Rudolf Hess, a life-long friend of Messerschmitt, also cannot be discounted. As has already been mentioned, Theo Croneiss was by then an SS Brigade Leader and had supported Messerschmitt with advice and financial aid for many years, although it is doubtful that he occupied a high enough position to influence the thinking of the Air Ministry.

Whoever was responsible and whatever the reasons, Messerschmitt was eventually invited to submit his design as a rival competitor for the fighter contract. Regarded as an absolute outsider by the majority of the German aircraft industry, a lesser man than Messerschmitt would have had little hope of a successful outcome.

It is reported that Milch said after a meeting with representatives of the companies competing for the fighter contract that he had no expectations of the Messerschmitt design becoming a serious contender. He added: 'Nothing much will come of it but, as a pike in a carp pond, Messerschmitt may be quite useful.' Although intended as a derogatory statement, it gives a fair indication of the respect with which Messerschmitt's design abilities were regarded by his competitors.

At an early stage of the competition Arado and Heinkel had been asked to proceed to the construction of prototypes, but Focke-Wulf had been eliminated. By the time that the two remaining competitors had started to build the prototypes of their designs, Messerschmitt also had received a contract to build three prototypes of his Bf 109.

The Arado aircraft soon dropped out of the contest, leaving the field open to the Messerschmitt Bf 109 and the Heinkel He 112 designs. The final decision as to which company would receive the production order was to be made on the basis of comparative flight tests by Luftwaffe pilots at the test centre at Rechlin.

The first flight of the new fighter took place at Augsburg in the middle of September 1935. It was immediately obvious to Messerschmitt that he had designed a winner. Its rate of climb was outstanding and its manoeuvrability was excellent. In particular, its maximum speed in level flight was better than predicted.

In view of the role that his fighter was to play in the Battle of Britain, it is ironic that because of delays in producing the promised Daimler-Benz engine, the first prototype, like the first He 112, made its initial flights with a Rolls-Royce Kestrel engine.

Because both the Bf 109 and the He 112 appeared to be promising contenders for the final contract, an additional order was given to each firm to produce ten aircraft of each type for evaluation.

Research into the background to this period of Messerschmitt's life throws up many adverse statements claiming that the Bf 109 was inferior to the Heinkel He 112 and that the adoption of the Bf 109 as Germany's only single-seat fighter was not based on technical merits. Unfortunately, all of these reports are written by people who were antipathetic to Messerschmitt for various reasons, or who had cause to feel cheated by his success. Heinkel in his autobiography is quite certain that his fighter was superior to the Bf 109.

Rüdiger Kosin who wrote an excellent book entitled *The German Fighter Since 1915* was one of the Heinkel design staff in the late 1930s. Judging by his exposition of the history of the competition between Heinkel and Messerschmitt for the fighter contract, he appears to share the opinion that the Bf 109 gained the victory over the He 112 by other than technical superiority. He quotes at length the reports of the Luftwaffe test pilots at Rechlin proving that the Bf 109 was inferior in many ways to the He 112.

The report of one pilot complained that he had great difficulty in getting the Bf 109 to perform a loop, a manoeuvre which must be one of the most basic necessities for a fighter. He also found the aircraft very difficult to land because one wing always stalled just before touch-down dropping the aircraft on to one wheel. The spinning behaviour also came in for criticism, although recovery was very easy.

The He 112 was endowed, in the view of the test pilot, with better handling characteristics than the Bf 109, but it was noted that the open cockpit of the He 112 was not regarded as an advantage. On 24 March 1936 the second prototype of the Bf 109 fitted with the 610 hp Jumo 210 was delivered to Rechlin, and flight testing of it started immediately. According to the same pilot already quoted, its basic handling characteristics were no different from those of the first prototype.

To the amazement of the test pilots, a decision was announced before the whole test programme had been completed. The aircraft selected as the only fighter for the Luftwaffe was to be the Bf 109 designed by a young man who was hardly accepted into the circle of Germany's greatest designers. The reasons given for the choice were that the Bf 109 had better performance than its Heinkel competitor, it was lighter and it would be cheaper to build in quantity.

The three criteria quoted above would be considered by most experts to be ample justification for the choice that was made. Messerschmitt's design principles had been proved correct. As a result of using the Handley Page slot and having a smaller wing, the Bf 109 was faster than the He 112. The simple trapezoidal plan shape of the wing had always been intended to make it much easier to manufacture than the semi-elliptical wing of the Heinkel.

Another beneficial design feature of the Bf 109 was the attachment of the undercarriage to the fuselage and not to the wings as on the He 112. This made it possible to remove the wings while the aircraft was standing on the ground without having to trestle up the fuselage.

In any case, the correctness of the final decision in favour of the Messerschmitt aircraft was proved by the fact that the Bf 109 was capable of continual up-grading throughout the war and eventually was produced in numbers approaching 35,000. Its total life in active service throughout the world extended over 30 years.

The principal deficiency of the Bf 109 was the narrow track undercarriage which was marginally adequate from a strength point of view. Throughout its career the aircraft suffered an unusually large number of undercarriage failures, sometimes during test flights before delivery to the Luftwaffe. The problem was exacerbated by the aircraft's tendency to ground loop on landing. This phenomenon, which is dealt with more fully in the next chapter, afflicted many otherwise successful aircraft. In the case of the Bf 109, this usually resulted in the aircraft coming to rest on one wing tip with a bent propeller.

In his book referred to above, Kosin recounts the story of the arrival of the first Bf 109 at Rechlin in preparation for the test programme. After a demonstration of aerobatics by the Messerschmitt test pilot who had delivered the aircraft, the Bf 109 made a landing which was described by all the onlookers as being a perfect 'three-pointer'. Despite that, the aircraft ground-looped and the undercarriage attachment failed. According to Kosin, the Messerschmitt company sacked the pilot instead of taking steps to correct the fault in the design of the undercarriage attachment.

Despite the deficiencies about which Messerschmitt's enemies made so much fuss, the Bf 109 was clearly superior to the Heinkel He 112 and a large production order was given. There then followed an extraordinary propaganda exercise by the Nazi government. The Bf 109 first made a public appearance at the Olympic Games in Berlin in 1936, when it flew overhead, crossing the stadium at a moderate altitude. The next move took place at the annual aviation meeting at Zürich-Dübendorf airfield from 23 July to 1 August 1937. In the previous 15 years Germany had not taken part in the meetings at Zürich, but Hitler determined to make an impressive debut with his new fighter.

When it was known that the new Bf 109 fighter and the Heinkel 111 bomber were to appear at the display, aviation journalists from all over the world flocked to Zürich to assess the abilities of the newcomers. The result was an unadulterated triumph for Germany and considerable worries for the Air Ministries of the other European countries who were already rightly apprehensive about Hitler's intentions in the long term.

The Alpine Race was won by the Bf 109 V 9 aircraft (the ninth prototype). The team prize in the same event was taken by a German team of three pilots flying the B-2 version of the fighter. A Rechlin test pilot won the climb and dive competition in another Bf 109. The only pilot whose fortunes were less encouraging was Messerschmitt's friend, Ernst Udet, who suffered an engine failure in flight. He was compelled to make an emergency landing which wrote off the aircraft and left Udet slightly injured.

As Hitler had intended, the outside world was stupefied and not a little perturbed by what it had seen. There was no doubt that Germany had a fleet of fighter aircraft superior to the best anywhere else in the world. Foreign policies would need to be modified to take account of this fact. In fact, the whole display had been an immense confidence trick. The Luftwaffe was desperately short of high speed fighters at that time. The display had been managed by putting into service all of the prototype Bf 109 aircraft available.

Encouraged by the success of his efforts at Zürich, Hitler was planning further surprises for his future enemies. Messerschmitt proposed fitting a Bf 109 with a much higher powered engine and taking the world speed record. An aircraft was fitted with a specially developed Daimler-Benz DB 601A engine capable of producing 1650 hp for a very short period before it burnt out. On 11 November 1937, Dr Wurster, the chief test pilot of the Messerschmitt company, set up a new world speed record of just over 620 kph (384 mph) in that aircraft. The official story was that the aircraft was a perfectly standard Bf 109 fighter identical with those in service with the Luftwaffe. The message to Hitler's potential enemies was clear to read.

Rivalries within the German aircraft industry were now coming to a head. Heinkel had been bitterly disappointed by his failure to obtain a contract for the He 112 as the Luftwaffe's standard fighter. He was even more disappointed by seeing the world speed record go to Messerschmitt. He set about designing another fighter, the He 100, which would be faster than the Bf 109. Messerschmitt soon became aware of Heinkel's plans and was taking steps to thwart them. There had never been any love lost between the two designers.

On 22 January 1938 the prototype He 100 took off on its maiden flight. After some development it was transferred on 1 April of the same year to the Luftwaffe test establishment at Rechlin. A second aircraft was by then being built for an attempt on the speed record. By a peculiar turn of events, Udet arrived at the Heinkel works at about the time that the Heinkel test pilot was about to set up a new world speed record. He insisted on getting into the aircraft to try it out. By some strange almost unbelievable coincidence, the official FAI observers were present so that when Udet completed the required course over 100 km at an average speed of 630 kph (391 mph), it could be registered officially as a new world record.

Messerschmitt was making sure that he was not too far behind. He had already completed the design and was engaged in the building of an aircraft the correct designation of which was the Me 209. This was not a modified Bf 109 but a completely new aircraft intended only for the speed record attempt. However, as part of Hitler's propaganda campaign it was to be announced as a slightly modified Bf 109 with the intention of again deceiving the world about the capabilities of the Luftwaffe's standard fighter.

The Me 209 flew for the first time on 1 August 1938 and immediately showed a whole range of undesirable flying characteristics which made it completely unsuitable as a military aircraft, even if it had been intended to use it as such. However, as we have seen, the Me 209 was not intended to be a fighter; its sole purpose was to stand in for the Bf 109 when the record was broken.

On 30 March 1939, Heinkel considerably extended his lead in the record stakes. An He 100 flown by his chief test pilot, Hans Dieterle, set up a new record of 746.6 kph (463 mph). Messerschmitt was now firmly in second place.

Messerschmitt confidently and patiently awaited the coming hour of his triumph. Work on the Me 209 was well advanced and he was certain that Heinkel's success would be short-lived. On 26 April, hardly four weeks after the Heinkel establishment of the new record, Fritz Wendel took off from Augsburg in the Me 209 in an attempt to win back the record for his company. Among the observers on the airfield was Willy Messerschmitt, anxious to see his rival defeated yet again. In front of the official FAI observers, Wendel flew at a speed of 756.1 kph (469 mph) and wrested the record from Heinkel by a margin of only 9.5 kph (6 mph) — just enough to establish a new record.

The record was officially acknowledged by the FAI and entered in the record book. The only error in the registration of the record was the statement that it had been won by an Me 109R aircraft, in other words, a special research version of the standard fighter. The entry in the record book still stands unaltered in those words today. Once again, Hitler, with Messerschmitt's assistance had succeeded in misleading the world as to the capabilities of his growing Luftwaffe.

Heinkel was furious at the loss of the record. He pointed out that the FAI rules required the record flight to be carried out at a height of 75 metres (246 ft) above the ground. Both he and Messerschmitt had complied with this regulation. However, the regulations said nothing about the altitude of the ground over which the record flight was made. His attempt had taken place at sea-level whereas Messerschmitt's successful attempt at Augsburg had been at an altitude where the lower air pressure would have given an advantage of about 13 kph (9 mph). He now announced plans to repeat his record attempt at a similar altitude to the Me 209 and was confident that he could regain his ascendancy over Messerschmitt.

To his surprise and dismay, Udet forbid him to make any further attempts on the record. On 12 July 1939 he received a letter from the Air Ministry which made it quite clear that he must abandon all hopes of regaining his superiority:

> It has come to my notice that negotiations are in progress between yourself and the Daimler-Benz company which are aimed at undertaking a repetition of the world record attempt for the highest speed close to the ground.
>
> I inform you herewith that there is no interest in a repetition of the record flight since any slight increase in the present world record which is held by Germany would not repay the costs and labour involved. I request you not to allow any work to be done to this end.

The reason for this attitude was explained to Heinkel by Udet in person when he told the disappointed designer:

> For God's sake! It really cannot be shown in front of foreigners that a fighter which, like the He 100, is not being put into series production, can fly the absolute world speed record, and the Bf 109 fighter, which everybody knows is our standard fighter, cannot. Things must stay as they are. And your plans for a new attack on the record do not please me at all.

In truth, the Luftwaffe's Bf 109 could not fly at a speed approaching anywhere near the world speed record, but the masquerade had to be kept up.

Messerschmitt's triumph was complete. He now held the world speed record and a lucrative contract to produce the Bf 109 in quantity. At one stroke he had become the foremost aircraft designer in the world. He was still only 40 years old.

CHAPTER 8

Problems with the
Bf 109

Messerschmitt was justifiably proud of the Bf 109, and he never tired of proclaiming its superiority over any aircraft possessed by the Allies. He was equally proud of the fact that he had succeeded in designing and building the aircraft despite the relative immaturity of his company in comparison with larger and longer-established aircraft companies.

In February 1940 he was asked to contribute a letter to the soldiers' newspaper *Front und Heimat*. He readily seized the opportunity to publicize the achievements of his company in designing both the Bf 109 and the Bf 110:

Dear Comrades!

When the Führer, after the seizure of power, gave the order for rearmament and militarization, we were still one of the small German aircraft companies without any national, let alone international, renown.

With only a few workers and designers, we built aircraft for various non-military purposes in quite small and modest numbers. Few people in Germany or abroad then knew of the Bavarian Aircraft Company, and nobody foresaw that Augsburg would one day be the birthplace of the best and the fastest fighter aircraft in the world.

Within the framework of the order for the reconstruction of the German Luftwaffe, on the basis of schemes for a fighter aircraft submitted by myself, the Air Ministry allocated to us the task of developing and building this type of aircraft.

The trust placed in me gave us the responsibility of achieving something extraordinary. The task was enormously difficult in so far as at that time in Germany we had no experience worth mentioning in the construction of warplanes.

Today we can declare with satisfaction that we have fulfilled the task placed on us by the Führer. The operation of the Bf 109 in Poland and, particularly against the Western Powers has shown clearly that the Bf 109 is superior to all enemy aircraft.

In the course of further development, the Bf 109 has recently had an even more powerful brother in the Bf 110.

The Bf 110, thanks to its great range and heavy armament, can carry out fighter duties which have to be performed deep in enemy territory. Like the Bf 109 it has become the terror of the enemy. Even when today our enemies abroad are trying vainly to establish the inferiority of our fighters relative to their own aircraft, they are still faced with the fact that the Bf 109 and the Bf 110 have shot down 36 Englishmen within a few hours in the great air battle over the Bay of Heligoland.

Even if his assessment of the qualities of the Bf 109 had been correct, his estimate of the effectiveness of the Bf 110 was far from accurate. The aircraft was inadequately armed and proved an easy victim for the Royal Air Force. So much so that it could only be used with an escort of Bf 109s to protect it. As the range of the Bf 109 was very limited, the supposed range advantage of the Bf 110 was unable to be of benefit to the Luftwaffe since it had to be restricted to that of the escorting fighters.

The Bf 110 only came into its own some time later as a night fighter, in which role it was very successful against the RAF heavy bombers.

Despite the praise which its designer lavished upon it, the Bf 109 was also destined to have its problems. Messerschmitt was to suffer many years of worry about the aircraft. The deficiencies in its design led to demands for a series of improvements which continued until the end of the war. The development of more powerful armament also made increasing demands on the ability of the designers to accommodate heavier and more bulky guns inside the contour of the aircraft.

Because of the requirements for ever more speed to cope with the parallel developments of the Spitfire in particular, a series of more powerful engines of ever-increasing weight and complexity kept Messerschmitt and his colleagues busy with modifications. The story of the development of the Bf 109 into a series of variants with different engines and armament has been told many times already by other authors.

Two problems in particular will be dealt with here on the basis of the documents preserved in the Imperial War Museum. Probably the most consistent problem with the 109 was the weakness of the narrow-track undercarriage. In the initial assessment it had been considered a positive advantage that the wings could be removed without the need to cradle the fuselage during the operation. Unfortunately, it also dictated that the top ends of the undercarriage legs had to be attached to the sides of the narrow fuselage. As a result they were too close together, and this made the aircraft unstable in roll when it was taxiing, taking off or (more important) landing. A modification was introduced at one stage to cant the legs outwards from the original nearly vertical attitude, but this served only to reduce the problem, not to eliminate it.

The problem was compounded by the tendency of the Bf 109 to perform 'ground loops'. This was a common problem in many aircraft with tailwheels, and at that time all aircraft did have tailwheels. Some aircraft suffered more than others, and the reasons for the defect were then not clear. The most common time for the problem to occur was during landing. If the pilot succeeded in carrying out a three-point landing when the mainwheels and the tailwheel touched the ground simultaneously, the tail would suddenly swing sideways, apparently for no distinguishable reason. The movement could sometimes be held in check by the use of the rudder and by applying the brakes on the wheel on the outside of the turn. Aircraft which regularly suffered damage from ground looping were usually deficient in rudder or braking power.

If the ground loop were not restrained, the aircraft would turn in such a tight circle that the side load on the undercarriage from centrifugal forces would cause a structural failure either of the undercarriage itself or its attachments to the airframe. Such was the case of the Bf 109.

In March 1940 before the Battle of Britain, therefore, a letter arrived on Messerschmitt's desk from the office of General Udet. The subject was the intolerable number of aircraft being immobilized by undercarriage failures because of ground looping. The letter contains alarming statistics:

From: Head of Flight Safety

19 March 1940

Experiences with the Bf 109 Undercarriage

I. According to reports submitted to the Head of Flight Safety, about 255 aircraft were damaged in 1939 because of ground looping. In 240 cases there was damage to the undercarriage, whilst 15 cases led to damage of other kinds. The number of reported cases is so extensive, even considering the number of aircraft engaged in flying operations, that maintenance failures alone can no longer be regarded as the only cause. (In September and October 1939, the number of aircraft unserviceable as a result of ground looping was about twice as high as that from enemy action; of the total number of cases only about 14% occurred in training.) In the present report, therefore, the intention is to collect together briefly the experience gained from the damage reports and thus to serve as the basis for the elimination of the existing situation. The fact that some remedy is required here is shown by a consideration of the cost of repair work. The average repair costs in the cases quoted are of the order of roughly 15,000 Reichsmarks, so that the costs for the year stand at about 4 million Reichsmarks. Since the material costs form the smallest part of this sum, it shows that the capacity of the repair workshops is being unnecessarily highly loaded because of the above-mentioned characteristic of the Bf 109 type alone.

II. Summary and evaluation:

1. Extent of faults in the different versions

Version	B	C	D	E	Number	In period
Aircraft in service	12%	2%	23%	63%	—	1.10. to 1.11
Faults	18%	3%	19%	60%	100	1.8. to 1.11
Aircraft in service	16%	3%	34%	47%	Average	1.1 to 1.1
Faults	20%	4%	27%	49%	222	1.1 to 1.1

2. Type of ground loop:

Ground loop	To the right	To the left	No information	
On take-off	57	8	2	67
On landing	59	39	4	102
When taxiing	5	6	2	13
No details	1	3	—	4
	122	56	8	186

3. Type of damage:
105 cases were evaluated. Of these there were 12 instances of damage of the same kind which did not occur because of ground looping. In detail, the following failures were identified:

Latch	10	Shock absorber head	11
Latch hinge pin	3	Shock absorber head and latch	2
Latch and lock plate	7	Undercarriage lug	22
Lock plate	27	Undercarriage lug and plate	3

A further 125 reports evaluated above did not contain any further information regarding damaged components.

III. Pilots' Reports.
In the majority of cases the pilots agreed in reporting that it was not possible to keep the aircraft straight despite braking and fully deflecting the rudder. In some cases the position of the pedals was criticized as it made it difficult to apply greater foot loads. Overall, the reports give the impression that the braking and rudder power are not sufficient to prevent a rotation about the vertical axis at average or lower speeds as soon as castoring of the tailwheel occurs.

IV. Summary
255 cases were investigated more closely in which aircraft of the type Bf 109 ground looped. Since the share of the cases in which ground looping can be attributed to the previous occurrence of other damage (tyre, wheel rim, locking failures) is only about 10% of the total number, it is justifiable to speak of a tendency of the Bf 109 type to ground looping. Various previously recognized defects and complaints were assembled and discussed. In this respect, reference was made to the characteristics and lack of locking of the tail wheel, since this is the most easily modified component of the critical parts.

Oberst Reithel

In fact, Messerschmitt and his colleagues eventually came up with a modification which introduced a lock on the tailwheel to prevent it castoring during the landing.

Because of the failure of the Bf 110 as a 'destroyer' aircraft — that is as a fighter-bomber — as a result of its vulnerability to attack by British fighters, it was decided by the German Air Ministry that the 109 should be fitted with bomb racks in an effort to fill the gap in the ranks of the fast daylight light bombers. The main problem was that the 109 did not have sufficient range to penetrate very deep into Britain. This difficulty would be solved later by fitting drop tanks to increase the fuel capacity. Messerschmitt received an instruction from the Technical Office to install bomb racks in June 1940 when the problems with the 110 were first becoming obvious:

Telex from Air Ministry

Ref: Bf 109E and F with bombs
It is intended to equip your types Bf 109E and F in series production with release gear for one 250 kg [550 lb] or one 500 kg [1100 lb] bomb. What needs clarification is whether the faired ETC 500 bomb rack, as on the prototype aircraft, Works No. 1361, is to be rigidly attached to the aircraft or whether when used as a fighter it can rapidly be jettisoned. The latter is the more desirable solution. In this connection, you need also to investigate whether instead of the ETC 500, four ETC 50s can be installed, so that different missions can be carried out with the same aircraft.

Please let me have detailed proposals with the associated weight schedules. The fitting of the Bf 109E type with bomb release gear will follow in the present production run. Retrospective fitting of a large number of aircraft in the Luftwaffe is not intended.

Messerschmitt cannot have been entirely encouraged by this news. After all his considerable efforts to design an aircraft with minimum drag to achieve maximum performance, he was now being asked to add excrescences which would make its performance inferior to that of the Hurricane or Spitfire. Not the one to refuse a challenge, though, Messerschmitt soon came up with a scheme for carrying bombs on the 109 which proved very effective in the later stages of the Battle of Britain.

A strange proposal from the Air Ministry arrived on Messerschmitt's desk in May 1941. It does not appear to have been treated by him with any real interest. In any case, it hardly affected him personally apart from the need to provide a radiator for the trial installation. His reaction is contained in a memo which he dispatched at the time to a Ministry official.

The Air Ministry has given a contract to Daimler-Benz to install a DB 601 N in a Spitfire. Basically, it is intended to determine how high the service ceiling is. For that purpose it is obviously necessary that the sizes of the radiators are adjusted to correspond to the 109 F radiators, not the improved E installation but as the radiator is actually installed in the Spitfire.

On the other hand, the oil cooler of the 109 E or F must be installed on the engine cowling. Airscrew DB 601 109 F or E.

At much the same time, Daimler-Benz had similar ideas of their own, but this time it was a two-way exchange. Messerschmitt's memo summarizes the situation but seems sceptical about the purpose of the exercise:

Installation of the DB 601 engine in the Spitfire

The Daimler-Benz company is making the following exchange: they are installing the DB 601 engine in a Spitfire and the Rolls-Royce Merlin engine in an Me 109. I have no objections to this trial.

Daimler-Benz are carrying out the exchange to demonstrate that the Spitfire is better with their engine and that the Me 109 with the Merlin engine is worse.

There is no further mention of the idea in the Messerschmitt correspondence. There is no surviving record to say whether the exchange ever took place, and what the results were if it did.

As an interlude to his serious concerns about the Bf 109, Messerschmitt received a request in July 1941 from the magazine *Deutsche Technik*. The editor was interested in obtaining from him an article on the topic of the future development of aircraft. Messerschmitt did not in the end find the time needed to write the article, but two pages of rough notes which he compiled are preserved. Even at that early date he was thinking about supersonic flight and the problems which it would entail. His notes cover the whole field which would be developed in the next ten years:

On the Future Development of Aircraft

Depends in first place on solution of high speed problem. At higher speeds air can no longer be regarded as incompressible; on reaching speed of sound (e.g. at certain places on wing upper surface) occurrence of compression waves (shock-waves). Associated with these phenomena, sharp increase in drag and other unpleasant accompanying effects yet to be considered. These phenomena are decisive for aerodynamic design of high-speed aircraft. Therefore, in all relevant countries high-speed wind tunnels for more detailed investigation. In order to reduce sharp increase in drag mentioned earlier, thin aerofoil sections of special shape better suited than conventional thick sections. Nevertheless, constructional difficulties, since with thin sections available structural depth very small, so that carrying of bending and torsion demands considerable expenditure of weight (move towards steel construction?). Carrying of torsion particularly difficult since on the one hand at higher Mach numbers large movements of centre of pressure and hence large torques; on the other hand torsional stiffness particularly important for reasons of flutter and to avoid 'aerodynamic divergence' at high speeds. Increase in drag can also be reduced by use of larger sweepback so that, apart from aerofoil section and structure, plan view of wing also is affected by high-speed problem.

From the aspect of flying characteristics, increase of downwash at high Mach numbers and hence a worsening of stability to be expected; also change of trim through movement of centre of pressure. In addition, on cambered sections (control surface movement!) Mach number effects occur earlier. Deterioration of control surface effectiveness, increase of control loads. Therefore, change in design of tail surfaces to be expected as far as flying characteristics are concerned, or total disappearance of tail surfaces (tailless construction). For high-speed flight at high altitudes significant decrease of speed of sound with altitude, so that compressibility effects occur at lower speeds than when flying at ground level; also increase of surface friction with altitude as a result of Reynolds Number. Since, in addition, the induced drag increases with altitude (importance of wingspan!), the maintenance at a constant level of engine power up to high altitudes is extraordinarily important for high-speed flight at high altitudes despite reduced density of air. On engine development, see below under altitude chambers.

The big difference between take-off and landing speed on the one hand and flying speed on the other ('speed range') will bring further difficulties with it, e.g. the necessity of being able to reduce control movements in flight. Auxiliary thrust rockets required for take-off. Boundary layer control (sucking, blowing) for landing to increase maximum lift. Use of airscrews for braking on landing.

Airscrew development going in direction of multi-blade propellers for high performance so as to reduce peripheral speed of blade tips. Contrarotating double propellers (on one shaft) to eliminate reactive torque, gyroscopic effects and slipstream moments on tail surfaces.

Since efficiency of airscrews at higher speeds falls off considerably, probable move over to jet propulsion. Efficiency of jet propulsion increases with increasing speed.

For the moment, Messerschmitt had more trivial but pressing needs to consider. One of the best features of Messerschmitt's design of the Bf 109 was the installation of the radiator. A radiator was obviously necessary to keep the liquid-cooled engine at the correct operating temperature. To act efficiently, as large a volume of air as possible had to pass through the radiator in flight but, if the installation were poorly designed, it could add considerably to the drag of the aircraft. So efficient was the design of the Bf 109 radiator that it was one of the outstanding features which made the Messerschmitt aircraft superior to its Heinkel rival.

Despite the high regard which his design of the radiator installation enjoyed in the Luftwaffe, Messerschmitt seems to have had doubts in his own mind about whether he had achieved the best solution. In particular, he was concerned that, as the power of the installed engines increased, his own arrangement would prove inferior to that in the British Spitfire. Accordingly, the idea came to him to try to install into his own aircraft a radiator taken from a captured Spitfire.

In 1943, he wrote a letter to the Daimler Benz company proposing this trial installation:

22 July 1943

Dr Dipl. Ing. Fr. Nallinger
Daimler Benz

Dear Herr Nallinger,

I propose to you that, if you are in agreement, we install a genuine Spitfire radiator in an Me 109 using the original fairing so that we can determine the exact relative conditions. Since your engine needs only 238cal/HP and the Merlin-45 268 cal/HP, the radiator must be adequate since your engine cannot in any case produce 14% more power.

Messerschmitt

As might be expected, the Daimler Benz engineers were not enthusiastic about this proposal and a suitable reply was soon despatched:

3 August 1943

Dear Professor Messerschmitt,

In your letter of 22 July 1943 you propose to install a genuine Spitfire radiator in an Me 109 and, indeed, with the original fairing. This test is certainly very interesting in itself. However, whether sufficient cooling is obtained cannot be predicted today and certainly does not accord with my view, for apart from the radiator and its fairing, the place in which it is situated, and above all the flow conditions in the intake are critical. In my opinion, the latter are extraordinarily important. How the radiator is situated here relative to the installation in the Spitfire, I cannot assess at the moment. It may happen, therefore, that this test produces no useful result. If it turns out to be unsuccessful, at least it will show that the intake flow conditions could be at fault.

Nallinger

That appears to have been the end of the idea as there is no mention of any trial installation having been carried out.

As the war proceeded and the Allied bombers reduced the output of raw materials for German war factories, the shortage of aluminium alloy became more and more acute. It was obvious that before long the production of fighter aircraft, so urgently needed by the Luftwaffe to stem the attacks on the German homeland, would be impeded by the lack of aluminium.

Messerschmitt saw as a solution to this problem a reversion to the use of other less strategic materials for the construction of airframes. He had a long experience in the use of wood and could easily return to designing in that material. The appearance of the Mosquito bomber over Germany had, in fact, provoked Goering into asking Messerschmitt why he could not design aircraft from wood. Steel was also in better supply than aluminium and that, combined with wood, could prove to be the solution to the materials problem.

Messerschmitt was also engaged at this time in developing the Me 209, a high altitude fighter, not to be confused with the spurious 209 which took the world speed record while posing as an Me 109R. The new aircraft was intended to be produced as a variant of the Me 109. It had the same wing as the 109 but the span was increased by inserting a parallel section protruding from each side of the fuselage. Its development did not progress smoothly, and the project was finally abandoned in favour of work on the Me 262 jet fighter.

Following the initial idea of using non-strategic materials in aircraft design, Messerschmitt's design office was before long producing schemes for redesigned wings for the Me 109 and the 209 using steel and wood. A report to the Air Ministry dated 16 April 1943 gives details of the results of the investigation carried out to date:

Ref.: Conversion of Me 109, Me 209

For the conversion of the Me 109 and Me 209, two differing arrangements for the wing and tail structure have been investigated.

I. Wing with spar flanges of steel with ribs as well as covering of light alloy; tail surfaces of light alloy.
II. Wing with spar flanges of steel, ribs and covering of wood; tail surfaces of wood.

In addition in both arrangements there are further converted structural components. The aluminium required for the individual arrangements is:

Aluminium required	Me 109	Me 209
Before conversion	898 kg	— kg
Arrangement I. Final stage 2nd quarter 44	608 kg	670 kg
Arrangement II.	300 kg	330 kg

The following reasons support the arrangement with a wooden wing and wooden tail surfaces:

1. On the assumption that the decision regarding the mass production for the wooden wing is taken before 30 May 1943, 4000 sets of wooden wings and 19,560 sets of wooden tail surfaces can be built in accordance with Programme 223 for the Me 109 before it runs out. Associated with this is a saving of aluminium of the order of 2490 tonnes relative to the latest conversion plans which provide for Arrangement I. For the Me 209, if all the aircraft are converted to Arrangement II in accordance with the present programme up to September 1945, there will be 13,000 wooden wings and 15,000 wooden tail surfaces and an additional saving of 4620 tonnes of aluminium.

By changing to the wooden wing and the wooden tail surfaces for the Me 109 and Me 209, the total saving of aluminium in the third quarter of 1943 to the fourth quarter of 1944 would amount to 7110 tonnes.

2. The manufacture of the wooden wing and the wooden tail surfaces is generally possible by bringing in idle factories in the woodworking industry which will make corresponding manufacturing capacity free on the metal side. Moreover, the wooden wing needs only half the expenditure of the man-hours available today for metal construction.

3. The design with a steel spar, wooden ribs and wood planking is particularly promising from an engineering point of view and deserves special encouragement in view of the future position regarding raw materials. If it proves successful, its extension to other types of aircraft is urgently desirable.

The following doubts can be raised against the wooden wing and the wooden tail surfaces:

a. A test wing can only be got ready for the test in September, so that the first results of the strength test to failure cannot be available before

October 1943. However, since the strength test, as far as can be seen, will produce no basic modifications to the design, it seems reasonable to begin preparing Production for the planned mass production immediately.

b. The resistance to battle damage of the wooden wing may be somewhat lower than that for metal wings whereas, according to the tests carried out to date, there is no difference on the tail surfaces. Against this disadvantage there is the large saving of aluminium which is indispensable for the realization of the aircraft programme according to investigations made to date.

c. The construction of assembly lines is necessary for the starting up of the wooden wing and the wooden tail surfaces of the Me 109 at the right time. For this the Messerschmitt company needs, according to a preliminary estimate, 1000 tonnes of iron. A more exact check on this requirement is being made by Messerschmitt at the moment. When procuring this equipment these can be used later after modification for the wooden wing and wooden tail surfaces of the Me 209.

In view of the extremely large saving of aluminium of 7110 tons in all, this iron requirement can be regarded as small.

Since the wooden wing is designed with the steel spar, the initial deliveries of the steel spar as they are planned today, must be fully guaranteed.

For the wooden design of the Me 209 wing, Messerschmitt AG needs 15 designers and draughtsmen, two stressmen and three weights controllers for a period of about four months. For the subsequent development a further five designers, one weights controller and one stressman are needed until further notice.

In addition, Messerschmitt needs for the design of the tooling of the Me 209, ten designers for four months, for the production preparations about 16 jig assemblers, for the tools about 30 tool makers, for a period of six months.

The manpower resources requested from the Hirth Company through the F.2 special committee must be made available immediately.

On the basis of the reasons quoted, it is proposed that a decision is made immediately to start on preparing for the production of wooden wings and wooden tail surfaces for the Me 109 and Me 209 so that the indisputably necessary relief of the aluminium requirements can take effect promptly.

The Me 109 G did enter service with a wooden tail structure, but the wood and steel wing never reached the production stage.

CHAPTER 9

The Hess flight

As recounted earlier, one of Messerschmitt's closest friends in the 1930s was Rudolf Hess, who had been Hitler's private secretary at one time and was involved in the innermost circles of the Nazi party. He was a great flying enthusiast and a very capable pilot.

As Hess had been active in sporting aviation circles for many years, it is probable that he first met Messerschmitt at some flying meeting where the young designer's aircraft were being flown. Their common interest in flying led to a closer friendship which lasted until Hess's sudden departure for Scotland in May 1941.

They must have met not long after the First World War, because in 1926 Rudolf Hess bought from Messerschmitt an M 17 sporting aircraft in which he scored some notable triumphs in flying competitions. This served to strengthen their friendship as the two men shared a common aim in attempting to win one prize after another — the older man by his skill as a pilot, the younger by the continuing refinement of his designs.

When the BFW company went bankrupt in 1931 there was an immediate danger that the works would be taken over and sold to repay some of the debts. In fact, one report has it that the local council in Augsburg intended to use the Messerschmitt factory as the city's tram depot.

Hess at that time was the chairman of the Augsburg city council. He intervened to ensure that Messerschmitt did not lose his production base. This must have strengthened the ties between the aircraft designer and the up and coming politician.

In May 1941 Hess shook the Nazi hierarchy to the core by flying to Scotland in an Me 110 with the intention of negotiating a separate peace with Britain. In doing so he was believed to be carrying out the unspoken wishes of Hitler, but the actual result was a propaganda triumph for Britain. Hess paid dearly for his initiative. From the day that he landed in Scotland he was never to live another day as a free man — eventually dying as the last occupant of Spandau prison in Berlin.

The technical background to Hess's flight has never been explained. In the first place it was necessary for Hess to get access to a military aircraft which would certainly not be available for any amateur pilot to fly. It can only be that Messerschmitt made an Me 110 aircraft available to his friend. Hess was the second or third most powerful man in Germany at the time, so there is no possibility that Messerschmitt could have refused to provide an aircraft if Hess insisted that he do so.

In the correspondence quoted below, the aircraft used for the flight to Scotland is referred to by Messerschmitt as 'Herr Rudolf Hess's Me 110'. It was clear, therefore, that the aircraft was regarded as the one regularly used by Hess, if not actually owned by him.

In fact, it seems that Hess persuaded the aircraft manufacturer to lend him an Me 110 so that he could familiarize himself with the aircraft by carrying out practice flights, without ever actually stating what was the real reason.

Some modifications must have been required to equip the machine for its long flight. The Me 110 had a limited range of not much in excess of 700 miles. In order to fly safely from Germany to Scotland it would have been advisable to install modifications to increase the fuel tank capacity. However, that would have revealed too clearly what was afoot and there is no evidence as to whether such a modification was actually fitted.

Included in the Messerschmitt papers in the Imperial War Museum are two documents which cast some light on the subject and which appear to exonerate Messerschmitt from any direct complicity in Hess's venture.

There had always been problems with the temperatures in the cockpit of the Me 110 and Hess soon discovered that on flights much shorter than his planned flight to Scotland, the heating was too effective for comfort. Messerschmitt was asked to improve the controls of the cabin heating. A memorandum from Messerschmitt to his design staff early in 1941 deals with this problem:

Me 110 of Herr Hess
Herr Rudolf Hess's Me 110 has an old heating system without cut-off cocks between the radiator and the heating system. I consider it necessary to install the cut-off cocks retrospectively.
Please check the possibilities and make proposals for their incorporation.

Messerschmitt

A few weeks later another memorandum was issued by Messerschmitt to his designers. From the wording of this, it appears that Messerschmitt himself was puzzled about what Hess had in mind:

Herr Caroli 2 May 1941
Please sort out the following and as far as possible give me an answer next Monday.

1. Reichsminister Hess is asking what radius curve is flown if the auto-pilot is fully displaced, and also within what accuracy the radius is assumed to be correct and how big the effect of wind could be in certain cases. I cannot

understand what the whole thing is about but I forgot to find out in more detail what he wants.

2. Please arrange for the observer's oxygen bottle in his aircraft to be connected over to the pilot's oxygen bottle, if that is not already the case. Also, there is to be an oxygen mouthpiece as well as an oxygen mask installed in the aircraft.

3. He wants a calibration of the static pressure and an associated set of curves showing what a reading of 410 and 450 kph at 500-600 metres (altitude) respectively is in reality.

Messerschmitt

From the above note it can be assumed that Hess had some idea of locking the auto-pilot at full travel before baling out over Scotland and was investigating all the things that could go wrong. The provision of additional oxygen for the long journey, by using both the pilot's and the observer's supply, is also catered for in paragraph 2.

The need for accurate navigation over such a long range required an exact knowledge of the accuracy of the airspeed indicator readings. This accounts for Hess's interest in the static pressure which affects the reading of the instrument.

It is surprising that an aircraft engineer of Messerschmitt's experience did not realize which way all these queries were leading. There is no record that in the aftermath of Hess's flight on 10 May 1941 Messerschmitt was suspected of wilfully collaborating in the venture. There must have been intense questioning of everyone who had been concerned either deliberately or innocently in the preparations for the flight.

Within a few days of Hess's flight an order arrived on Messerschmitt's desk from General Udet. Its purpose was to ensure that there was no repetition of the incident which had so severely embarrassed Hitler and the Nazi hierarchy:

From: Generalluftzeugmeister   Berlin, 24 May 1941

Order No. 376

I am taking the opportunity to point out yet again most strongly that during the war any use of aircraft must be justified on official grounds. There is no such thing as unofficial or private flying. The Reichsmarschall [Goering] has charged me particularly to forbid any agreements made by third parties, especially personalities of the state, party and armed forces, with aircraft establishments regarding the provision or loan of aircraft. For this, my approval must be obtained in advance in every case. The Reichsmarschall will punish ruthlessly any offences of this sort.

In addition I repeat the most important regulations for the operation of aircraft by aircraft establishments:

1. Official flights from all aircraft establishments to the central government, to occupied territories and abroad are each subject to my approval. In special cases I reserve the right to issue a standing order permitting flights.

Excepted are delivery flights to the front line from the test centre.

2. For each official flight previously approved by me, a flight sheet is to be made out as in the attached example.

3. The loading of an aircraft, apart from the approved passengers each with 25 kg luggage, can consist only of official goods, (this applies also to the flight crew).

4. The carrying of female persons in aircraft with military markings is forbidden.

I expect the leaders of my aircraft establishments to support me energetically in the correct carrying out of the whole of the flying operations of my department.

Signed: Udet

There the matter rested. Messerschmitt was subjected to no further enquiries as to his part in Hess's flight. What could have been a very awkward affair for him passed over with no ill effects.

CHAPTER 10

The Me 210 disaster

The Me 210 was the most unmitigated failure in Messerschmitt's career as an aircraft designer. The aircraft had been intended as a replacement for the Me 110, although design of the new machine had started in 1938, two years before the shortcomings of the Me 110 had been demonstrated in battle. The aircraft was to be designed as a fighter-bomber 'Zerstörer' with a range of 2000 kilometres (1240 miles). Because the German military hierarchy were still obsessed with the supposed effectiveness of dive-bombers, a capability of performing in that role was also imposed on the aircraft. The engines to be fitted were Daimler-Benz DB 601s, identical to those fitted to the Me 110.

The layout of the 210 was similar to that of the 110. The most obvious difference was the more forward position of the cockpit and the generally sleeker lines of the new machine. It shared with the 110 the twin-engined monoplane layout and the twin fins of the tail unit.

So great was the faith of the Air Ministry in the eventual success of the latest of Messerschmitt's designs, that 1000 aircraft were ordered off the drawing board before the first prototype had flown. This was to prove a costly mistake for the Luftwaffe, for Germany as a whole and, not least, for Messerschmitt himself. The first flight took place on 2 September 1939, the day before Britain declared war on Germany. From the beginning the aircraft displayed undesirable handling characteristics. The longitudinal stability was a cause for great concern and the tendency of the aircraft to go into a spin did not endear it to the pilots.

It was reported that, after the first flight, the test pilot told Messerschmitt that the fuselage needed to be lengthened by at least a metre. Messerschmitt is supposed to have replied that such a modification would mean the scrapping of millions of Reichsmarks' worth of jigs which had already been built preparatory to the large production order. As a result no fundamental changes were made to the geometry of the aircraft.

Because of the obvious deficiencies revealed by flight testing of the first prototype, Messerschmitt was besieged by questions from the Air Ministry. In reply he dispatched reassuring reports on developments, with no intimation that any really serious difficulties were involved. What in fact were most difficult fundamental problems were dismissed as temporary setbacks, the elimination of which would require very little time or effort.

This had been a characteristic of Messerschmitt's response to criticism throughout his life. Because of his unshakable faith in his own ability to solve any technical problem, he inevitably underestimated the effort and time required for the solution of what were often serious setbacks. Really difficult problems were dismissed as being of minor importance. The estimates made for the effort involved in the rectification of any design faults were far below what eventually turned out to be necessary in fact.

This attitude is obvious from a typical letter which he sent on 15 July 1940 to an official in the Technical Office of the Air Ministry:

SECRET!

Dear Herr Lucht,
As you requested, I am sending you the required information on the state of the Me 210. You will see from the enclosed summary that there are still a number of smaller difficulties to be overcome, but that the start up of series production can in no way be regarded as endangered by them. Unfortunately, because of a mishap and not least due to the bad weather conditions of last winter, we have had some set-backs in the testing.

From the flight tests carried out today, the aileron loads, which were giving us some trouble, are now satisfactory.

It has also been possible to test the dive-brakes to the extent that we can already review the shortcomings still to be removed and we will have eliminated them in a very short time.

The flights showed that the feared aileron buffet with dive-brakes out does not occur and that the required terminal diving speed of about 600 kph [372 mph] is achieved.

We have not quite reached the required level for the control forces but are of the opinion that they are absolutely adequate for a first series production run since they are in part smaller than those on the Me 110. We will, of course, continue to work to reduce the control loads.

In order to overcome the programme difficulties caused by the dive-brakes not yet being fully tested and the radio sets still not being installed, I have arranged for this equipment to be delivered as a self-contained installation and to be installed subsequently in the aircraft.

What is important for series production is that the material is delivered to the subcontract firms on the planned programme dates. In order to ensure this in every instance, the material procurement group, which has to look after no less than 72 firms, is being reinforced in the next few days by three people. They will look after the delivery of fixtures in accordance with the programme.

I would be pleased if you could come here and see for yourself the state of the work.

Yours sincerely,
Messerschmitt

It was less than eight weeks later that the second prototype crashed. Udet lost no time in demanding an explanation from the designer. The reply came within a few days, and again conveyed a reassuring picture of the continuing development of the aircraft; although for the first time Messerschmitt does admit to some slight misgivings on certain aspects:

13.9.1940

Dear Udet,

You called me recently and asked me to what could be attributed the failure of the tail unit of the Me 210. Since no other reason for it could be found, there is no doubt that the horn-balance on the elevator, which lies within the propeller slipstream, must be being excited. Before the horn-balance was used, there was no knowledge of any flight conditions which led to vibration. Only since the horn-balance has been introduced have continual difficulties of such a nature occurred. I have decided, therefore, to do without the horn-balance and to redesign the tail unit accordingly so that the desired low aerodynamic forces are achieved by different means. The present state of the aircraft is as follows:

Of the control surfaces, the rudder is perfectly all right. In the meantime the aileron has also been made perfectly all right, so that the effect is better and the forces are smaller than on the Me 110 with the reduced loads. The characteristics in a dive with and without the dive-brakes, even with the bomb-doors open, are now, and always were, all right. Essentially, on the aircraft the tail unit has still to be got right since the control surface loads were too big. The Luftwaffe test establishment did agree, however, that the old controls would be approved for the initial production run. I assume that the first series aircraft, like the aileron, can be put right. The weapons installation was checked and is all right. The rear weapons, the remote-controlled Borsig guns, are still causing some problems but these can probably be eliminated. In the worst case, the initial production would have to be with a standard Mg 15 gun as in the Me 110. The performance has been checked and agrees with the guaranteed performance when it is converted for the engine output used as the basic assumption.

I can assure you that you need have no fears concerning the airframe, but I am a bit worried about the following points:

The DB 601 engine refuses to come up to scratch. So far I have not received a single engine which has not had to go back to the works after a few flights, so that there is no way of thinking about performance test flights. Moreover, the engine performance figures obtained do not agree with the performance guaranteed by the manufacturer. Then Herr Hentzen is complaining to an unusual extent that the raw materials for the series production of the Me 210 cannot be obtained in time. After many struggles, we have obtained material order forms but on these forms the material cannot be obtained in time. The material that we need in August and September, we will receive on the basis of the allocation system in December or the beginning of January at the earliest. As we have not stockpiled any material at all, this late allocation has particularly adverse effects for us.

Nine months later the frustration of the Air Ministry and the Luftwaffe was becoming more evident. Time was passing by and there was still no evidence of early deliveries of the aircraft to the Luftwaffe. Udet found it necessary to write again to Messerschmitt on 27 June 1941:

Dear Messerschmitt,

The problems which have arisen in recent years with your designs of the 109, 110 and 210 have resulted in significant delays and loss of life. I feel constrained to be absolutely open with you on this occasion. Much as I am aware of the outstanding performance of your designs, I feel compelled to point out that you are, in my opinion, going in the wrong direction. It is necessary to design military aircraft with an adequate safety margin, particularly in times of war. It is essential to avoid having to incorporate modifications later because that wastes time.

A month later Messerschmitt received another letter from Udet. Another problem which the Me 210 shared with the Me 109 was the fragility of the undercarriage. As usual, in an all-out attempt to save weight, Messerschmitt had pared the undercarriage and its attachments down to the absolute minimum, or possibly below the absolute minimum. As a result undercarriage failures on landing were a common occurrence during the testing of the prototypes. In this latest letter Udet complains about undercarriage failures caused by designing too close to the bone.

Messerschmitt replied with a letter which admitted that he took risks, but making the excuse that, in the absence of adequate research facilities, he had no alternative but to push on blindly into the darkness:

But I could wait, as is perhaps usual in engineering, until all the possibilities of research are exhausted and then start on the construction of a new aircraft. In that case I would today have to wait until a series of wind tunnels are in operation and until detailed tests are carried out on present day high speed aircraft with service pilots. You will agree with me that the responsibility would not be bearable since the loss of time could not be recovered. Therefore, in the future, as in the past, we must take risks and build aircraft which are pushing into unknown territory, and learn from the bitter losses of life and equipment. It is obvious that the maximum care is needed in all risky ventures, and unnecessary risks in testing must be avoided. But who will set himself up as the judge after the event and declare: 'But surely we should have known that?'

By the beginning of 1941 14 prototypes had been produced and the first pre-production models were beginning to appear. A number of changes had been made to the initial design in attempts to eliminate the handling problems which still persisted.

One fundamental design change concerned the tail unit. The original lay-out had included a tail with twin fins similar to the Me 110. The armament was to include remotely controlled machine guns mounted in turrets on each side of the fuselage, and firing rearwards to protect the aircraft against attack by fighters diving on to its tail. The two fins restricted the field of fire for these turrets, and a modification was introduced to fit a single fin mounted on the fuselage.

This period of stress for Messerschmitt was relieved by his re-election to the German Academy of Aviation Research. Only the best brains in German aviation circles were invited to join this august body which regularly organized meetings for the exchange of information on aeronautical subjects. Membership was granted for five years.

Messerschmitt had first been invited to join the Academy in 1937. On 26 November of that year, on the occasion of his inauguration, he had presented at a meeting of the Academy a very wide-ranging paper entitled 'Problems of High-speed Flight'. In it he reviewed the progress made to date on the development of high-speed aircraft. The paper also summarized the thinking on which the design of the Me 109 had been based and which eventually led to the Me 210 and his later high-speed aircraft.

A lot of water had flowed under the bridge since then. In view of the disaster in which he was now involved with the Me 210, the current which was flowing in 1942 was obviously muddied. A less confident man than Messerschmitt might have seen cause to be concerned.

Because of the resulting reduction of his popularity, with Hermann Goering in particular, he might have felt insecure in his membership of the Academy. It was reassuring, therefore, to know that he was still considered to be a leading expert in aviation matters. As evidence of his membership of the Academy he was presented with a certificate printed in black and red on thick, vellum-like paper with the bold signature of Hermann Goering, the President of the Academy, at the bottom.

The text of the certificate reads:

The German Academy of Aeronautical Research founded by decree of the Führer and Chancellor of the Reich, Adolf Hitler, on 24 July 1936 in Bayreuth, nominates:

Armaments Industry Leader Professor Dr-Ing.E.h. Dipl.-Ing. Willy Messerschmitt

as a Full Member up to 28 February 1947.

I effect this document in the expectation that the person named, by his cooperative efforts in the duties of the Academy, will contribute to extending the scientific and technical base of aeronautics, in so doing indicating new paths for future progress, and by applying himself fully in the spirit of scientific solidarity and respect for all the members of the Academy, will co-operate in the wider aims of aviation to conquer space and time.

Berlin on 1 March 1942
The President
Goering
Reichsmarschall of the Greater German Reich
Minister of State for Aviation
Supreme Commander of the Luftwaffe

It might have been expected that the recipient of this prestigious award would have had it framed for display over his desk. In fact, it was filed away among Messerschmitt's office papers where it remains today in the archives of the Imperial War Museum.

Messerschmitt felt that he had no need of commendations from his fellow men to convince him of his own worth. He was fully aware of his unique qualities as an aircraft designer developed over many years of sometimes arduous effort. No doubt he enjoyed the admiration of others, but his self-confidence was in no need of external reinforcement.

However, his self-confidence was just about to suffer the most painful assault of his life. The Me 210 problems refused to go away and a major crisis was inevitable in the immediate future.

Despite the continuing difficulties with the Me 210, there was considerable reluctance on the part of the Air Ministry or the Luftwaffe to cancel the project. Large manufacturing resources had been diverted from other aircraft in order to speed up the production of the Me 210; resources which could have been more profitably used in manufacturing the Me 109 or the Me 110, which despite its limitations did not suffer from the severe problems of the Me 210.

However, a decision could not be long delayed. The longer that production went on, the more of the aircraft industry's resources were being wasted. Luftwaffe pilots in the few front line units which had received Me 210s were refusing to fly them, and were reverting to the Me 110.

A meeting was held with Goering on 9 March at which the decision was finally taken to cease any further production of the Me 210. The resulting gap in the resources of the Luftwaffe was to be filled by increasing as quickly as possible the production of existing aircraft.

On the next day Messerschmitt received a telegram from the GL/C-E, the body overseeing the technical development of all aeronautical equipment. It read as follows:

SECRET
10 March 1942

To: Professor Messerschmitt, Augsburg.
Copy to: Major Croneiss, Messerschmitt Company, Regensburg.

On the basis of the discussion on 9 March, the Reichsmarschall has decided that further building of the Me 210 is to be stopped. After test flights have been made by the test establishment and service personnel, a decision will be made about starting production of a new type of aircraft with a lengthened fuselage, elevators with internal balance, slats and the elimination of all the complaints which have resulted from test flying by the Luftwaffe.

As a substitute, an increase in the production of the Bf 110 and Bf 109 is envisaged. The Reichsmarschall expects from the Messerschmitt company that it will fill the gap left by the failure of the Me 210 by increasing production of the Bf 110 and the Bf 109 with all conceivable means. For a discussion of the consequences arising from the foregoing, I expect Professor Messerschmitt, Director Hentzen and Major Croneiss on 12 March at 11 o'clock in Oberst Vorwaldt's office.

Please bring with you as accurate plans as possible regarding personnel and materials so that decisions about future deployment of the staff can be taken.

Please also bring a set of drawings of the change in position of the tailplane.

The dating of the various communications at this stage of the career of the Me 210 is somewhat puzzling. As we have just seen, Messerschmitt had been informed on 10 March of the decision to stop production of the aircraft, but correspondence regarding the shortcomings of the Me 210 was still being passed back and forth some weeks later.

What is surprising is the fact that the news of the aircraft's cancellation does not seem to have been revealed to the workforce two weeks later. Nevertheless, the realization that something was seriously wrong had obviously penetrated to all strata of the factory and the local community. Despite the fact that over 300 aircraft had already been built, and that components for hundreds more were arriving in a continuous stream from outside contractors, nobody could have had any doubts that disaster was impending.

So great was the unrest that Messerschmitt felt compelled to address his workforce on 25 March in a speech which was transmitted over the factory loudspeaker system.

Comrades!
As rumours about the situation of the Me 210 are being spread in the factory and in the city which do not correspond to the facts, I consider it necessary to give some explanations in so far as it is possible on the grounds of security.

On Monday, 9 March, a meeting took place with the Reichsmarschall of the Greater German Reich [i.e. Goering] at which the services representatives produced a list of desirable modifications to the type of aircraft in question. These considerably exceeded the modifications being worked on at the moment in Landsberg. The Reichsmarschall has decided that these modifications must immediately be initiated, tested and incorporated. In order to prevent unnecessary delay and consequent larger and later modifications, some of our comrades for this reason have been displaced to work on other types of our design.

Naturally, in the interests of secrecy I am unable to inform you about the details of what is the nature of these modifications and for what purposes they are being introduced.

I can only say to you that the rumours which have been spread do not correspond to the facts. In particular, rumours that I have personally fallen out of favour with the Reichsmarschall are utterly and completely figments of the imagination, and you can see that from the fact that the Reichsmarschall has ordered that I am to get more manpower in the design office to carry out my plans.

I ask you, comrades, to ensure as far as you have the opportunity, that the rumours which have been spread are rectified.

Added in pencil to the bottom of the typewritten text which Messerschmitt used for this broadcast is a manuscript note by another hand than that of Messerschmitt himself:

Every member of the workforce has been made aware of the regulations regarding security and, as a consequence, of the need to take steps to suppress untrue rumours. Anyone who impedes this and, in particular, makes public any matters concerning the factory, renders himself in some cases guilty of treason for which, as is well known, the most severe punishments are prescribed.

I demand, therefore, that you act accordingly and, in particular, that you produce the names of such rumour-mongers.

Presumably the pencilled addition was added to Messerschmitt's typed draft of the speech by a fellow director because it was thought that the original message was not forceful enough.

By that time Messerschmitt had been forced to accept the fact that most of the problems could be cured by lengthening the fuselage as had been suggested by the test pilot immediately after the first flight. One of the prototypes was modified by inserting an extra section into the rear fuselage. Slots were incorporated in the leading edge of the wing in an effort to improve the disastrous stalling characteristics. The testing of the modified aircraft showed that the main problems had been eliminated by the new configuration. Some unpleasant characteristics still remained, however, as is indicated in a letter which Messerschmitt wrote to an engineer at the Rechlin test centre on the same day as his broadcast to the workforce:

SECRET

25 March 1942

Flieger-Oberstingenieur Franke
Rechlin Test Establishment.

Dear Herr Franke,

You certainly know already that the service pilots are having difficulties with the Me 210 and that, against all expectations, these can be attributed in the first instance to the stall.

As a large number of aircraft are already built and are still being built, it is absolutely necessary for the aircraft to be got right as quickly as possible. The defects identified up to now (swing on landing, ugly characteristics of the elevators) have been taken care of by lengthening the fuselage and installing a balanced elevator, both of which have already been accepted by the test establishment and have been considered satisfactory after a few flights by service pilots and the test establishment. The other complaints about the undercarriage, hydraulics, weapons, etc. are essentially engineering jobs which can be cleared up in the not too distant future. The most critical point has become the one that we all feared the least. The difficulty consists essentially of the fact that a bottom limit on the speed, in accordance with which the aircraft must be flown, has not yet been determined. Obviously we cannot today lay down and rapidly confirm the requirement that the aircraft, if it gets into a spin, must recover just by centring the control column at a certain number of turns. This requirement has not so far been imposed on any modern aircraft, and in some circumstances it could take a long time before such tests were completed.

However, I am of the opinion that at least the technical standards of roughly the Me 110 must be attained in this condition.

An indication of the atmosphere prevailing by then among the works test pilots who had had the daunting task of flying the Me 210 during the test programme can be gained by an addendum which Messerschmitt added to his letter. This asks that Luftwaffe pilots at Rechlin should carry out any further flight tests as Messerschmitt's own test pilots 'have no experience'.

The 210 with the extended fuselage and other modifications, including the DB 603 engines, proved so successful in test flights that it was immediately decided to put it into full production. In order to sever any associations of the new aircraft with its unfortunate ancestor it was decided to rename it the Me 410.

The Me 210 debacle was the most damaging episode in Messerschmitt's career as an aircraft designer, the damage being inflicted on Messerschmitt himself, his company, the Luftwaffe and, ultimately, on Germany. As a result of this failure the Luftwaffe was deprived of over 600 aircraft, the lack of which became increasingly devastating as the war progressed. There was a continuing shortage of aircraft to attack the fleets of American daylight bombers which proceeded to destroy the German armaments industry.

To the Messerschmitt company the Me 210 represented a loss of more than 30 million Reichsmarks. The Air Ministry insisted that as the mistake had been made by the Messerschmitt company, it must purchase from subcontractors the components already manufactured for incorporation into the 1000 aircraft on order.

Messerschmitt may have convinced his employees that he had not been alienated by the Reichsmarschall. Nevertheless, Goering is alleged to have declared that his epitaph would record that he would have lived longer if the Me 210 had never been produced.

The disaster led to demands by Milch, with the support of Goering, that Messerschmitt be removed from the managing directorship of his company. The Air Ministry insisted that this change in the organization of the Messerschmitt company should take place without delay. Although still a major shareholder, Messerschmitt was to be deprived of control over the company which he had built up with so much effort. In future he was to be restricted to acting as a designer, whilst leaving the running of the company to others. This seems a strange decision since the primary fault with the Me 210 had been in the design of the aircraft. It is more likely that it represents the final triumph of Milch over the man with whom he had disagreed for over ten years, and whom he honestly believed was responsible for a devastating loss to the power of the Luftwaffe.

Milch's victory was tempered by the knowledge that Hitler still had a high opinion of Messerschmitt, but he could console himself with the thought that he had managed to strike a deadly blow at the object of his dislike. The whole Me 210 affair must have been a distressing experience for Willy Messerschmitt. He had had failures before in his career, as every aircraft designer has, but none as humbling as this disaster. He had lost a great deal of money through the cancelled order, his ability as a designer had been exposed to public ridicule, and he had lost control of the company which he had founded. He was still complaining about his lack of power to direct company policy two years later.

CHAPTER 11

The Me 262 jet fighter

Although the Me 109, in its day, had been an outstanding step forward in the art of designing fighter aircraft, the Me 262 jet fighter could be regarded as an even greater advance over contemporary standards of technology. The Me 109, with all its innovations, was an assembly in one aircraft of the best of existing knowledge and experience. The Me 262 was a completely new concept using a hitherto untried method of propulsion — the jet engine.

The most important advantage of a jet-propelled aircraft was its higher speed relative to that of a machine of similar layout powered by a conventional piston-engine. Messerschmitt had made his views on this topic clear in the address which he gave to the German Academy of Aviation Research on 26 November 1937. After reviewing the progress made in the previous 20 years in raising the speed of aircraft, he pointed out that at that date the fastest aircraft was flying at about six tenths of the speed of sound. He went on to say:

> The possibilities of progress of that order of magnitude cannot be anticipated in the near future if I neglect extremely-high-altitude flying and jet propulsion. Man-carrying aircraft which fly at speeds approaching or exceeding the speed of sound are the dream of the aircraft designer. I have, however, little hope that we ourselves will live to see flight above the speed of sound, although it will certainly come one day. Every extra ten per cent of the speed of sound brings greater difficulties, and so it might appear that it is no longer profitable to spend a great deal of effort on it. But we should remember that we are talking about the small advantage of speed by which we must defeat our enemy.

Messerschmitt was now having to face up to those 'greater difficulties' since his new fighter was, at one fell swoop, going to eat up far more than the ten per cent of the speed of sound to which he had referred.

The first German jet engines had been designed and built by Hans von Ohain in the late 1930s. Ernst Heinkel had sponsored Ohain's early work and had designed an aircraft, the He 178, to incorporate the engines which he had invented. The first flight took place on 27 August 1939. It is to Heinkel, therefore, that the honour of designing the first successful jet aircraft must be awarded. Because of bureaucracy in the Air Ministry, Heinkel was prevented from developing his ideas further. Instead, Messerschmitt was selected as the designer of the first military aircraft to enter service with a jet engine.

The original proposal for a jet fighter was issued by the Technical Office of the Air Ministry in January 1939. This called for an aircraft with only one engine. Messerschmitt was justifiably doubtful about the reliability of jet engines at such an early stage of their development. He was also aware that their power would be limited in those early days. As a result he thought it better to design an aircraft with two engines.

These doubts about the practicality of jet engines persisted in his mind for several years. As late as 1943, when instructing one of his senior designers as to the correct attitude to adopt at a Ministry meeting to discuss single-engined jet fighters, he made his views quite clear:

> My attitude to the single-engined jet fighter is the same as it always has been: that with the power of present day engines it would not be adequate to keep up with the ever-increasing demands for the armament of fighters with anything like satisfactory performance.

The first scheme drawings for Messerschmitt's twin-engined fighter were ready in May 1940, and the Air Ministry allotted the official designation Me 262 to the project. Work on the construction of the first prototype was started shortly afterwards so that the airframe was ready for its first flight less than a year later. Unfortunately, Messerschmitt was to suffer yet again from the problem that beset him throughout the war, the shortage of suitable engines to power his aircraft.

At that time the rival Heinkel jet-powered machine was also grounded awaiting an engine. Heinkel himself had been ordered by the Air Ministry to stop the development of the Ohain engine. In its place, BMW had been given a contract to produce a jet engine with a thrust of about 600 kp. Setbacks in producing a reliable engine led to unexpected delays, so a date for the first flight of the Me 262 could not be fixed with any certainty. It was decided to fly the aircraft with a piston engine installed in the fuselage nose. Messerschmitt could not have been happy with this decision, but it was necessary to get the aircraft into the air by some means so that any deficiencies in the handling characteristics could be discovered as soon as possible.

A Junkers Jumo 210G powerplant was mounted in the nose of the prototype aircraft. On 18 April 1940 test pilot Fritz Wendel took off for the first flight. The aircraft's behaviour in flight proved to be satisfactory, but no further progress could be made until jet engines became available. The delay exceeded Messerschmitt's worst fears. Two years were to go by before any further development of the aircraft could take place.

Meanwhile, Junkers had also been busy developing a jet engine as a rival to the BMW design. This also ran into difficulties which seriously delayed its appearance as a usable power unit. One of the problems encountered was the need for the development of a suitable alloy capable of standing up to the very high temperatures existing in the engine. When such an alloy was eventually produced, the acute shortage of critical alloying metals was to delay series production of all German jet engines throughout the war.

By the beginning of 1942 the BMW 003 engine had managed to produce a thrust of about 450 kp. Although far below the specification value, it was sufficient to get the Me 262 into the air. Two engines were at last installed into the prototype, but it was decided to leave the piston engine in place in the nose for the time being. The first flight was made on 25 March 1942. Shortly after the aircraft had taken off, both jet engines failed. In this drastic way, the decision to retain the piston engine was fully justified, and the aircraft managed to land safely.

It was 'back to the drawing board' for the BMW design team. Another year elapsed during which extensive modifications were introduced on the engine. Junkers now announced that they had brought their engine, the Jumo 004, up to a thrust of over 600 kp. Two were fitted in the Me 262 in place of the BMW units. The first flight in this configuration was again made by Fritz Wendel on 18 July 1942.

By the spring of 1943 four examples of the Me 262 were being test flown. In particular, on 22 May, Adolf Galland flew the aircraft and was immediately convinced of its outstanding qualities and its potential as a war-winning aircraft. Galland had no difficulty in taking the aircraft up, and he was amazed by its performance and its handling characteristics. After his flight in the Me 262, Galland sent a telegram to Milch:

> The 262 aircraft is a very great hit. It will guarantee us an unbelievable advantage in operations, as long as the enemy adheres to the piston engine. From an airworthiness point of view it makes the best impression. The engines are absolutely convincing except during take-off and landing. This aircraft opens up completely new tactical possibilities.

As a result the decision was made to manufacture a pre-production batch of 100 aircraft. The only modification required by the Luftwaffe was a tricycle undercarriage as it had proved extremely difficult to lift the tail off the ground during the take-off run with the conventional tail-wheel undercarriage. There had also been serious damage to the surfaces of concrete runways due to the impingement of the jets. The concrete had been broken up into large pieces which had been thrown into the air with effects not entirely beneficial to other aircraft in the immediate vicinity.

It might have appeared at that stage that the technical difficulties had all been overcome. However, problems of a different sort were soon to cloud the horizon.

Hitler was not entirely convinced of the feasibility of the Me 262 as a jet fighter and insisted that further trials be carried out on the prototypes. He also envisaged the aircraft as being a fighter-bomber despite its having been designed as a pure fighter. This produced further delays in reaching a decision on the version to be produced.

These delays in producing the Me 262 were having serious effects on the strategy being developed for the defence of the German homeland. By the end of 1943 things were going far from well for the German armed forces. It was obvious that an invasion of Europe from the British Isles could not be long delayed. Hitler planned to use the Me 262 for the first time as a bomber against the bridgeheads of the invading forces. He imagined that these unique fast-flying aircraft screaming over the heads of the American and British troops would reduce them to panic and make it an easy task for his defending forces to repulse the invasion.

Arguments have raged ever since as to who convinced Hitler of the suitability of the Me 262 for bombing missions. When asked by Hitler if the Me 262 could carry bombs, Messerschmitt assured him that it could be modified to do so. Whoever was responsible, Hitler had the idea firmly fixed in his mind that the Me 262 was a 'lightning bomber' — so much so that he would not tolerate any reference to the aircraft's use in any other role. As a result an order went out that any future reference to the aircraft as a fighter was unacceptable. That meant that aircraft already built as fighters could not be used until modifications had been incorporated to enable them to carry bombs.

The resulting indecision proved catastrophic. By the time the invasion of France took place not a single Me 262 was in service, either as a fighter or a fighter-bomber. The opportunity had been lost for ever, never to be recovered.

It was not only indecision that delayed the Me 262. Messerschmitt had been trying for months to get more labour to work on building the aircraft. He even proposed closing down the production lines of other aircraft manufacturers so that their labour forces could be made available to him for accelerated production of the Me 262. Not unnaturally, this proposal was not welcomed by other aircraft manufacturers and it did little to endear Messerschmitt to them or to the Air Ministry.

Even so, Messerschmitt himself does not appear to have been entirely convinced of the superiority of the jet aircraft over conventional piston-engined machines in all circumstances. In a letter to Herr Seiler, his managing director, he expresses some doubts on the subject:

> An aircraft with jet engines like the Me 262 will not for a long time, perhaps never, replace the conventional fighter, particularly because of the take-off and landing conditions and because of the very high fuel consumption. In spite of the good climb performance of the 262 up to altitudes above 10 km [33,000 ft], it has not yet been demonstrated whether these new types of engines are suitable for higher altitudes. It is known today that altitudes of up to 17 km [56,000 ft] can be reached with conventional engines, whereas this is absolutely impossible with the jet engines in the 262 in their present form. For this reason, the conventional form of fighter must be further pursued.

With his usual careful eye on the strategic situation, Messerschmitt knew that the Allies were also developing jet aircraft. If they got into service before the Me 262, there was no doubt the war would be lost. He was relying on his jet fighters to put an end to the devastating daylight bombing missions being continued by the American Air Force.

To make matters worse, engines were not coming off the line fast enough to satisfy the demands of Messerschmitt's own rate of production. On 20 April 1944 he wrote to the managing director of the Junkers concern:

Dear Herr Cambeis,

I would like to make contact with you personally yet again with regard to the jet engine programme.

You must have heard in the meantime that, according to reports from our agents, the English and Americans intend to equip large units with jet aircraft in the autumn of this year. It is, therefore, a matter of life and death for us all to step up the numbers of Me 262s with your engines as rapidly as is in any way possible. I will try to accelerate the increase in the rate of airframe production, but I can only do this successfully if I know that we are getting the corresponding number of engines.

I would be grateful to you, therefore, if you could let me know, naturally without any guarantee, the expected numbers in the programme until the spring of next year. If you have bottlenecks with which you might hope that I could be useful, I beg you to name them to me.

Messerschmitt

When the Me 262 did eventually enter service with the Luftwaffe it scored some notable successes, particularly against the American daylight bomber raids. Messerschmitt was not slow to write letters of congratulation to the airmen responsible for the first victories. As always he regarded victories scored in aircraft of his own design as vindications of his thinking, and he obviously took great pleasure in hearing of their successes.

On 4 September 1944 he writes to Oberfeldwebel Baudach:

You have flown our latest jet fighter in its first engagements, and under your control the Me 262 has victoriously withstood its baptism of fire.

I congratulate you on this great success which for me too means the joy of knowing that our latest design has been proved, and the certainty that air supremacy over our homeland can be regained.

In this sense I couple with my congratulations on the third victory in the Me 262 my best wishes for many further successful air battles.

The Me 262, despite being an aircraft far in advance of its time at its conception, was destined to play only a minor role in the Second World War. However, if its development and that of its engines had been pursued with more intense application it could easily have altered the outcome of the conflict.

That the Me 262 did not realize its promise was attributable to the lack of forward thinking of a number of influential officials in the German

Air Ministry and the Luftwaffe. When he was interrogated by Allied officers in June 1945, Rakan Kokothaki, who had been in charge of Me 262 production, wrote the following devastating report revealing the tragedy of the world's first jet fighter:

Difficulties and Obstacles During the Manufacture and Introduction into Service of the Me 262.

The story of the development of the Me 262 is recorded in a separate report, so that I can only describe my experiences from the time when the Air Ministry had decided to put the Me 262 into series production. At that time the Ministry expressed the desire to produce 60 aircraft a month for delivery starting in January 1944. In this connection a proposal was sent to the Air Ministry by the company management on 15 June 1943 in which were laid down the conditions which were necessary for the fulfilment of such a requirement. The company had decided on this step despite the fact that in earlier programmes the conditions had been only poorly met, or in a very dilatory way. Above everything it was necessary, if series production were to start on time, for the whole of the production facilities (jigs, templates, tools, etc.) to be made as quickly as possible. As at that point of time Messerschmitt had only a very small jig and tool department, a considerable build-up of it was the most urgent requirement. The granting of contracts to outside firms for the manufacture of jigs had in the past produced poor results both as regards programme and quality, because Germany required an enormous number of manhours for the manufacture of jigs as a result of the large number of aircraft types being built (about 40 basic types).

I had made my mind up, therefore, that at the same time as jig building was evacuated to Kottern, this jig and tool department would be constituted so that it was in the position to produce unaided the essential jigs at least — and, in particular, the templates — in an acceptable time.

In order to achieve this aim, a certain degree of concentration on one single task would have to be instituted within the company itself. Because I personally was of the opinion that the Me 262 would represent a revolution in aerial warfare, I regarded it as essential on the company's part to refuse the simultaneous production of other types along with the Me 262 and to concentrate on the Me 262 alone. Unfortunately, in doing so I was in opposition to Professor Messerschmitt, who at that time considered it necessary to design an aircraft with a piston engine in addition to the Me 262 which would be put into series production. That was to be the Me 309.

Subsequently, it turned out that my train of thought had been correct because the jigging capacity for the Me 262 could not effectively be produced, so that the jigs necessary for the start-up of production were delivered after considerable delay. The start-up of production had to be undertaken, therefore, with makeshift jigs (partly of wood) as a result of which the accuracy of the construction and with it the interchangeability suffered severely. Since the Air Ministry also only provided the promised 1800 jig builders for Kottern after a very long delay, and then only in the form of unskilled and semi-skilled manpower from other trades, 2.8 million manhours were lost to jig construction at Kottern within a period of nine months.

Nevertheless, by exerting the utmost efforts, it was possible to test fly the first aircraft in February and deliver it in March. Feldmarschall Milch did not even acknowledge this special achievement but expressed his surprise that, although the requirements had not been fulfilled, the company had been in the position to achieve this. He ordered that a military court should investigate the matter, apparently with the purpose of demonstrating to the company that it had laid down unjustified conditions. In reality, however, the situation was that the first aircraft had indeed been produced at something like the right time, but that the lack of the proper conditions was bound to have a strong effect on the following deliveries. The investigation by the military court did not lead to any conclusion because, while it was going on, the Speer Ministry had taken over aircraft production. Speer immediately stopped all investigations by military courts.

During the Speer period the Me 262 programme was pushed along quite vigorously after the importance of the Me 262 had finally been recognized. During the many discussions of the programme we pointed out again and again that the unusually high number of aircraft ordered could not be produced in the shortest possible time unless the Speer Ministry gave us unlimited support in the procurement of really expert staff, material, means of transport, etc. We would also need a priority to be given to the building of the Me 262 to make it possible to carry out the task in the face of continually increasing difficulties in some areas of the armaments industry.

The Speer Ministry first of all created the so-called 'Jägerstab' (Fighter Staff) which functioned well right through the first two months, since it could draw on its earlier sources in the Armaments Ministry. The Jägerstab was, however, employed in all areas of armaments and, as a result very quickly lost its impetus and effectiveness. The assurances we were given about fulfilling the requirements were in no way implemented. Herr Saur allowed no discussions on this point. In fact, in opposition to the facts, he adopted the position during discussions that the Ministry had done everything that it could do.

A discussion of whether the requirements laid down by the company, which had previously been checked by the Armaments Ministry and defined by mutual agreement, had or had not been satisfied was always refused out of hand by Herr Saur. The result was that the deliveries naturally did not match up with the numbers specified in the programme. Because nobody wanted to find that the fault lay with the Ministry itself, the blame continued to be attributed to the company. Works officials, production officials, sponsors and special commissars were installed, and a turmoil of mutually confusing organizations created. That of itself was bound to throw the company organization out of gear.

There is no denying that mistakes were made by the company also, but this one-sided pushing of all the blame on to the company by the Armaments Ministry, particularly the official of the Airframe Section, Herr Lange, had no justification at all.

Neither the Armaments Ministry in the person of Herr Saur and Herr Lange nor the Aircraft Committee in the person of Herr Frydag were clear about the fact that significantly more men than they already possessed must be allotted to the Messerschmitt factories, including its sub-contractors. We pointed out that in the second half of 1944 more than 50% of the German aircraft programme was Messerschmitt machines, which were being built by the Messerschmitt company together with the Messerschmitt sub-contractors. Of the labour force available to the whole of German aircraft production, however, the Messerschmitt company and its sub-contractors had only between 25% and 30%. Neither the Armaments Ministry nor the Airframe Committee had succeeded in bringing about the transfer of labour from the remaining aircraft industry to such a degree that it would have removed, even to some extent, this great disparity. When we pointed this out, it was remarked, of course, that Messerschmitt aircraft were only small aircraft which would require significantly less manhours to be expended than bombers. Since it had been decided, however, to cut back bomber production severely and, in fact, to stop it altogether towards the end of 1944, this argument no longer had any justification.

This lack of proportion was even worse in the area of design. Messerschmitt, who designed the most efficient aircraft from the aerodynamic point of view and whose types occupied up to 50% of the total production, as mentioned above, had only about 10% of the total German aircraft design capacity at his disposal. In all the years from 1933 to 1943, the Messerschmitt company never had the opportunity to build up the numbers of its staff, since it always had to suffer because of the enmity of Feldmarschall Milch towards Professor Messerschmitt, resulting in Milch doing everything in his power to hold back Messerschmitt and his factory.

Milch also gave the express order that the industry was forbidden to make contact with the Luftwaffe. As a result it was understandably difficult to control the design by direct contact during the development stage in such a way as to prevent significant modifications having to be introduced later at the request of the service personnel.

If, despite all these difficulties, it was possible to deliver 1445 Me 262s by the end of April, that was to a great degree attributable to the extraordinary application of all the staff and employees in the Messerschmitt factories, who really did their utmost to bring out the aircraft. It was all the more incomprehensible to all these workers and staff that the Me 262s, which had been produced with so much effort, never went into action. On two occasions I myself from personal experience on the airfield at Memmingen and also on that at Neuburg a/Donau, saw, when the air-raid warning sounded, that there was a large number of Me 262s prepared for action on the field (in the first instance, about ten machines, in the second case about 35 machines).

The whole of the flying personnel, however, took themselves off to safety far away from the airfield together with their cars and transport vehicles. The attacks could then be carried out, as for example at Neuburg a/D, by the American Air Force completely undisturbed. The result was always the loss of a large number of Me 262s. It went so far, for example, that the Chief Pilot of the Messerschmitt factory at Regensburg, Herr Tränkle, who saw an enemy reconnaissance aircraft over the airfield and shot it down in an Me 262, was later brought up in front of a military court because he had received no orders.

When a number of fighter pilots who flew the Me 262 were asked why they did not climb up in defence against the attacks on Lechfeld, for example, the answer was that they had had no orders to attack. The impression for me, as one outside the Luftwaffe, was that the German Luftwaffe did not have a general staff which was even partially competent.

The two of his aircraft of which Messerschmitt was most proud were the Me 109 and the Me 262. In later life he was immensely satisfied that they were both to be seen displayed in the aeronautical section of the Deutsches Museum in Munich as examples of outstanding aircraft design. His conversations on aircraft design matters were punctuated by recommendations to visit the Deutsches Museum to examine some example of his design on one of his two favourite aircraft.

Messerschmitt himself always regarded the Me 262 as the one great missed opportunity of his life, not because of his own shortcomings but through the indecisions of those who should have recognized earlier the potentialities of his design.

CHAPTER 12

The America bomber

A part from being an aircraft designer, Messerschmitt took a great and well-informed interest in the strategic implications of the war's campaigns. His various writings show a persistent worry over a number of years about the potential of American industry when the USA became seriously involved in the fighting. Some extracts from his observations on this topic are given in Chapter 17.

His particular worry was the inability of the Axis powers to strike at the United States. There exists an undated report by Messerschmitt which, to judge from its contents, must have been written in early 1942. It provides a most clear exposition of Messerschmitt's awareness of strategic matters and is remarkably prophetic in its realization of what the future would bring:

> The English have known for a long time that on their own they would lose the war. Faced with the choice of accepting this and concluding a peace with Germany or delivering themselves up to the United States they have decided on the latter. It is a waste of time arguing whether the English or the Americans are delivering Europe up to Bolshevism. I am convinced that England and America would not think of allowing the Russians to become powerful, but they greet the war with Russia as a welcome opportunity to play off Bolshevism and National Socialism against each other. In the most favourable case they reckon, at the end of this war with Russia, to be able to easily finish off two battle-weary enemies, and also to eliminate both Bolshevism and National Socialism, and Germany along with the latter. In the worst case they reckon that Germany in the war with Russia will so weaken itself that, after the end of the campaign in the East, the balance of armaments is established or, indeed, that their own superiority in armaments is achieved. That is the great danger for Germany. The Europe that we dominate is surrounded by bases of the USA which are available to them directly or indirectly. The USA has the possibility of launching against Germany a future strong Air Force from Iceland, Ireland, England, from many bases in Africa and from Asia. It can also in addition establish a powerful land front from Asia, the intention to do this being illustrated by the occupation of Iran. A land front against us

96

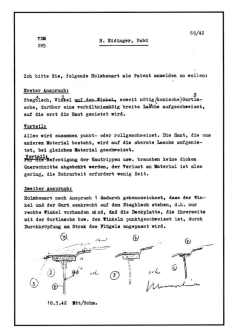 

Above left *The sketches made by Messerschmitt of a proposed patent method of attaching wing spars to the outer skin of a wing.* (Imperial War Museum)

Above right *A post-war portrait of Messerschmitt in a relaxed state of mind.* (Gero Madelung)

Below *The reverse of the sheet of sketches made by Messerschmitt during his interrogation shows the development of the Me 323 'Gigant' from the Me 321 glider and two proposed ways of extending the wingspan of the Me 109 to produce the Me 209 high-altitude fighter.* (J.M. Ramsden)

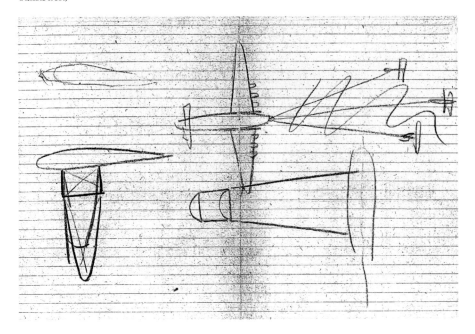

Top *The Me 328 was powered by two Argus tubes similar to those used on the V1 flying bombs. The jettisonable undercarriage is seen falling away after take-off from the launching pad. The pilot's headwear does not appear to be quite what is expected of a test pilot.* (Messerschmitt Archives)

Above *The last resting place of Willy Messerschmitt and his wife, Lilly, in the family vault of the Michel-Raulino family in the cemetery at Bamberg. On the memorial tablet the scant particulars of his life are squeezed in below those for his wife. There is no reference to his distinguished career or the fame which he once enjoyed.* (Janet Vann)

Below *The Porticusgruft in the cemetery at Bamberg. The grave of Messerschmitt and his wife can be seen near the centre of the picture.* (Janet Vann)

could become dangerous if the enemy advances with technically advanced equipment in superior quantities. We can always interfere with transport to the British Isles, but that island is not so important for the Americans. On the other hand, we can today do virtually nothing to interfere with the way to the Persian Gulf. The U-boats have no bases; we unfortunately also lack long-range aircraft which could make the whole ocean unsafe.

This thought had worried him before the actual entry of the United States into the war. He was even then making plans to counter the American threat. In 1941 he had already embarked on plans for a long-range aircraft capable of dropping bombs on New York. He realized that, with the limited bomb load that the aircraft would be able to carry over such a long range, this would only be a token gesture, but he believed that the psychological effect would be formidable.

The result of these plans was the Me 264 bomber with an operational range of about 9000 kilometres (5580 miles) and with a bomb load of 3 tonnes. The aircraft, as originally designed and built, had four engines, but plans were soon in hand for a stretched version with six engines and an even bigger bomb load.

The Me 264 was a handsome aircraft with a circular section fuselage and a tapered wing of 43 metres (141 ft) span and an aspect ratio of 14.5. It had two roughly elliptical fins set at the tips of the tailplane. The project drawings show gun turrets installed in the fuselage nose and tail as well as on the upper and lower sides of the fuselage amidships — a similar arrangement to that adopted in the British 4-engined bombers. One unusual feature for the time was that it was equipped with a tricycle undercarriage, the nosewheel retracting backwards behind the nose gun-turret.

A diagram contained in the Messerschmitt report on the aircraft shows that the aircraft could take off from Germany and, with a range of 8575 kilometres (5320 miles), could carry out missions beyond the coast of California. It could, therefore, attack targets on the whole of the North American continent and a large part of South America. It could penetrate beyond the Cape of Good Hope in a southerly direction and reach Japan to the East.

On the afternoon of 23 December 1942 Messerschmitt sent a telex to his Berlin office to announce the first flight of the prototype Me 264. In it he says that 'everything went well and the pilot's comments are very favourable'. Messerschmitt's own ideas on the aircraft are contained in a letter which he wrote to Claudius Dornier on the same day. Because of the heavy load on the Messerschmitt Design Office from the unsolved problems with the 210 among others, the contract for further development work on the 264 had been given by the Air Ministry to the Dornier company. Messerschmitt was never pleased to see any other designer interfering with his work and he was obviously not happy about the modifications to the design that Dornier was intending to introduce.

As usual, Messerschmitt has the overall strategy of the war in mind, as can be seen from his letter:

I acknowledge with thanks the receipt of your letter of 9 December 1942. From it I gather that, contrary to my own view, you are considering extensive design modifications from the third prototype Me 264 V-3 onwards. As a result, I would like to explain a bit more fully how I myself regard the whole project. The reason for the development of this aircraft was originally the intention to produce a long-range aircraft capable of dropping propaganda material over America and showing the Americans that they would have to set up a civil and military defence organization in the case of war. From the beginning it was quite clear to me that the big step in the development of long-range aircraft could not be made all at once, but that the end-result could be attained by the planned introduction of intermediate stages. Of course, these intermediate stages would not only be prototype aircraft but pre-production models fit for action, which on the one hand would ensure early testing of the basic type by the forces, and on the other would satisfy the requirements of the high command for fast long-range maritime reconnaissance aircraft.

Before the entry of America into the war it was not possible for me to get from the Air Ministry the urgently needed support in the provision of design staff. Since the entry of America into the war my earlier view of the necessity of such an aircraft is daily increasingly confirmed. If today the U-boat war cannot be conducted with greater success, despite what should be possible with the very large number of U-boats available, this is solely because of the lack of reconnaissance of convoys in the Atlantic. Despite initial successes, the attempted maritime reconnaissance, particularly with the Condor, was unfortunately soon no longer possible since the speed of that aircraft remained substantially below that of the enemy fighters carried in the convoys. Because of the continuing perfection of the enemy defences against U-boats, it is only a matter of time before U-boats will cease to be able to effectively attack enemy shipping. In order to employ the U-boats with the greatest effectiveness in the remaining time available, the lack of maritime reconnaissance must be made good.

In the present Air Ministry development programme this requirement can be met in the short term only with the Me 264, since this aircraft is the most advanced in its class in design and construction. This was also the reason, probably, which prompted Generalfeldmarschall Milch to grant the aircraft increased urgency and to transfer the further development of the aircraft to your company. I consider a clear explanation of the immediate objectives in the Me 264 development to be urgently necessary, since only then can decisions be made regarding the necessary modifications relative to the state of the Me 264 V-1 prototype.

As a remark in passing, it is worth noting a strange coincidence which relates the Me 264 to a project of the First World War. When the Allies entered Cologne at the end of 1918 they discovered the remains of a huge aircraft, the Poll Giant Triplane. This enormous contraption was to have had ten engines, a wing span of over 50 metres (164 ft) and a fuselage almost 46 metres (151 ft) long. Its duration of 80 hours would have given it almost the same range as the Me 264.

The remarkable feature is that that aircraft was also said to have been designed to drop propaganda material over New York before the United States entered the conflict. The stated purpose was to warn the Americans of the danger to them if they became involved in the war. The

German Navy is also said to have been interested in the aircraft as a long-range bomber.

The similarities between the intended uses of the Poll Triplane and the Me 264 are sufficiently surprising to make one wonder whether Messerschmitt had heard of the earlier machine and the purposes to which it was to be put.

Six months after the above letter to Dornier, despite the fact that the development work on the Me 264 had gone to Dornier, drawings had been prepared in Augsburg of the 6-engined version of the aircraft. The outer wings were to be moved out unaltered. A long centre-section whose leading and trailing edges continued the lines of the outer wing was to be introduced at the wing root. This centre-section would carry an extra engine on each side.

Messerschmitt was by then more convinced than ever that the most effective role for the aircraft was as a long-range maritime reconnaissance aircraft. In a memorandum which he issued to his designers in May 1943 he explains that the aircraft is to be introduced into service gradually in order to ensure steady development:

The aircraft is to be introduced in the following stages:

1. As a pure long-range reconnaissance aircraft without armament and with no bomb bay, but with the necessary armour; similar to the English 'Mosquito' which also flies without armament as a reconnaissance aircraft over Germany. With the speed of the Me 264 and the speed of the enemy fighters and fighter-bombers expected over the sea, the aircraft can certainly be sufficient.

2. Introduction of bomb bay and armament, as intended until now.

3. Design of the modification kits, wing inserts and fuselage extensions so that the aircraft can fly as a 6-engined aircraft. In addition, introduction of a suitable tail turret.

4. In parallel, the large modification kits necessary for the extremely long ranges, such as the auxiliary undercarriage, etc., are being developed and tested.

By this continual development it can be ensured that the services obtain a usable aircraft very quickly which by continual development over a long time will be superior to all other aircraft of this type.

In fact, the 6-engined version was never built. The 4-engined version was already in limited production when the Air Ministry decided to cancel the order. A rival had appeared in the shape of a Focke-Wulf project fulfilling the same role.

Messerschmitt soon had his staff preparing detailed reports intended to demonstrate the technical superiority of the Me 264 over the Focke Wulf FW 400 design and pointing out the delay in introduction into service if a new project was substituted for the Me 264. From the cover sheet to one of the surviving reports it is apparent that Messerschmitt could not or would not understand why his aircraft was being rejected in favour of the project of another designer:

> The rejection of the Me 264 can only have happened because of a false basis for the comparison. For this reason the Focke-Wulf project and the Me 264 are compared below on the basis of a searching investigation.

There follows a long and detailed comparison of the performance figures for both aircraft which succeeds in demonstrating the superiority of the Messerschmitt design.

In the end the Focke-Wulf project was never built and production of the Messerschmitt aircraft was confined to three prototypes, none of which survived the war. Germany had, therefore, lost its last opportunity of producing a successful 4-engined bomber in time to be of real use. This was despite the fact that at a conference of leading aircraft designers with Goering in March 1943, the Reichsmarschall criticized the German aircraft industry for failing to supply the Luftwaffe with 4-engined bombers. Messerschmitt attended this stormy meeting. His full report of the proceedings appears later in Chapter 14. It contains one particular reference to the subject of 4-engined bombers:

> The Reichsmarschall complained in particular that we had no usable 4-engined bombers, whereas the English could fly daily into Germany with their Stirling bombers with no difficulty.

Looked at in retrospect, the Me 264 was a remarkable design. It was far in advance of any contemporary aircraft in respect of range and bomb load. However, even if it had been produced in quantity, it is doubtful that it would have had much effect on the outcome of the war. The damage which it could have inflicted on the United States was limited and would not seriously have impeded the American war effort. Nor is it likely that the propaganda effect of a direct attack on the United States from a European base would have been as effective as Messerschmitt had hoped.

It might have had a significant effect on the war in the Atlantic, but it was probably even too late for that. The only official mention of the Me 264 in the German Press appeared in a news report in 1944, at the time of the threatened putsch by some of the German generals. According to the report, an Me 264 had been standing ready to fly Hitler to Japan if the coup had succeeded.

CHAPTER 13

Military transports

Because Messerschmitt's greatest achievements as a designer were the
Me 109 and Me 262, his two most ungainly creations the Me 321 and
Me 323 'Gigant' transport aircraft have been considered as aberrations
unworthy of a designer of high-speed fighters. Most of the many books
which deal with Messerschmitt's aircraft dismiss the Me 321 glider and
the Me 323 powered version as virtual monstrosities which proved inef-
fectual in service, being no better than clumsy leviathans which formed
an easy prey for Allied fighters. In fact, far removed in their design — as
they undoubtedly were — from the high speed fighters, they were outstanding aircraft in the light of the daring of their design and the amazingly short time in which they progressed from proposals to actual
flying aircraft. As will appear later, from service reports on its operations, the Me 323 was not by any means useless in its role as a supply aircraft for the Afrika Korps in its North African campaign.

In his book *Fighting Gliders of World War II*, James E. Mrazek suggests
that the idea for a large transport glider was discussed by Messerschmitt
and Voigt, one of his senior designers, early in November 1940. The first
thoughts were, however, already in Messerschmitt's mind in April 1940,
as can be seen from his correspondence with Udet.

A draft of a letter to Udet in Messerschmitt's handwriting and a
number of carbon copies of the typed original are filed in the Imperial
War Museum's collection. Along with the letter is a sketch by
Messerschmitt of the arrangement of the glider he is proposing.

The letter reads as follows:

14.4.1940

General Ernst Udet
Air Ministry, Berlin W.8.
Leipzigerstr. 7.

Dear Udet,
Enclosed is a document from my company with a proposal. If the landing in

England is really to take place in the early part of next year, it would in my opinion be of great importance if, simultaneously with the sea landing and the airborne troops, units of heavy and very heavy tanks with all the associated equipment were to be transported to the rear of the enemy.

I have spoken to Professor Georgii who has no doubts about the manner of towing and would be ready to begin immediately with the trials and the training. With a reasonable organization, a large quantity of such gliders could be produced in four months. The size of the wings will perhaps raise some eyebrows but the solution to the problem is so simple that there is no cause for any doubts.

I believe that the idea is still of value even if it were too late for England. Please let me know whether I should do some further work on it.

With cordial greetings and Heil Hitler!
Yours
Messerschmitt

Accompanying the letter is the following proposal for converting tanks into gliders. Included with the proposal is a sketch of the towing arrangement using four aircraft.

Arrangement for towing large loads, particularly heavy tanks

It is extraordinarily effective to drop behind the enemy lines airborne parachute troops and military units in gliders towed by metal aircraft. In general it is a question in those cases of lightly armed units. It could be very much more effective if it were possible to drop the heaviest weapons, particularly heavy tanks behind the enemy lines.

The new proposal is as follows:

1. The heavy tank is provided with bolted on fittings to which wings and a rear fuselage with a tail unit can be attached, i.e. in the case of rigid bodies the structure of the object being towed is included as a load-carrying part of the aircraft.

2. Wings, tail unit and rear fuselage are scaled up proportionately in size from well-known gliders and heavy-load tugs so that any aerodynamic risk is eliminated.

3. The assembly of the separate parts with the tank takes place at the take-off site.

4. The tank receives on each of its tracks a strong wooden skid for the landing, which is torn off by the starting of the tracks.

5. For the take-off, a jettisonable axle with two suitably dimensioned wheels is provided.

6. The Ju 52 is available to us as the towing aircraft. Since one is not enough, several (probably four) are coupled together as shown in the accompanying sketch. Three cables are used. One cable is attached to the tank by a pulley; the two other cables are attached to the ends of the first cable, again by means of a pulley. A Ju 52 is pulling at each of the four ends of the last two cables. Four Ju 52s can easily take off side-by-side in

a slightly staggered formation. In this way, theoretically, even more aircraft can be used as towing aircraft. Differences of speed between the individual towing aircraft are balanced out through the pulleys. In the case of large mis-matches, one or the other of the aircraft can disengage.

7. With four Ju 52s, 40 to 50 tons can easily be got into the air in a towed aircraft in one unit, and be towed to a sufficient height.

8. Following discussions with the Gliding Research Institute, at the moment in Einring, there are no doubts about the method of towing. Practice flights with smaller towing aircraft could begin immediately.

9. In general, pinewood and thick plywood are used as the materials for the parts of the glider, in addition to simple welded steel fittings. Only simple wooden jigs are required.

10. Since the equipment of the glider is small, and the aerodynamic shapes of well-known gliders are adopted, the design could be ready in a few weeks.

11. Since the construction of such a glider is very much simpler than that of other aircraft, the run-up time and the throughput time can be kept so low that, with proper organization, a large number off can be produced in a few months.

12. Naturally, other heavy and bulky objects can be transported through the air in this way. In some cases, however, the method of transport requires a fuselage to accommodate the parts, e.g. heavy guns. (The tank does not need such a fuselage.)

We ask you to check the proposal and, if it is of interest, to let us know the loads, the weights and sizes of the tanks which it is required to transport, whereupon we will prepare more accurate information for you.

Messerschmitt AG

The seeds of the Me 321 Gigant glider are clearly contained in item 12 of the above proposal.

The towing of these large aircraft always presented a problem, as was found when the Me 321 was first flight-tested. The proposal, contained in item 6, for the use of pulleys to cope with differences of speed between the towing aircraft hardly bears up to examination as a practical proposition unless the cables were extremely long and the differences in speed were extremely small. The carefree suggestion that one of the towing aircraft could 'disengage' in case of problems arising would have resulted in a fairly rapid movement of the cable through at least one of the pulleys, to say the least.

Hitler was impressed by the idea of the giant glider as an aid to the imminent invasion of Britain, and production orders were issued. The aircraft was built at Leipheim and Obertraubling, and flew for the first time only 15 weeks after the order was placed. This was a remarkable feat in itself in view of the size of the aircraft. To have completed all the aerodynamic assessments, to have performed all the stressing calculations for the airframe and to have produced the necessary drawings in so short a time scale was an achievement rarely equalled in the field of aircraft design.

The first flight of the Me 321 'Gigant' took place on 25 February 1941, the towing aircraft being a Junkers Ju 90, which was just about capable of raising the enormous aircraft into the air with a reduced payload.

The original proposal for the method of towing was luckily abandoned in favour of the 'Troika-Schlepp', which consisted of harnessing three Me 110s to the glider by individual tow-lines. Even so, the flight trials cost the lives of many test pilots. The final solution for a towing aircraft was the production of the He 111Z (Z = Zwilling = twin) composed of two He 111s joined together by an intermediate wing with three engines, making five engines in all. This aircraft on its own was adequate to tow the glider into the air.

Although 175 were built, the Me 321 was by no means an unlimited success. It was difficult to get into the air. Later versions were fitted with rocket-assisted take-off to facilitate getting them off the ground. Once they were in flight the towing aircraft could keep them aloft. The 'Gigant' was also difficult to handle on the ground after it had landed. Without engines, it could not be taxied and had to be manhandled off the landing site. If a prepared airstrip was being used to land a succession of gliders, it was not easy to get one Me 321 off the runway quickly to make room for the next arrival. Nor could one glider delay its landing until the runway was clear of earlier arrivals.

There were problems too with the aircraft in flight. Although the 'Gigant' was surprisingly manoeuvrable, the control loads were exceedingly high and it proved an exhausting exercise to pilot the aircraft for any distance. A better solution was urgently needed, and it was decided to equip the Me 321 with its own engines. This resulted in the Me 323, a powered version which still retained the name 'Gigant'. To avoid having to use valuable engines of German manufacture, it was proposed that another source of power-plants should be sought in the occupied territories.

Surprisingly, the problems with the Me 321 had been anticipated before the first flight of the prototype. A solution was being proposed before the problem had occurred in practice. The idea surfaced for the first time at a meeting held in the Air Ministry in Berlin early in 1941, at which Messerschmitt was present. The official minutes of the discussion are contained in the archives of the Imperial War Museum:

Secret!
Official Memorandum

Visit to General Udet in Berlin on 21 January 1941

Present: General Udet
Major-General Ploch
SS Brigade Leader Croneiss
Professor Messerschmitt

The following questions were discussed:

1. Regarding the further development of the Me 321, General Udet reserved his decision until after the test flights of the first aircraft.

2. The fitting of the Me 321 with captured engines (in German 'Beute-Motoren'). General Udet agreed that some of the aircraft being built will be fitted with engines, and that captured French engines will be used for this. He has asked Herr Mahnke by telephone to send to Messerschmitt AG about 20 captured engines for this purpose. In order to clear up the question of which captured engines are suitable, Messerschmitt AG will immediately send a man to Berlin who will settle the matter of the captured engines and obtain the documentation about them in Berlin and/or in France.

Messerschmitt's representative, in his subsequent travels through occupied France, visited the factory in Merignac where Bloch 175s were being built in quantity. These aircraft were powered by Gnome-Rhone engines, four of which — it was hoped — would produce the required power for the motorized version of the 'Gigant'. Instructions were given that the engines should all be removed, together with their airscrews, and despatched to the Messerschmitt factory at Leipheim. Messerschmitt and his team were soon busy designing a powered version of the huge glider using four of these spare engines. The first flight of this version of the Me 323 took place on 21 April 1941.

Flight trials showed that the aircraft was under-powered. The design team were immediately back at their drawing boards adding two more engines to the four already installed. This 6-engined version of the Me 323 first flew in March 1942 and proved so satisfactory that full-scale production was ordered. Over 150 aircraft of this type were built between 1942 and 1944, although most of them were not built from scratch but modified from existing Me 321 gliders.

With a wingspan of 55 metres (180 ft), the 'Gigant' was one of the largest aircraft ever built up to that time. Capable of carrying a payload of more than ten tonnes, it outclassed all of its contemporaries.

Although extremely vulnerable to enemy fire, the Me 323 proved very successful, particularly in the North African theatre. Messerschmitt was very proud of the aircraft, as is revealed by a letter which he wrote in January 1942 to the Luftwaffe officer in charge of Me 323 operations.

Dear Major Mauss,

Many thanks for your kind message and the report on the introduction into service of the Me 323. You will understand that this report was the finest Christmas present that I could receive.

Years ago I pointed out the necessity of a transport aircraft and, in the face of the greatest opposition, I managed to win permission to develop this aircraft. Because of a lack of manpower resources it was extraordinarily difficult to carry out the task.

I know the many deficiencies still associated with the aircraft and am aware that all sorts of things need to be done to make it operationally suitable for any weather and for blind flying.

You, Major, have rendered the greatest service by demonstrating in practical operations, despite all the deficiencies, that something useful can be made of it, and I hope that the successes that you have had will lead to the Heavy Transporter no longer being treated as a stepchild, and its significance being widely promoted in the future.

Messerschmitt

He was even more delighted later to receive the following 'Christmas present' from one of his own staff at Christmas 1942:

Regensburg

30 December 1942

The Obertraubling inspector, Broll, who as you know is stationed with the Me 323 unit in Naples, has given some interesting information about the use of these of our aircraft in North Africa which I would like to pass on to you immediately.

He has reported that, after the operations from Crete to North Africa, he was transferred to Southern Italy immediately after the 8 November with the Me 323s in question, and experienced the first operations to Bizerta and Tunis. The first Me 323 flew with an assault gun and the necessary ammunition to Bizerta immediately after our landing in Tunis. It unloaded there without any trouble and returned to its home base without any damage. It was this assault gun that we have to thank for being able to break through the ring of American tanks drawn up in a circle of 12 km diameter around Bizerta. On the very first day eight tanks were destroyed by it and on the next day that total went up to 28. More assault guns were flown over with the Me 323 and these opened up for the troops the possibility of driving the Anglo-Americans even further back so that now the nearest enemy positions are to be found at a distance of 80 km from Bizerta. The transport of the assault guns was necessary because the straits of Otranto had been completely mined by the enemy. This had the result that one of our transport ships loaded with tanks was blown up. In the meantime, the mines have been swept by Junkers which are fitted with a large ring charged with current and fly at low altitudes over the sea. The effect is that the mines release themselves, rise to the surface and explode. Now, transport ships can again operate without danger.

As a result of our unprecedented assistance in establishing the Bizerta bridgeheads, the troops are very enthusiastic about the Me 323, which moreover exceeds the Ju's quite notably in its economy. They really cannot get enough of these aircraft. As soon as one is delivered to Southern Italy it is immediately taken over by a crew and sent into action. The airframes are beyond praise up to now, and there are no complaints in this respect; only a few about the engines. The Ratier airscrews are the cause of some complaints, and it is hoped soon to get other airscrews.

Major Mauss, who is running the operation, is just as enthusiastic as his men and is looking for a significant increase in our aircraft. It is interesting that the Me 323 up till now has had no interference from the enemy. Enemy machines have often been sighted already but they always turn away.

Apparently, a quite massively powerful armament is feared! The outward flights have taken place up to now in a convoy of a large formation of Junkers; the return flight was usually unaccompanied.

Indeed, the aircraft proved so successful that a developed version, to be known as the Me 323g, was urgently required in 1943. Because the Messerschmitt design office was too busy with the problems of the Me 210, the design work was transferred to the aircraft design section of the former Zeppelin company in Friedrichshafen, now effectively a part of the Dornier concern.

Early in October 1943 Messerschmitt received a letter from the Air Ministry telling him that Goering had taken a hand in the proceedings, and asking him to establish the new arrangements:

Dear Professor,

I have just received the following telegram from the Reichsmarschall:

Ref: Me 323g

1. The development of the Me 323g has to be pursued with the greatest urgency.

2. To ensure that this happens I have asked Professor Dornier on the grounds of his great experience to undertake with his colleagues the appraisal of the intended actions for the Me 323 and the carrying out of the work.

3. I ask you to set up the contacts with Professor Dornier from your end and to charge Herr Stender with the responsibility of making all the information available to the team of workers named by Professor Dornier.

4. Professor Dornier will make every effort to overcome any bottlenecks which may occur by employing his own designers wherever possible.

Reichsluft GL/c-e Chef

Messerschmitt was once again confronted with the unpleasant prospect of another designer tampering with one of his projects. His letter of 19 October 1943 to Dr Hugo Eckener does not bode well for future co-operation on the Me 323:

Dear Dr Eckener,

I have only today got round to answering your kind letter of 7 October. Until now I have not had an opportunity to speak on the subject in question at the Air Ministry, and I believe that there is little point in undertaking anything. I am also of the opinion that the Air Ministry would have done better to discuss the whole issue in the first place with you and myself. At the moment I am so occupied with the Programme for the Defence of the Reich that I really cannot bother myself with the Me 323.

Nevertheless, I would be grateful to you if you would keep me in touch with what is going on, since I must fear that the Dornier Company, who naturally are not very conversant with the aircraft, will demand modifications to such an extent that they can hardly be implemented.

Messerschmitt

By the later stages of the war the inevitable defects in the concept of the Me 323 were becoming too obvious to be ignored any longer. Although they carried out some remarkable missions in evacuating German troops of the Afrika Korps from North Africa after their defeat there, the losses of Me 323s due to enemy fighters had been too high to be acceptable.

Messerschmitt still believed in the need for the Luftwaffe to have heavy transport aircraft at its disposal, and was clearly disappointed when the decision was made to discontinue the use of the Me 323.

On 10 July 1944 he writes again to Major Mauss, who had commanded the Me 323 operations throughout:

Dear Major,

My most hearty congratulations on the 2000th operation with the Me 323.

I, too, regret that this undertaking has been stopped, as I believe that it is absolutely important to maintain a strong fleet of transports.

Before leaving the 'Gigant' story, there is one final touch which would surely have appealed to Willy Messerschmitt's sense of humour.

At almost exactly the same time that the Luftwaffe was giving up its operations using the Me 323, because of its vulnerability to attack by fighter aircraft, consideration was being given by the British military authorities to the employment of the gigantic Messerschmitt transporter as part of the Allied forces in the Far East. With the possible necessity of an invasion of Japan when Germany had been dealt with, the military planners were looking forward, as Messerschmitt himself had done in 1940, to the possibility of landing heavy equipment behind the enemy lines. With no aircraft available on the Allied side with anything like the load carrying capacity of the Me 323, consideration was given to the use of captured 'Gigants'. Possibly consideration was even being given to the manufacture of the aircraft by British constructors.

This surprising state of affairs is recorded in documents preserved in the Public Records Office at Kew. In the archives are two pages containing a very detailed specification of the aircraft and its performance capabilities, compiled by British experts. Particularly significant points are underlined in pencil, and marginal notes such as 'V. good' are appended to features which favourably attracted the attention of the War Office.

Items which appear to have been regarded with the greatest favour are:

1. The ability of the Me 323 to carry bulky loads. The paragraph which describes this notes that:

The freight space covered by the fixed floor in the new Messerschmitt 'Gigant' exceeds in its area that of a normal goods wagon of the German State Railways and its height corresponds with the loading clearance gauge of the State Railways. Thus, all bulky loads which can be borne on a railway truck, can be stored in the loading space of the Me 323, e.g. two medium motor lorries.

Carrying, as it does, 12 tons useful load, the Me 323 'Gigant' is capable of conveying the two motor lorries with a freight of 2.5 tons. For example, it can carry tanks, small motorized units, an 8.8 flak gun in combat conditions, enormous quantities of provisions (abt. 8700 loaves), fuel (52 barrels of 250 litres each) or fully equipped crews up to 130 men. As an ambulance it can carry 60 wounded men in beds. Bulky goods are loaded in through the gates in front of the fuselage (which open up the full cross-section of the fuselage) and over a one metre high ramp which is carried by the aircraft and which can be adjusted to different track widths. When the gates are closed, access to the loading space may be had at each side through a door through which small piece goods can be loaded in and out. Special locking devices are fitted for securing vehicles and piece goods. These prevent the load from slipping and facilitate rapid unloading.

2. The take-off run of the loaded aircraft amounts to about 800 metres (875 yd). (This distance is heavily underlined in the report.)

3. The description of the undercarriage and its ability to operate over all kinds of terrain are also underlined as items of special interest.

This detailed description of the abilities of the Me 323 apparently so impressed the War Office that the following reply, revealing what was envisaged as the purpose for which the British Army intended to use the aircraft, was sent to the Air Ministry:

SECRET

From: War Office (D. Air)
To: Air Ministry (D. Ops. (Tac))

German Aircraft – Me 323

Reference your CS.22346/D. Ops (Tac) dated 7 August 1944.

The information given is most valuable and still further enhances my interest in this aircraft for the war against Japan.

I understand a party from the Ministry of Aircraft Production are examining one of the aircraft in the Mediterranean theatre. I shall be interested to hear of their conclusions.

(Sgd) K.N. Crawford
Major General
DIRECTOR OF AIR

The unexpectedly sudden end to the war against Japan obviously made any requirement for the Me 323 no longer valid.

As it was, the only Messerschmitt aircraft which saw service with the Royal Air Force were two or three Bf 108 Taifun communications aircraft captured from the German Embassy at the outbreak of the war.

CHAPTER 14

Differences of opinion

It is obvious from his many statements and writings that Messerschmitt had very little doubt that he was usually, if not always, right in what he said and thought. When his views were challenged he was quick to spring to his own defence and to stave off any criticism made against his decisions. No doubt, if he had not possessed those qualities his name would still be unknown to the world at large today.

One of the constant targets of his annoyance was the RLM (the German Air Ministry). He was compelled to deal with its officials, and they could obviously dictate to him the types of aircraft which they required, and they could lay down the programmes for manufacture of the aircraft which they selected. Messerschmitt was to fight many battles with the Ministry during the war years. He claimed with some justification that he was never allocated staff in sufficient numbers or of adequate quality to perform all the tasks demanded of him. He was also annoyed by the intervention of Ministry officials in design matters.

For instance, Messerschmitt was irritated by the continual requests for modifications to his aircraft raised by the Technical Office of the Air Ministry. His testy reply to one request patently reveals his annoyance:

Please convey the following to
Herr Malz in the Technical Office:

Propose lightly armouring the inflatable dinghy at the rear end. The probability that it will be hit is equal to zero because nobody aims there. The armour plate can only be made very weak because hardly anything more is acceptable for weight and C.G. reasons.

After all, everything that the Air Ministry wants can be done. Whether the aircraft can fly afterwards is another question.

Any complaints from the Ministry about late deliveries were met by sharply worded rebuttals of their arguments. A typical example of this sort of defence is provided by a letter to an official in the Air Ministry who had been maligning the Messerschmitt company for failing to make use of manpower which they had available for him:

13 March 1940

Dear Herr Tschersich,

The works manager of Messerschmitt AG, Herr Schmidt, who has attended a discussion of our programme in Berlin, informs me that you had got yourself worked up about the fact that we had pulled in firms like Daimler-Benz, Drauz and Steyr as subcontractors whilst you were having difficulties in keeping the aircraft firms (Weser) fully occupied.

I consider it correct to state my attitude to this.

You know that at the start of the war we got a new programme which had undergone a considerable increase. In order to satisfy this programme, we asked for the relevant workers and machine tools. I was repeatedly in Berlin with Herr Hentzen on this topic, also with General Udet.

We complained that because of inroads by the Ju 88 we were having difficulties in obtaining workers, machines and materials, and that our previous subcontractors were being strongly adversely affected by the Ju 88. General Udet explained to us that we were a bit too easy-going and, as a result, had been outmanoeuvred by Koppenberg (of Junkers). We drew the obvious conclusions from that and secured the three companies, Daimler-Benz, Drauz and Steyr against opposition from Koppenberg, who tried to wrest Daimler-Benz away from us again.

You should have come in at that time and told us that you had capacity free at Weser. We would then have gone willingly to Weser and would not have had the struggle of training the companies in aircraft construction. You missed that opportunity. You have no right at all now to reproach us for employing firms which were not brought in by the Air Ministry and that, on the other hand, firms which were brought in by the Ministry are underemployed. Any change now is naturally out of the question since a considerable dislocation of the programme would be unavoidable.

I would propose, therefore, that people who are free in other aircraft firms such as Weser should be made available, for the time being, to the companies which are still short of staff. I remember, for example, that at the moment I require personnel for the test and jig and tool departments, that I am still having very great difficulties in carrying out on time the tasks continually being put upon me and am under the greatest pressure. You know that the demands of the war are always bringing new tasks and that the design companies are having to introduce modifications from one day to the next, or to introduce additional equipment in aircraft for which the services are calling out. I would remind you of the current new versions of the Bf 110 as a short-range and long-range reconnaissance aircraft.

My company would be in the position to convert a few aircraft relatively quickly, if it had the personnel available.

I have gradually got the impression that the greatest difficulties in producing and equipping aircraft on time arise because of the lack of planning in the work of the Air Ministry. I remember the immense number of changes to the programme and, what is more serious, the unco-ordinated changing of the firms building aircraft under subcontract which presents the main contractor with unheard of difficulties, which in the long run must unavoidably lead to delays in delivery dates. You only have to see what changes the

Bf 109 F and the Me 210 have been subjected to in the last six months, and you only need to check what outlay has had to be devoted to the provision of new jigs and templates, and if you know how difficult it is to get good workers for templates, then you would also understand why in the end no programme dates are being maintained.

I would be grateful if you would sometime try to eliminate this lack of planning in the Air Ministry, or reduce it to a sensible level, and not make reproaches to companies about things for which the Air Ministry itself is responsible.

No hard feelings, but for once the truth has to be told.

Messerschmitt must have had some doubts about whether he had over-done the plain speaking in this letter. He felt it necessary to send a copy to Theo Croneiss with the following note:

Dear Theo,

Enclosed is a carbon copy of my letter of today to your friend Tschersich. The letter is hard and bitter but, if you consider it necessary, I leave it to you to ring Tschersich some time.

His readiness to take up arms in a just cause was not only displayed in his professional world of aircraft design. On a number of occasions he intervened in political matters in a way which might have caused a less confident man considerable worry about the possible effects on his own safety in the Nazi environment. The appeal to Hitler for mercy to be shown to Dr Langbehn cited later in Chapter 23 is an outstanding ex-ample of this.

He was particularly sensitive to criticism of his own design even when the criticism was justified; indeed, it was very rarely that he con-sidered any criticism of his activities as being justified. This did not pre-vent him from springing to the aid of other aircraft designers and manufacturers when he considered that they had been unjustly attacked. Despite his touchy relations with some of his contemporaries in the field of aircraft design, he was quite prepared to stand up and defend the whole aircraft industry against what he regarded as unjusti-fied criticism. The most notable example of this is provided by the memorandum which he wrote on 20 March 1943 for his fellow directors following what appears to have been a savage meeting with Hermann Goering and Erhard Milch at the Reichsmarschall's villa, Karinhall, ear-lier in the month.

SECRET

The Reichsmarschall, in a $1^1/_2$ hour-long agitated speech, ran down practi-cally everything that the industry produces. First the aircraft: He claimed, for example, that the 109 and the 190 have today been overtaken by the Spitfire. Admittedly with a 2200 hp engine. He mentioned again the 210 failure and that of the [Heinkel] 177 which were still not yet ready for service.

The Reichsmarschall complained in particular that we had no usable 4-engined bombers, whereas the English could fly daily into Germany with their Stirling bombers with no difficulty. He will get the German industry to build copies of the Stirling (which of course makes no sense since the English with their radar techniques and anti-aircraft armament would certainly more easily shoot these down than our own bombers).

He criticized the aircraft industry in the most barbed words. It did not consist of people who could be taken seriously, but of jugglers and sorcerers. It appeared to him like a circus; e.g. two years ago in Augsburg he had been shown the plans for an aircraft which could fly to the east coast of America and back. Now he had to allow himself to be convinced that such a requirement was technically not achievable. In addition, the aircraft was certainly not capable of entering service from a military point of view because it had a fuel tank which was riveted and not bullet-proof.

Since I was being attacked on this wide front I began to speak. First I defended the aircraft industry as a whole, with words such as: 'It is true that the aircraft industry and I myself have made mistakes, but it is not true that everything that the industry makes is bad. There were very many good things and, as far as the 264 was concerned, he is apparently ill-informed. In the first place, the aircraft does not have a riveted tank but bullet-proof tanks spaced out along the wing similar to those in the Stirling mentioned earlier. In the second place, it is not true that the requirement is not achievable technically, but that the requirement is very easy to achieve. Such an aircraft is flying in an unfinished state and will achieve a range of about 15,000 km [9300 miles] and thus fulfil the requirement.

Secretary of State Milch interrupted to shout out that that was not true, the aircraft would have a range of 10,000 km [6200 miles] at the best. Whereupon I insisted that I must certainly be better informed on the matter, and I emphasized again that the 15,000 km will be able to be flown with this aircraft in its finished state. If the aircraft is not already there today, that was not the responsibility of our company but of the fact that the promised capacity of designers and skilled workers has not been provided.

Following this, the Reichsmarschall complained again about the 210 and wanted to know from me whether the 410 was now satisfactory in performance and flying characteristics. I explained to him that I personally would not express my opinion here since the aircraft is being assessed by the Luftwaffe and he can allow himself to be informed there about the flying characteristics and performance. The grant of the order for series production depends on the satisfactory quality of these aspects. I mentioned in addition that the 410 aircraft was nothing more than the 210 with which there is already adequate active service experience available. It is only the installation of the DB 603 engine that has led to the better performance. At this point Milch butted in, rather abruptly, and declared that my statement was not true. In the case of the 410 it was more a question of a completely new aircraft. I replied that Secretary of State Milch must in all likelihood have been wrongly informed. It is in accordance with the facts that the 410, in essentials, is identical with the 210, but with a different engine, of course.

The Reichsmarschall now asked whether the 410 now actually had the contra-rotating airscrews installed on safety grounds, whereupon I answered that at the moment that was not the case. This severely shook him. I was able to console him, however, that the Luftwaffe finds that the aircraft meets the intended requirement (for service ceiling). Two cases where pilots fell asleep from lack of oxygen at great heights prove this. I emphasized, however, that the flying characteristics with contra-rotating propellers would be so much improved that these would have to be introduced later.

The Reichsmarschall then went on to talk about the 209 and claimed to be informed on the subject that this new aircraft was being developed because the performance of the 309 had not been attained. I put him right on this and explained that the performance of the 309 agrees very well with the required performance and that, with the same equipment and armour, the performance of the 209 was no greater than that of the 309. The company had decided, therefore, to offer the 209 instead of the 309 since the former is developed from the 109 and, as a result, a considerable amount of jigs were saved which the Air Ministry could not provide for the 309, and for the lack of which the possible deliveries of the 309 had foundered.

Secretary of State Milch then declared that this also was not true. Rather the 209 was a completely new aircraft. In Germany we were unable to build fighters. Since the Italian fighters are better than our German ones, in future he will have Italian fighters built. I declared that, of course, the best aircraft must be built. But you can only talk about a better aircraft if all the flight performance figures are weighed one against the other and if you know what performance the services lay particular emphasis on. For the industry it is possible to match the required performance with that of the Italian fighters by modifications to the existing 109 and 190 fighters. To get an aircraft with a better rate of climb it is not necessary to immediately make everything new starting with the control column mounting to the whole machine. In this context, I proposed building for one type of fighter basically two different-sized wings and two engines which are interchangeable so that the aircraft, as a high-speed aircraft, has the best performance for ground-level and moderate heights, and as a high service ceiling aircraft — with a larger layout and a high altitude engine — has the best performance there too. The Reichsmarschall agreed with this.

After about a five hour session, the Reichsmarschall became more conciliatory and invited us, with a few friendly words, to have lunch together. As we were breaking up, Secretary of State Milch, in a smiling but threatening manner, spoke to me again and told me that he had been so furious with me that he would very much have liked to tear out my last remaining hairs; whereupon I suggested that it would be a good idea if we at some time talked the whole thing over again personally. But I could not tolerate the industry being continually attacked, and I had considered it necessary, therefore, to set the record straight.

I consider it proper that the Reichsmarschall, after it has so clearly been shown how wrongly he is informed, should receive a short report from our company or from myself, in which the reasons for the delay of the 323 and the 264 are explained and in which we point out that contracts which could be particularly important in the future, such as the 262, are being excessively delayed. We must also point out today that we are not to blame for this delay.

Messerschmitt was able to rectify the situation a few weeks later when he was invited to an interview with Hitler, who was beginning to realize that all was not well with the Luftwaffe despite Goering's blusterings. The Führer was anxious to hear the views of the main aircraft designers on the existing situation. Since neither Goering nor Milch were present at the discussion, it provided an opportunity to register some complaints with Hitler directly without the danger of being shouted down.

Messerschmitt gave a report on the proceedings to his own Board of Directors on 2 July 1943, as was recorded in the minutes:

Herr Messerschmitt reported that on 27 June he was ordered by the Führer to attend a discussion on the Obersalzberg. The invitation had been given also to other aircraft designers, to Herr Tank of Focke-Wulf and Herr Hertel of Junkers. The Führer had received each man separately. During the discussion with him, apart from the Luftwaffe Adjutant, Group Captain von Below, Reichsminister Speer was called in. The Führer explained to him that he placed great value on hearing the opinions of the leading designers. This led Messerschmitt to ask whether he could express his opinions without reservations as he thought that it was right to do. The Führer, referring to the seriousness of the situation, explained that he must set forth his thoughts quite openly. Messerschmitt first reported on his meeting with the Reichsmarschall when he had criticized the industry with the most cutting words causing him, Messerschmitt, to intervene positively on behalf of the aircraft industry. The leadership of the Luftwaffe by the Reichsmarschall, in his opinion, made the great mistake of not keeping directly in touch with the industry. The Reichsmarschall allowed nobody from those circles to approach him to ask him what developments were in hand and what possibilities of further development there still were. He had now been able to report in detail to the Führer on these topics.

When explaining the fighter problem, he had propounded the further development of the Me 109 into a high-altitude fighter, the Me 209. The Führer was very interested in a high-altitude aircraft that would be fully ready for service in the next three months and with which it would be possible within that time to fly into England undisturbed. Messerschmitt also reported on the basis of the plotted curves on the demonstrated performance figures flown with the Me 262, results which the Führer did not yet know of and which greatly surprised him. Reichsminister Speer then pointed out that special arrangements had been made for the production of this aircraft, which was far superior to any other. Messerschmitt then indicated that the Me 262 could be used later as a bomber.

The Führer had then gone over to the Me 264, from which Messerschmitt deduced that this question was the real reason for the discussion which had been ordered.

Herr Messerschmitt commented in this connection that, on Monday 21 June, Gauleiter Wahl had visited the Augsburg factory to clarify some information that had been given to him regarding the future of the Me 264. According to this information, there was a serious danger that this type would not get as far as being introduced into service despite its decisive advantages and its significantly advanced design, because of wrong decisions in the Air Ministry. In the interest of the state he felt himself duty bound to bring the affair directly to the attention of the Führer, Gauleiter Wahl had been informed immediately about the Me 264 affair and then had expressed the view that the Führer demanded the strictest secrecy on the subject.

The Führer got from Messerschmitt the most detailed exposition of the performance of the Me 264 and of the measures needed for its production. Messerschmitt forcibly expounded all that was necessary and explained the continuing criticism of the machine. The Führer had, there and then while still at the meeting, given the order that Oberst Rowehl should be sent a telegram ordering him to the Führer on the next day. *In addition, an order was given by the Führer that every effort should be made to continue the building of the machine.*

He, Messerschmitt, had talked to the Führer about further developments, among them one that was at the moment being tested in Peenemünde [presumably the Fi 103 (V 1) flying bomb], which caused the Führer to say that indeed a lot more was going on than he knew about. This caused Messerschmitt to remark that it appeared as if there was not the necessary interest in the Air Ministry for the important future developments. If there was an important new development, the support in the Ministry, which had so far been lacking, must be secured by an imposed programme. He had at the same time brought up the point that Generalfeldmarschall Milch had performed the decisive service of greatly increasing the number of aircraft being built.

On the other hand he had complained about the Chief of the General Staff who had so far not understood the necessity of contacts with the aircraft industry. In the interest of controlling developments, the industry must know the plans of the General Staff. On the other hand, the General Staff must be accurately informed about forthcoming developments in the interest of its plans. Since there was no contact here, he considered it to be a prime reason why the urgently needed equipment came too late. The Führer expressed himself as being very surprised about what developments were actually in hand, that these were not being properly promoted and that the measures indicated by Messerschmitt were being neglected.

The Führer also asked about the armament of the Me 109 with the MK 108 cannon, to which he answered that so far 30 machines were being tested at Rechlin with this armament. He also informed the Führer about the jet engine, about which he knew nothing as yet. Messerschmitt then explained that this engine was not so complicated that we could believe that the enemy powers had no similar development. Indeed, in the English aircraft test establishment such a machine was already being flight tested. This was news to Reichsminister Speer also.

Herr Messerschmitt finally stated that the talk had conveyed the most valuable suggestions to the Führer which, there was no doubt, he would make use of. In any case, because of the order by the Führer, the particularly important question of the continuing construction of the Me 264 had been clearly decided.

Unfortunately for Messerschmitt, as we saw earlier in Chapter 12, the Führer's orders must have been countermanded somewhere along the line, because the Me 264 did not enter production.

CHAPTER 15

Employment of prisoners-of-war and concentration camp inmates

A somewhat shady episode in Messerschmitt's career is that concerned with the employment of forced labour in his factory at Augsburg. Among Messerschmitt's personal correspondence there is a letter sent by him to the Commandant of the notorious concentration camp at Dachau. The letter is, unfortunately, not one which enhances one's regard for Messerschmitt as a private individual.

20 July 1943

Sturmbannführer Weiss
Commandant of Dachau Concentration Camp
Dachau

Dear Sturmbannführer Weiss,

My people inform me of the considerable increases in output which have been achieved through the employment of concentration camp prisoners in the Augsburg factory, and also of the outstanding results which have been obtained within a very short time by transferring a part of our electrical manufacture into the camp at Dachau. I am aware that these successes were achieved thanks above all to your personal initiative and readiness to help in these new tasks, and that the spirit of close co-operation, which reigns following the surmounting of the initial difficulties between your workers and mine, is to a very special degree thanks to your personal influence.

As a result, I would not like to fail to express my most heartfelt thanks for your most co-operative attitude and energetic support, and I join with them the request that our co-operation in the future also will be ever closer and more understanding and may help us to even greater joint successes. As a modest sign of my thanks please accept the enclosed picture.

Messerschmitt

There can be no doubt, therefore, that concentration camp prisoners were employed at Augsburg and that, surprisingly, sub-assemblies were being put together by workers inside the Dachau camp itself. It would be very interesting to know what were the 'initial difficulties between your workers and mine'. Presumably Messerschmitt was aware of the difference in the living conditions between his employees and the 'workers' of Sturmbannführer Weiss.

The fact that this letter was sent by Messerschmitt at all is surprising. At the time in question, Messerschmitt had been ordered to confine his activities to design. The overall responsibility for the running of the company had been transferred to Herr Seiler on Milch's insistence following the disastrous failure of the Me 210. Why then should Messerschmitt have signed a letter dealing with matters lying outside his responsibility? Surely Seiler himself or the production director should have been given the task of thanking Weiss for his assistance. A possible explanation is that, despite his nominal confinement to design work, Messerschmitt's name still symbolized his company, and probably he was asked to sign the letter as a public relations exercise.

That is not the only document dealing with the employment of prisoners of one sort or another. Prisoners-of-war were also employed in many German armaments factories, including those belonging to Messerschmitt. Evidence of this is distributed throughout the company documents over the whole of the period of the war.

When the subsidiary Messerschmitt factory was set up in Kematen in the Tyrol, prisoners-of-war were employed in the plant. The company reports of 1941 and 1942 include statements on the situation.

In the report for 1941:

Welfare of Foreigners and Prisoners (1941)

For the accommodation of the foreign workers and the prisoners, an encampment of huts has been made available consisting of 11 huts, of which one hut is used for the building foremen and one for the kitchen and canteen. Two further huts are fitted out as washing and toilet huts. All the other huts are used as living quarters. The number of occupants of the huts on 31 December 1941 was 167, of whom 33 were Germans, 41 Italians, one French civilian and 92 French prisoners-of-war. The number of workers occupied on building who were accommodated in the huts was ten Germans and 18 Italians. The building workers and the prisoners are fed in the canteen.

With seven huts allocated as living quarters for 167 people, the average number of occupants of each hut was 24 approximately.

Another company report includes detailed plans drawn to scale of all the accommodation on the site, down to and including the bicycle sheds. It also contains photographs of the interior of one of the huts showing the bunks in which the workers slept.

The company report for 1942 shows that the accommodation had been extended. Moreover, a considerable number of Russian prisoners-of-war had now joined the ranks of the impressed labour force, together with a few Poles and a scattering of other assorted nationalities. That they were not all employed by common consent of both parties is indicated by the inclusion of eight guards among the occupants of the huts.

Once again, with typical attention to meticulous detail, the statistics are quoted in the annual report for the year:

Accommodation of Foreigners and Prisoners-of-war (1942)

The hut encampment was extended from 11 to 18 huts in which the following personnel were accommodated:

27 Germans	1 Dutchman
30 Italians	9 French civilians
1 Russian civilian	91 French prisoners-of-war
2 Slovaks	260 Russian prisoners-of-war
3 Poles	8 guards.

In the canteen for prisoners-of-war the following meals were served: 40,950 breakfasts, 42,340 lunches and 41,074 evening meals.

From the statistics quoted in this report, the number of people in each hut has now increased to roughly 31.

Although it looks impressive at first sight, the number of meals served in the canteen is surprising on closer examination. The total number of meals served during the year is quoted as 124,364 comprising breakfasts, lunches and evening meals. Yet there were 351 prisoners-of-war in all. The arithmetic, therefore, is 351 prisoners x 365 days = 128,115 man days — or an average of less than one meal per man per day. Presumably, to put the best light on it, the numbers of prisoners quoted were those applying on the last day of the year. The average for the year may have been less. Even so, the number of meals served is surprisingly low, unless the prisoners were restricted to only one hot meal a day and had only bread or some such basic food at other times during the day.

Prisoners were certainly employed in the construction of the bomb-proof underground factory for the Messerschmitt company at Landsberg. The details given in the Combined Intelligence Objectives Sub-committee report written after the war contain the following information:

> Adjacent to the area a concentration camp had been built and filled with political prisoners. This provided a pool from which to draw labour.
>
> The labour personnel consisted of 600 to 800 Germans, 200 volunteer Russians and 1500 political prisoners, mostly Jewish, from the adjacent concentration camp.

It is necessary to point out, however, that this was labour for the construction of the plant only. There is no evidence that concentration camp labour was employed in the factory, which in any case had hardly started up production by the time that the war ended.

Another interesting document in the Imperial War Museum collection is a table dated April 1945 giving the composition of the work-force at Regensburg arranged according to nationality. The figures quoted are as follows:

Messerschmitt GmbH	Work-force broken down according to nationality		As of April 1945
German	Male	4880	38%
	Female	1540	12%
Hungarian	Male	250	2%
	Female	80	0.6%
Russian	Male	1600	12.5%
	Female	450	3.5%
French	Male	400	3.1%
Belgian	Male	700	5.4%
Italian	Male	900	7%
Prisoners of war	French	120	1%
	Russian	1850	14.5%
TOTAL		12,824	100%

This indicates that only half of the work-force consisted of Germans. The remainder were foreign nationals who had been recruited or impressed from the occupied countries of Europe or were prisoners-of-war of whom the main part were Russians.

Another report issued by the Combined Intelligence Objectives Sub-committee entitled: 'Survey of Production Techniques Used in the German Aircraft Industry' contains the following assessment of the situation:

An outstanding feature of German production methods was the extensive use of slave labour. Among these people were relatively few possessing skills. The 'Ausländer', as they were called, were handled in various ways — ranging from extreme cruelty and neglect to attempts to secure co-operation and good work by more favourable treatment. In the larger government-controlled plants, such as the Mitteldeutsch Motoren Works and the Nordhausen V-plants (i.e. those producing the V1 flying bomb and the V2 rocket), the slave labourers were badly mistreated. In the small privately-controlled plants their lot was comparatively good, and efforts were made to properly feed and house them.

The 'Ausländer' were paid wages, said to be the same as German workers, but they were heavily taxed and no opportunity for spending was provided as all the workers were kept inside barbed wire enclosures, except during working hours.

The majority of the heavy unskilled work was done by these virtual prisoners.

Turnover among slave labour was very high in places where cruel treatment was reported in order to increase output. At the Nordhausen plants, the total number of 'Ausländer' employed at any one time was approximately 14,000, and the death rate was 17,000 per year.

In general, the 'Ausländer' were required to work in 12 hour shifts, while the Germans worked only eight hours.

(In all fairness it must be said that this report seems to be unduly biased. There can be little doubt that German aircraft workers during the war worked similar hours to their British or American counterparts. Seventy hour weeks were by no means unusual in British aircraft factories during the war and it is hard to believe that the German workers were less hard pressed. In fact, among the papers relating to the Messerschmitt plant at Oberammergau, there are details of special rations being awarded to workers who worked excessively long hours.)

The reports on the war crimes trials in the Public Record Office give a horrifying account of the treatment of slave labour in some parts of German industry. In particular, the foreign workers and prisoners at the Heinkel plant in Oranienburg were starved, housed in inhuman conditions and frequently taken to the neighbouring concentration camp at Nordhausen where they were brutally flogged by members of the SS if their efforts were regarded as inadequate.

It is to the credit of Messerschmitt's company that there is not one recorded case of ill-treatment of prisoners in any of their factories. As any allegations of the wrongful handling of prisoners were vigorously pursued by war crimes investigators after the war, it is a virtual certainty that any such cases would have come to light if they had existed.

Messerschmitt himself mentioned the subject of foreign workers briefly in his address to the work-force at Christmas 1941:

> We have had new and greater responsibilities placed upon us. As in this year, we will in the coming year have to work together with the different races of Europe. I beg you always to be conscious in these circumstances that you are Germans. I am counting here also on the harmonious co-operation of the German Workers' Front of our company in the arrangements.

Messerschmitt himself was not happy with the conditions under which French prisoners-of-war were employed in his factories. In a letter dated 17 January 1942, he writes to the Industrial Adviser of the Reichsmarschall (Hermann Goering) for the Production of Luftwaffe Equipment concerning his need for more labour in his factories. After complaining about the fact that some of his highly-skilled staff are being called up for military service, he goes on to say:

> We could envisage the following measures to improve the situation and prevent too great a fall in the level of output.
>
> 1. Permission to allow us to employ foreigners from friendly nations also in the final assembly stage of series production.
>
> 2. Release of French prisoners-of-war to civilian status, under a commitment at the same time to stay at their place of work (by which means getting them to work would be made much easier).

3. A general relaxation of the very strict security measures associated with the employment of foreigners.

4. For the increased employment of foreigners we need to have barracks available to house them, since the calling up of building workers has stopped all building work, otherwise the engagement of any further foreigners would be impossible. In our opinion it must be possible to move out the training of recruits mainly into barracks in the occupied countries in order to make free additional accommodation here.

The letter is signed by Messerschmitt, the Chairman of the Board and the Works Manager.

That all sounds very different from the conditions of foreign workers in the Heinkel works at Oranienburg where they were accommodated in unheated underground cellars with no protection from Allied air-raids, and were inhumanly treated by their overseers.

Another letter from Messerschmitt to one of his managers is dated 10 April 1942:

I am asking you urgently to obtain permission for foreign workers and prisoners to be allowed to work in the jig building/test department on condition that this is separated from the factory by a fence.

Please let me know if difficulties occur so that I can eliminate them personally.

The matter is extremely urgent.

As the end of the war approached in 1945 there was quite naturally some concern among the German personnel about the activities of the foreign workers. It was not unreasonable to expect them to rise up at a convenient time and wreak revenge on their German employers.

A pedantically worded secret memorandum was circulated to all the supervisory staff in the Oberammergau works in March 1945:

Oberammergau, 27 March 1945
Secret!
Circular to all Departmental Heads and Section Leaders!

Subject: Supervision of foreigners

Because of the tense situation I am giving the following order:

All Departmental Heads and Section Leaders must immediately instruct the shop supervisors responsible to them to prevent any unlawful assemblies of foreigners. An unlawful assembly is considered to be any standing around of foreigners in groups of more than three men in a place which is not necessary for their work and/or where no German supervisor is present.

The preventive measures will consist until further notice in that a supervisor who is nearby asks the foreigners what they are doing there and orders them to go back to their work immediately. If the foreigners should refuse to follow the order (which is not to be assumed if the approach is correct), the works police are to be informed immediately by telephone giving the place or the shop.

The Security Officer,
Signed: von Plottnitz

Although Messerschmitt was interrogated after the war on suspicion of being a war criminal, he was not charged with any offence and can be presumed to be innocent of the ill-treatment of prisoners or slave labour in his factories. Some of them may have fared better in his employ than they would have in other factories. It is obvious, however, from the correspondence quoted above that he was aware of the employment of prisoners-of-war and concentration camp prisoners in his factories.

CHAPTER 16

Messerschmitt as an employer

Messerschmitt was in no way an unsympathetic employer of men. There is ample evidence of his interest in the personal well-being of his employees. Examples of his concern for his staff are not hard to find in his correspondence. His Christmas address to the workforce at Augsburg in 1941 is a typical example of a combination of understanding for personal problems with firmness in the face of any attempt to revolt against the enforced less pleasant wartime conditions of working in his factory.

> Sometimes perhaps a decision which the works management has to make must appear hard, perhaps even unjust, when viewed as an individual case. I can assure you, however, that I always have the wish that justice should be predominant in our community.
>
> This year the Führer has again indicated to us the magnitude of the sacrifices which the soldiers at the front are making. When victory comes we would not like it to be said that we were not worthy of these sacrifices. For many of us today it leaves an unpleasant taste to have to live far from our families. I know that the living conditions are frequently not such as to make life outside the factory a pleasant experience. I also know that many would rather be at a different place of work or wear the uniform of a soldier. Nevertheless, in staying here at your place of work you are making this sacrifice for the German people. We have tried, as far as is possible, to remedy the most acute cases of distress.
>
> Many comrades, in order to improve their position, want permission to take posts in other organizations. In such cases we must unfortunately be unrelentingly hard. In the same way as the soldier at the front cannot seek out the position that he wants, so must you during the war perform your work in the place where you are installed. I must in this respect proceed with unrelenting severity against those who deliberately set themselves up against the company and seek in that way to force us to release them.

Messerschmitt obviously took a particular personal interest in the well-being of his design staff and was kept aware of their problems. In 1942 he takes the trouble to write to a fellow director of the company regarding his concern for a member of his staff:

To: Brigade Leader Croneiss

Woltmann – Project Office

Woltmann was a senior section leader in the Project Office and has given excellent service there. Because of a severe illness, possibly a brain tumour, which the doctor says W possibly contracted in the service of the Company, Woltmann will presumably no longer be fully fit for work. In the worst case a progressive deterioration of his condition must be reckoned with. Woltmann is married. At the moment he has been given leave and I have advocated paying his salary in full for the present.

If Woltmann is only employable to a limited extent or not at all, a final decision must be made.

9 July 1942   Mtt

He was also concerned to ensure that his staff were adequately rewarded financially, especially those who had acted beyond the expected bounds of duty:

To: Frl. Angermaier, Bookkeeping

Because of their special services in flight I have approved a bonus payment of three thousand marks free of tax (the company will take care of the tax) for:

Feldwebel Gutsche
and Dipl. Ing. Ziegler.

Please pay these bonuses to Herr Caroli for onward transmission to the persons named.

26 March 1942   Mtt

Where he regarded their services to the company and to the nation as especially worthy of reward, he asked for them to be awarded a decoration as outstanding servants of the state:

To: Majorgeneral Ploch
Air Ministry
Berlin W.8
Leipzigerstr. 7

14 November 1940

War Service Crosses

Two of our comrades in the company

Flight Captain Fritz Wendel, born 21 February 1915 in Monzerheim and Alois Sdzuy, fitter, born 13 February 1898 in Hindenburg in Upper Silesia, have particularly contributed to the accelerated development of the Me 210 at the risk of their life and health, respectively.

We request, therefore, that the War Service Cross, II Class, be awarded to these comrades.

Although Herr Wendel had determined in flight tests that the tail unit has a tendency to critical vibrations at an increased speed, Wendel carried on the test at the risk of his life in the interests of clearing up these investigations. In fact, during one of these tests, because of the failure of the tail unit through buffeting, Wendel was forced to abandon the aircraft by parachute. As a result of the failure of the tail unit Wendel was unfit for work for a week.

When an Me 210 made a forced landing in very cold weather last winter, Alois Sdzuy occupied himself untiringly with the salvage of the aircraft. In doing so both his legs were frozen to the extent that, unfortunately, one leg had to be amputated. In that way he sacrificed his health for the accelerated development of the Me 210.

Messerschmitt

On this occasion Messerschmitt's efforts were rewarded when he received a reply from the Air Ministry:

12 December 1940

The War Service Cross 2nd Class has been awarded to the following members of your staff:

Flight Captain Fritz Wendel
Fitter Alois Sdzuy

Udet

Messerschmitt was also concerned about the salary levels which he was allowed to pay to his staff, particularly his most valuable designers. In this case it must be admitted that he appears to be more troubled by rival firms attracting away his workers than with the living standards of his staff.

15 February 1940

Dear Herr Cejka,

I am returning to the conversation which we had on the occasion of the last Board meeting concerning the increase of salaries, to which you took exception.

It is known directly and indirectly that the Heinkel company has given a contract to a man here in which he is guaranteed a transfer payment of 2000 marks, apart from an increase of salary from 850 marks to 1200 marks and, naturally, repayment of removal expenses. This contract was made without my approval, despite the fact that the rules of the Society of the German Aircraft Industry forbid the poaching of staff without the approval of the original company.

I can tell you of yet another case. The Junkers company is offering 800 marks to a man who is getting 600 marks here. In this case the man has been given notice by mutual agreement because I could not agree to an increase of salary here on account of his performance (the salary would fall outside our guidelines).

We also have the grotesque case that I cannot pay the 800 marks because otherwise I would have to raise the salaries of a large part of the other staff, but the Junkers company is in the position of paying that salary. This man cannot in any way be worth more to Junkers than to me.

From these two cases it can be clearly seen that our salary levels are certainly not too high in comparison with the rest of the aircraft industry but, in fact, lower.

I have already explained to you on the occasion of the Board meeting that I cannot put into effect the stand-still demanded by you on increases in the average salaries because otherwise I would unavoidably lose my good people to other companies. Because of the cases cited above and a great number of other salaries which have become known in the aircraft industry, I have for years had unrest among my staff, particularly engineering staff, because they are of the opinion that my company pays too small salaries compared with other aircraft firms. This state of affairs is gradually becoming unbearable and, in fact, is going so far that a falling-off in their work is noticeable. I will have to give way against your wishes and gradually bring the salaries up to a higher level.

There is only one way out here. In the same way that wages are firmly anchored in the whole of the German Reich in accordance with a wage-scale, and cannot be increased outside the limits permissible in that scale, so must a compulsory maximum wage-scale be forcibly introduced for the aircraft industry by the Air Ministry. I believe that it would be an easy matter to get the approval of General Milch for the introduction of such a wage-scale. The Air Ministry, the Society and a group of firms could work out such a compulsory wage-scale within a few months. Then, at least during the war, nobody on the staffs of the aircraft industry can or will object when an immediate increase in salary is forbidden, apart from when changing jobs, i.e. moving up into another sphere of activity.

I would be grateful to you if you would let me know whether there is a possibility of my proposal being adopted. I will naturally not put through any further salary increases until I have a report from you in my hands.

Yours faithfully,
Messerschmitt

Messerschmitt was never too busy to take an interest in the most commonplace details of the running of his design office. He obviously had a sense of order and was annoyed if even trivial matters were left in what appeared to him to be an unsatisfactory state of affairs. Typical examples of his intervention are to be found among his numerous memoranda issued to managers in his own design department or to others in authority who had an influence on the running of his office. He was particularly proud of the quality of the work done by his designers and draughtsmen. It is not surprising, therefore, that he reacted strongly when he personally received complaints from the Technical Office of the Air Ministry about the standard of presentation of drawings sent to them. His instruction to his design office manager was forthright:

Enclosed are two design documents.

It is a scandal that we allow ourselves to distribute such documents to the Ministry, and the Air Ministry is right to get upset about it. (I had the documents pressed into my hand personally in the Air Ministry.)

Please, when you have the chance, bring to me the person responsible.

6 February 1940   Messerschmitt

He was equally abrupt about the waste of paper and time involved in producing an excessive number of duplicates of documents:

Herr Bley - Drawing Office

Instructions for the performance of jobs in the shops

Instructions for the performance of jobs in the shops are produced in 27 copies. I am convinced that the same applies to minutes of meetings, office instructions, etc.

This state of affairs is in the long term quite unacceptable since it represents an amount of over-organization without equal. It must be possible surely, by laying down a specified channel of information for a specified job, to reduce the distribution to a fraction. Obviously, everyone who gets a copy also studies it, which means that, because of each of these instructions, a large number of valuable manhours are taken up.

I would be grateful to you if you would take steps to produce a proposal for considerable simplification.

Messerschmitt

Even the standard of the office cleaning was not below his notice as is shown by a peremptory memo to one of his fellow directors:

Charwomen in my area and in the Design Office

The cleaning has gradually sunk to a level below the dignity of our company. I urgently request, therefore, that some responsible authority is nominated within the management who continually checks the rooms and instructs or changes the cleaning women.

I will take this opportunity, while the present moves are going on, to ask for the parquet flooring in the Design Office to be stripped and properly treated so that it looks decent.

Messerschmitt

That the state of his own office was not beyond reproach is proved by a memorandum sent by his secretary to the Plant Department.

In Professor Messerschmitt's room there has been a large hole in the carpet for a long time already. I had reported this to the management who, however, cannot carry out the repair. I am requesting you to order a repair patch from the suppliers of the carpet or to provide a matching rug.

The thought that the great aircraft designer was compelled to resort to a rug to cover up a hole in his carpet is enough to shed quite a new light on his image.

He also was ready to criticize the design of the buildings in his factory. He seems to have been particularly annoyed by the configuration of a railing erected around the top of the Design Office:

16 May 1941

Herr Mayer, Planning

New Design Office Building

Does there have to be such a hideous railing on the new building for the Design Office next to Flight Test? My opinion is that an edging of 10 to 20 cm is perfectly adequate.

Messerschmitt

Messerschmitt took a great pride in the social services available to his workers. It was a particular source of pleasure to him that his company was given an award for the standard of its care for the employees.

A social gathering was arranged in the factory at which Messerschmitt made a speech to the assembled company:

My fellow guests!

I am pleased to be able to welcome you here on the occasion of a small celebration. We are gathered together to accept the 'Award for Outstanding Care of the Health of the People'.

Today, all the health facilities and social services, which make possible a great society, have become accepted as a matter of course. We can hardly remember any longer that it was once quite different. For that reason it is a good thing if we recall again the social improvements which the national-socialist movement has achieved in the last seven years.

Apart from the offices of the District Committee of the German Workers Front, which have assisted with advice and actions in the setting up of this social work, and for which we express our heartfelt thanks, my colleague, Director Kokothaki, has earned particular credit for the social arrangements.

I would not like to omit to thank also his colleagues, our friend Himmelreich, the adviser for social affairs, the men of the health services, the factory social workers, our efficient factory nurses, the canteen manager, Wagner, and finally our sports manager, Hummel. They all, in addition to many others, have helped to ensure that in difficult circumstances our comrades have been supported, that they get healthy and stay healthy.

I would not like to close, however, without remembering the man whom above all we have to thank for making possible this splendid social organization.

Our Führer, Adolf Hitler, Sieg Heil!

There exists a revealing outside assessment of the industrial relations existing within the Messerschmitt company towards the end of the war.

It is given in a report prepared for the Air Ministry by an inspector sent to check on the production and development of fighters in the company. Apart from giving an insight into the atmosphere prevalent in the firm at the time, it provides an interesting insight into the close working relationship between Messerschmitt and his employees.

The attitude with which work is performed to accomplish a task is decisive for its success. It seemed to me important, therefore, at the beginning of my report on the Messerschmitt Company to record the impression which I gained of the inherent attitude of both the management and the workers of this company.

Nothing can more graphically convey this impression than a description of the last hour that I spent with the responsible leaders of this enterprise on the evening of 27 October [1944].

We had broken off the final discussion in order to listen to the speech of Reichminister Dr Goebbels on the radio in Professor Messerschmitt's room. The set, which was fixed to the floor, was not working properly and could only be heard at a very low volume. So we all sat, the Professor, the Board of Directors, the engineers and the Managing Director, on the floor in close attention so as not to miss a word, until an official in a neighbouring room called out that his set gave better reception. The man who called out was unable to come himself because he had to replace the missing aerial by putting his hand on the set and he was not prepared to interrupt the speech for even a second. We then gathered around him and he stalwartly carried on as the aerial until it was possible to relieve the technical deficiency with door-keys and a paper-clip.

What I experienced in four days, besides this little occurrence, which was characteristic of the interest in contemporary events, was an endless succession of demonstrations of the fact that I was not in a commercial enterprise intent on turnover and profit, but in a fellowship of men who in deadly earnest are obsessed with their task of making every effort to make available the best in design and manual work for the Fatherland, without any concern for their health or private interests. With this inherent attitude, difficulties which bordered on the improbable were overcome without any serious loss of production. For example, the Regensburg concern operated in 36 dispersed sub-concerns which are accommodated in woods, road tunnels, caves, shot-up aircraft hangars, barns and other commandeered shelters.

I also considered it particularly pleasantly surprising that during my four day visit, not the slightest attempt was made to influence my opinion by any hospitality in kind which disregarded the wartime restrictions.

All the information requested was made available to me with the greatest readiness, sometimes with considerable overtime and overnight working, in the sheer hope of now being able, with the help of my minister to eliminate the restrictions on which until now the full exploitation of the production capacity has been wrecked, and which the works management have been unable to do by their own efforts.

In this respect, there was no show of arrogant infallibility on their own part, but faults were freely admitted which the management and workers had committed during the improvisation of the dispersal.

From all these observations I have gained the impression that our fighter production, in so far as it lies in the Messerschmitt Company, is in the best of hands, and that it is worthwhile following up the worries which are raised by this company with reference to production hold-ups.

That description of the somewhat eccentric circumstances in which the radio broadcast was received clearly reveals the camaraderie existing between Messerschmitt and his senior colleagues. With a few changes to the surnames involved, the scenario could easily be accepted as an anecdote about life in an English aircraft company at the same date.

CHAPTER 17

Assessment of the opposition

During the Second World War Messerschmitt kept a close watch on the aircraft being designed in other companies, particularly those being produced on the Allied side of the conflict. In his biography of Erhard Milch, David Irving includes a footnote which states that 'Milch complained at one meeting that Professor Messerschmitt showed no inclination to visit the displays of captured Allied aircraft.' Even making allowance for the fact that Milch rarely missed an opportunity to discredit Messerschmitt on some pretext or another, this accusation does not appear to be compatible with Messerschmitt's obvious interest in all developments taking place in the aeronautical world wherever they might be.

His close study of foreign design trends is evinced by the numerous comments which he produced throughout the war on British and American aircraft and on the American aircraft industry in general. He recommended his designers to take opportunities to inspect foreign aircraft, as will appear from the documents quoted later in this chapter.

It is ironic that Milch should have criticized Messerschmitt in that way, as the designer's efforts to keep abreast of developments abroad were not always helped by the Air Ministry. At the end of 1940 he had asked to be allowed to read a report compiled by the Ministry on British aircraft and engines. In reply he received a memo from Ernst Udet dated 30 November 1940:

Ref: Transmission of the report 'Aircraft and Aero-engines of Great Britain'.

The report requested by Messerschmitt AG is only intended for individual offices within the more confined range of the Air Ministry. Releasing it to Messerschmitt AG is, therefore, not possible. The communication of individual items of information is, however, possible at any time on request.

Without any knowledge of the overall contents of the report, Messerschmitt found it difficult to request 'individual items'. However, he did take every opportunity to find out whatever there was to be found out about British and American aircraft. He even appointed one of his staff to be responsible for organizing visits by his designers to the exhibition of captured enemy aircraft in Berlin. He would hardly have acted in this way if he had not himself inspected the aircraft in question.

His memo of 24 October 1942 makes this very clear:

To: All Departmental Heads, Type Designers and Section Leaders in the Design Office

Captured Aircraft
Herr Degel is charged with organizing a visit to inspect the captured aircraft at least once in every four weeks. The permanent exhibition of these captured aircraft is in Berlin-Adlerhof. Any requests must be communicated to Herr Degel.

I recommend everyone to visit this exhibition if they should be making a business trip to Berlin.

Messerschmitt's forecasts of the future ability of the American aircraft industry to produce aircraft in quantity, and of the effects of the American daylight raids on German war production were remarkable but, inevitably, his views were ignored by the Nazi hierarchy who expected the war to be over before the Americans got seriously involved.

As early as August 1941 Messerschmitt was issuing warnings about the potential of the American aircraft industry. One report which was sent to Ernst Udet reads:

In September 1939 the firm of Glenn Martin in the USA came out as the winners in a design competition with their projected bomber the B26. The result was an order for prototype aircraft. Because of the war which was beginning in Europe, Glenn Martin smelt a commercial success, made the aircraft ready for series production during the design and build stages and at its own risk embarked on large-scale production. About the turn of the year 1940/41, that is in about 16 months, not only could the first aircraft be test flown by the Air Force, but at the same time the production aircraft could be delivered. There was no actual prototype aircraft, no pre-production run, but the first aircraft was the first production aircraft. Modifications which were necessary were built in at that time. Non-essential modifications were simply not done. From the beginning of the design to the delivery of the first production aircraft took 16 months. That could be a record. Nevertheless, such achievements do not remain individual cases in the USA, but become the order of the day.

If we are to be sure of winning the war, they must also become the order of the day with us.

In another memo of about the same date to Udet, Messerschmitt returned again to this topic which appears to have been on his mind throughout the war years:

Unfortunately, I fear that the war will last for a long time yet. Because of the entry of the Americans, the struggle will shift even more than it has until now to the technical domain. The American is both a first-rate designer and an excellent organizer. In addition, he has resources which are not available to us, and unfatigued men in large numbers. His strategic position is far better than ours — he has bases close to us from which he can send bombers out against us. We do not have a single one close to him. Only the Luftwaffe can provide us with these bases. For that purpose we need high speed long-range aircraft which can rule the sea, and destroy enemy ships and transport aircraft before they reach their bases. The enemy will also build such aircraft. The enemy has long-range aircraft and we have none. There is a lot to catch up with here.

He was also aware of the work being done in Allied aircraft factories, and appreciative of the quality. There are numerous notes filed in his correspondence referring to copies of foreign aviation magazines and technical publications which his own design staff are advised to study.

For example, in January 1942, he issued a memorandum to his senior designers:

Please look at Interavia [the Swiss aviation industry magazine] of 20 December 1941, Pages 796/97.
Worthy of note are the fantastically good fairings between the engine nacelles, wings, tail unit and fuselage on the AVRO Manchester and on the Aer. Macchi C202.
Whatever happens, we must do something similar on the 309.

In July 1942 a new threat to Germany had appeared in the skies above the Continent. The De Havilland Mosquito was making its first appearances and frustrating the Luftwaffe by its superior speed and altitude.

Messerschmitt soon heard that one of the new aircraft had been shot down, and he issued a memo to Herr Voigt, the most senior member of his design staff:

Please enquire in the Air Ministry about where it is possible to see the English bomber built entirely of wood, one of which has been shot down.
It would be sensible to send a specialist to look at it who can find out all that is worth while knowing.

A few months later on the 26 October 1942, he writes to Karl Linder, one of his staff in the Regensburg factory:

I would recommend you to have a look at the American aircraft in the exhibition of captured equipment in Berlin. I believe that the American aircraft are better because at the moment they can still work with better operatives than we can.

In March 1943 Messerschmitt was still entertaining some slight hopes of Germany winning the war, despite his concerns about the superiority held by the American aircraft industry. In a report which he wrote at that time, he emphasized the advantages possessed by Germany because of its shorter lines of communication and the superiority of the German workers. It is very significant that by this time, Messerschmitt saw the role of the Luftwaffe as being no longer offensive but purely defensive.

In the course of this winter the initiative in the conduct of the war has surprisingly gone over to our enemies. It is not remarkable if, in the course of a long war, serious setbacks occur from time to time. If, however, like today, an excellently trained army, which was almost always used to winning and overcoming setbacks in a short time, is engaged on all fronts in the most difficult defensive battles, that must have unusual causes. Our first duty must be to identify these causes and then to do away with them.

For the conduct of the war we need men as soldiers, men as workers, raw materials in the form of foodstuffs and raw materials for the production of weapons and all the equipment such as means of transport, etc.

The Axis Powers and their allies have in Europe and Asia, including the occupied territories, about 600 million men, our enemies about 900 million men. Because of the better quality of the manpower available to us, on the one hand, and through its considerably more favourable concentration with resulting much better transport facilities, on the other, it must be possible for us to employ the men available to us with so much greater effectiveness than our enemies, that their superiority in manpower is lost. There is also the fact that we in many cases can dispense with offensive weapons since we can regard our position in the main as a defensive one.

We need far fewer men and much less material. U-boats are much smaller than merchant ships, cruisers and aircraft carriers. Fighters and fast bombers for relatively short ranges are much smaller than large bombers for long ranges. Transport aircraft for our short routes can be built with much less outlay than transport aircraft for large distances. Defensive weapons for use against tanks require much less material and maintenance than tanks. We need fewer weapons and fewer soldiers because we can move them about more quickly on account of the shorter distances.

This note is intended to reveal that the present inferiority in equipment and manpower can be eliminated by a tighter organization. It is amazing that a country like Russia, whose industry for the most part has fallen into our hands or been destroyed, has managed to keep on producing ever greater quantities of tanks and aircraft. It is amazing with how few men the USA produces aircraft in comparison with the numbers of employees that we need for a much smaller number of aircraft. The information available for 1942 shows that we, with 50% more people employed, produced only one third of the aircraft built by the USA. If it is assumed that the USA at the moment is building relatively more training aircraft than we are, but correspondingly more bombers as fighting aircraft, that shows that we need 4.5 times as many men per aircraft as the USA and that is at a time when they are only beginning. It is to be feared, therefore, that this ratio will get even more unfavourable for us when the USA is up to full power.

In Messerschmitt's view, if the quantity of aircraft produced was not to Germany's advantage, it was possible that quality would make up the difference. The German aircraft industry believed correctly that it had established a lead over the Allies in the development of jet aircraft. They were also aware, however, that work was going on in Britain, in particular, to produce similar aircraft. Problems with the early jet engines in

Germany had kept the Me 262 standing on the ground for two years, and there was considerable apprehension that the Allies might yet get a jet fighter into service ahead of the Luftwaffe.

A memorandum from Messerschmitt to his Chief Designer indicates that German intelligence was closely monitoring British developments in the field of jet propulsion and, incidentally, obtaining useful information about them from indiscreet prisoners of war:

3 November 1943

According to statements by prisoners, an aircraft without any propellers is flying in England. Its fuselage is very pointed at the front and cut off blunt at the rear. This leads one to the conclusion that it is a rocket-propelled aircraft similar to the Me 163. Nevertheless, it could be that a jet engine is installed which does not suck in air from the front but is installed behind the pilot's seat with the air conducted in at the sides through gills.

Worries about the Allied progress in developing jet aircraft, and the delays caused by shortages of German jet engines are displayed in the letter to the Junkers company in April 1944, already quoted in the chapter on the Me 262.

Messerschmitt's comments on the products of other German manufacturers vary from extremely negative, as in the case of the He 162 Volksjaeger designed by Heinkel — a long-standing rival — to very enthusiastic in the case of the Fieseler Fi 103 (V1) flying bomb designed by Robert Lusser, a former colleague of Messerschmitt.

In 1944, as the threat of the aerial destruction of Germany by Allied bombers became ever more imminent, the need for a jet-propelled fighter aircraft in the Luftwaffe was increasingly obvious. The Me 262 was being produced as fast as the circumstances allowed, but the Air Ministry saw the need for a cheap single engined fighter which could be rapidly turned out in large numbers.

Ernst Heinkel produced a design for an aircraft to satisfy the requirement — the He 162. Messerschmitt and other leading personalities in the German aircraft industry were asked to comment on this proposal which was to be known as the Volksjaeger (People's Fighter).

Messerschmitt was unrestrained in his comments, for if the proposal were accepted it would surely jeopardize orders for his far more sophisticated Me 262 jet fighter.

His report reads:

I summarize my opinion as follows:

The plan to build a cheap jet fighter with a BMW 003A jet engine, which is to be in service in quantity in the spring of 1945, I consider to be, at least in its present form, misguided.

1. The technical specification is wrong because the requirements for this fighter can be better satisfied by tested aircraft available today.

2. It is unlikely that a newly developed aircraft with all the risks it involves would permit us to throw large numbers of aircraft into the battle in the spring and summer of 1945. We can, however, produce at least the same number of aircraft of a proved type at the same point of time, without having to take account of the risks of a new development and its consequences, if we use the extra capacity earmarked for this project to increase the production of our present types.

3. In my opinion it is as good as completely out of the question to push ahead with the 'Volksjaeger' programme until the spring of 1945 to such a degree that the introduction into service of the aircraft in large numbers can be expected.

4. It is a delusion that the 162 can be developed and manufactured with 'extra capacity' without disturbing the current types, in particular the Me 262.

The Me 262, now as in the past, is on very shaky ground. There is still a shortage of jigs, skilled workers and inspectors.

Moreover, the capacity now identified for the 'special operation 162' is urgently needed for the further development of our present-day jet fighters and for the production of a new type which offers the assurance that we do not immediately lose to our enemies the technical superiority provided at the moment by the Me 262.

On the other hand, Messerschmitt was enthusiastic about the projected flying bomb which had been designed at Fieseler by his former associate, Robert Lusser. Lusser conceived the idea of using the simple propulsion device, the pulse-jet known as the 'Argus tube', to propel an extremely basic unpiloted aircraft carrying a ton of high explosive.

Messerschmitt was himself familiar with the potential of the Argus tube and had already designed an aircraft, the Me 328, which was to be propelled by this means. The first design had two tubes mounted one on each side of the fuselage. Trials showed that acoustic fatigue caused by the high noise levels at the exit of the tubes led to rapid structural failure of the fuselage.

In order to avoid that problem, a later version of the aircraft had the tubes mounted under the wings in a similar fashion to the engines of the Me 262. This aircraft was successfully flown in a test version at Peenemünde, giving it the distinction of being the first man-carrying aircraft to be powered by an Argus pulse-jet tube, but no further development of the Me 328 was undertaken.

While acknowledging the difficulties which he himself had experienced in the design of the Me 328, Messerschmitt realized immediately the value of the V1 which was to cause so much damage in London and the Home Counties in the last months of the war. Germany had failed to produce a heavy bomber, despite Messerschmitt's appeals to the Nazi hierarchy, and the fact had to be faced that the Allies now had such superiority in the air over Europe that it would have been impossible for the Luftwaffe to make any decisive use of bombers even if they had had any.

Messerschmitt had always been aware of the necessity of striking at

Britain if the tide of war was to be turned in Germany's favour. The V1 flying bomb now promised to be an effective weapon which, even at that late stage, could force Britain to call a halt to the war. So many bombs could be launched that it would be impossible for the British defences to protect southern England from widespread destruction.

So enthusiastic was he about the new weapon that he found it difficult to keep his hands off Herr Lusser's new project. This is demonstrated by the letter which he wrote to the designer on 23 August 1943:

Dear Herr Lusser,

I have asked Herr Voigt to come and see you about the interesting thing that you have developed. I consider the affair to be so extraordinarily important and significant — in my opinion it is much more important than the whole of the bombing operation with aircraft — that it cannot be produced quickly enough in huge quantities and brought into operation.

My first worries were the adequate reliability of the Argus tube. But I have been assured lately that these problems have been completely eliminated and the difficulty would not be with the Argus tube but rather with the airframe; apparently because of excessive lack of stiffness for the 15 g launching acceleration. A very large proportion of these aircraft would dive into the ground immediately after launching.

I really do not want to involve myself in your work but I believe that it is my duty, if I have some knowledge of that sort, to pass it on to you. I have, therefore, asked Herr Voigt, with whom you are personally very friendly, to come and see you and to support you with advice and practical help if it should be necessary. In view of the importance of the matter, I consider it to be my duty to assist in any way I can. It would be important for me if I could know the actual state of affairs, as apparently the highest authorities in Germany are adversely informed about the affair. If you give me the material to disperse the doubts which still exist today, you can be assured that I will do this at the highest level.

I ask you again to excuse my involving myself in an affair which has nothing to do with me, but I am only doing it in the interest of the defence of the country.

With all good wishes, yours

Messerschmitt

It is difficult to accept Messerschmitt's statement that he 'did not want to involve himself in Lusser's work'. Every line of the letter reveals that he was obviously itching to get involved. His excuse that he was 'only doing it in the interest of the defence of the country' only served to cover up his intense personal desire to contribute to what he regarded as an outstanding development in aerial warfare. There is, in fact, no evidence that Messerschmitt contributed anything at all to the design of the Fi 103.

Messerschmitt also included his opinions of the V1 flying bomb in a six page letter which he sent to Albert Speer a week later:

I would not like to leave unmentioned that the self-piloting aircraft, such as Fieseler has developed, must be further developed urgently for series production in very large numbers. This aircraft permits the carrying of the same amount of explosive to England as is possible with aircraft, without putting valuable manpower at risk and at a cost which is about 1/500th of that of a bomber aircraft of today. I am convinced that by the employment of real mass production methods it will be possible to build 100,000 units a month, when it is considered that the American car industry has produced nearly 4,000,000 cars of different types in one year. The range of this unmanned aircraft and its accuracy will certainly be capable of considerable improvement. How many advantages the A4 device [that is, the V2 rocket], which is intended for the same application, would have relative to the above-mentioned I cannot decide, as I know too little about the A4 device. I just have the impression that the A4 device is unacceptably expensive if only on account of the fuel costs.

Once again it is remarkable that Messerschmitt could be so accurate in predicting problems with a project with which he had no intimate dealings. His forecast regarding the failures of the flying bomb during the launch phase was to be justified in practice. In fact, 9300 of the missiles were launched against southern England before their launching sites were overrun by ground troops. About 2000 of them did not succeed in getting airborne because of failures of one sort or another during launch.

Luckily for southern England, Messerschmitt's proposed production rate for the weapon was never remotely approached.

CHAPTER 18

Messerschmitt's views on research

Because of his engineering training and his years of practical experience in solving aeronautical problems, Messerschmitt was keenly aware of the importance of research in furthering the progress of aircraft design. He himself had experimented with different structural layouts and innovative control systems in the early days of his career. He realized that it was no longer good enough to try out new ideas on an experimental aircraft in the hope that the results would prove satisfactory. By the late 1930s aircraft design had reached a stage where further progress was only possible with the backing of adequate results from research programmes, particularly into the problems of high-speed flight. One of his constant worries was that research in Germany was lagging behind the advances being made in the United States. The lack of wind tunnels of sufficient size and with sufficiently high air flow velocities was of particular concern to him as the age of the jet-propelled aircraft approached.

Throughout the war, and indeed even earlier, Messerschmitt had been concerned by the production capabilities of the American aircraft industry and by the depth and extent of the aeronautical research being carried out in the United States. In a lecture which he gave in Berlin on 15 March 1940 he used information about the wind-tunnel facilities available in enemy countries and the United States (who were not yet officially involved in the hostilities) in an effort to get more funding from the German government for better wind tunnels in Germany.

The most relevant parts of his speech are quoted below. Unfortunately, the slides which Messerschmitt used for his lecture have not survived, but their importance is clear from his address:

> Herr Betz in his lecture has explained the many tasks that a wind tunnel can perform for the development of an aircraft. He has particularly emphasized that it is not only a matter of producing the most modern and valuable research facilities. As in the front line, where the most modern equipment on its own will not bring victory without well-

trained forces under good leadership, so it is in the research sphere. Apart from the construction of facilities, the selection and training of the engineers and assistants, and their application to the simplest test procedures appropriate to the desired end result, are a particular problem. Nevertheless, the research facilities are such an important resource that I would like here to make a few short comparative statements about the present state of the most valuable wind tunnel research institutes in different countries.

In his lecture on 'Tasks and Methods of Aerodynamic Research' on the occasion of the General Meeting of the Lilienthal Society in Munich in 1937, Herr Betz has shown a diagram representing the development of the operating power of wind tunnels from the beginnings in 1908 up to 1936. On the basis of this diagram he drew the conclusion that further development would, in all probability, hardly continue to increase at the same rate in view of the enormous expense involved. I have now completed this diagram from 1937 on the basis of information coming from reliable sources on the state of expansion abroad. From it, it can be seen that the power consumption of these most up-to-date tunnels exceeds all expectations.

This first slide shows the enormous power that is already today considered essential abroad for the improvement of aircraft development. In the next two slides I have shown for two groups of wind tunnel installations the dimensions and wind velocities as characteristic parameters, as well as the power requirements.

In the first group we are dealing with the so-called giant wind tunnels which are distinguished by the large dimensions of their working sections. German aircraft engineering has for years deliberately stood back, in much the same way as the French and more lately the Russians, from imitating the construction of the American giant wind tunnel with low speeds. The only large facility of this kind in Brunswick can be seen in the last column from which the difference in the dimensions of the working section is apparent above everything else. Much more thought-provoking on the other hand is the representation of the test facility at Wright Field with 40,000 hp and a speed of 150 m/sec with a working section of 6 metre diameter. This installation is being taken into operation in 1940 and will be an extremely valuable resource for the American aviation industry, particularly for the testing of engine installations. German designers will certainly fully confirm the usefulness of a test facility of that type. Indeed, I believe that — apart from the construction and running costs — every aircraft and engine factory would like to have such a facility in its own concern.

The second group of test facilities occupying the forefront of interest are the so-called high-speed wind tunnels. In this field the United States have been in the lead with the tunnel represented in the first position which, in the last two to three years, has provided extremely valuable results in the field of present-day high-speed flight. The two other USA wind tunnels shown are projects agreed last year for the expansion of the new test centre of the NACA in Sunnyvale, California. There is no doubt that these installations will be completed within a considerably shorter time than would be possible in Germany with the extraordinarily long delivery times for the detail manufacture of motors and fans, etc. The construction of the high-speed tunnel was agreed last year for the Japanese test centre shortly to be set up. Its completion is to be expected perhaps in 1942/43.

The building of the high-speed tunnel of the Soviet Union had already started in 1937. It can be assumed that it is already in operation or at the least will be put into operation in the very near future. Its operating power is, nonetheless, double that of the largest German installation. The wind tunnel in Brunswick, referred to above, was designed in 1936/37 and will be put into operation in 1940/41. It is intended to make possible tests above the speed of sound at 'modest' cost. The Americans have already provided for three to four times its power for that purpose. It is already obvious today that the permissible dimensions for a model in this tunnel are hardly adequate for the planned developments of the next few years.

When considering the three German high-speed wind tunnels in Adlershof and Brunswick, it should be noted that their construction started in 1936, but because of difficult circumstances they were not completed until 1939/40. It follows therefore, that even if construction starts immediately, a large tunnel equivalent to the aforementioned foreign installations certainly could not be available before 1944. We can say with justification and pride that at the moment we, together with the United States, stand at the head of all the nations carrying out aeronautical research.

The above review, which is based on reliable information, makes it appear necessary, however, to look forward to further developments in the future. It is known that American aeronautical research is directed very strongly to practical needs and to an immediate use of the first test results. It must, therefore, give cause for thought that it is just there that such an enormous expenditure is envisaged for the next few years. Characteristic of the attitude of the American industry to this question is the opinion of the responsible technical leader of the Curtiss-Wright Corporation, T. P. Wright. He expressed this in the following words in an article of June 1939 about the attitude of the American aircraft industry to national defence, as an adjunct to his remarks on the production capabilities of the American aviation industry: 'A more rewarding safeguard for the future would be to put increased value on the possibilities of research today. Research which concerns itself with quality is and remains the foundation stone for a good air force.'

The many years of predominance of the Americans in the field of high-speed research has shown us all how serious the lack of information of that kind can be for development. As a result it appears necessary, whilst appreciating fully the existing circumstances in Germany, to follow with the most careful attention this continuing development abroad.

Messerschmitt was constantly worried by the lack of aeronautical research being carried out in Germany. As has been seen, this stemmed partly from the belief of the Führer and his close followers that the war would soon be over and that there was no need to plan too far ahead. The decision to abandon all projects which would not be in service within 18 months is further evidence of this mistaken thinking.

On several occasions in public lectures and correspondence with influential personalities, Messerschmitt returned to the need for adequate research to maintain Germany's superiority in aircraft design. A particularly interesting example is the letter which he sent to Ernst Udet on 22 January 1940. This was provoked in the first place by the proposal to call up research workers for what were considered to be more important duties in wartime. Once again, because it was expected that the war would be over within a few months at the utmost, the German authorities saw no purpose in tying up valuable manpower in research work which could easily be postponed for a year at the most until victory had been achieved.

Messerschmitt's evaluation of the relationship between research and practical engineering and of the employment conditions required for the workers engaged in both spheres is still as relevant today as it was then:

Applied Research and Pure Research in Wartime

I am taking the decree of the Generalluftzeugmeister (according to which the research institutes are to give up 50% of their specialists), and the resulting questions to me from the research institutes, as the excuse for speaking briefly about the necessity of research in wartime and about the concentration of all resources. Applied research for industry and pure research are perhaps even more important in wartime since the problems have to be overcome in a much shorter time. But in my opinion we can also achieve a lot by concentration of effort in this area.

In industry, particularly since 1933, we have had a considerable number of wind tunnel measurements carried out. Part of these measurements could still be lying unevaluated since there was often a lack of the necessary time and personnel needed for that. Moreover, for private commercial reasons, a considerable amount of duplicated effort was used because the measurements were kept secret. In wartime, these private commercial interests must take a back seat. I propose, therefore, that all the available research material in the industry should be gathered together and evaluated in a united effort. In this way a series of new contracts in the research institutes could be dropped.

In addition, a whole series of research projects can be deleted as they partly deal with scientific problems which have long since been made meaningless by the advance of technology. In this connection, I remember research work on the stressing of frameworks with regard to welded steel structures after we have been designing for years in monocoque. Research projects whose use in engineering is not possible for structural or other reasons can also be deleted. As an example, I would mention the 'Standard Sets of Joukowsky Airfoils'. We are not in the position to produce their slender trailing edges in practice and, therefore, cannot make use of this family of sections.

I also consider it necessary, on the other hand, to check the necessity of the projects newly formulated by industry since, in the interest of the overall good, this or that special question can certainly be put back.

On the occasion of a Lilienthal Symposium it was pointed out by Herr Tank that we in Germany must carry out considerably more systematic tests. I can only urgently support this requirement because we have to rely on the Americans for the only really systematic tests. The evaluation of the raw material in the NACA reports is often excellent, and the test material is systematically arranged, illuminated from several sides and critically examined. In addition, the reports are collected in a sensible external form and available to a wide circle because of their cheapness. I know very well that in the area of systematic measurements the first beginnings are on hand with us, but I must point out that they are unfortunately only the first beginnings. I consider it absolutely necessary to plan these research projects in co-operation with industry.

Naturally, the war must not be allowed to become a reason for stopping long-term research projects. For we must not repeat our experience in the area of the effect of high Mach numbers where, with our maximum speeds, we are breaking into areas which have not been explored either theoretically or by tests. I have often pointed out that we urgently need high-speed wind tunnels in order to study the effects of Mach number. Unfortunately, the processes are so poorly understood to date that we have to clarify them in practice by tests with full-size aircraft, and hence involve a high risk in material and men.

In the theoretical domain we engineers cannot be satisfied with the solution of a couple of special cases. With the effect of Mach number, we are interested, for example, in the first place with the transition from the subsonic to the supersonic region. Those are questions which should already have been cleared up by research. But as that has not happened, we have helped ourselves and have advanced so far in the area that we have found a general solution which theoretically represents this transition.

As far as the research is concerned, it must be made clear that the theoretical work for the greater part is intended for us engineers. It is necessary to write the proceedings in such a way that the engineer can read and understand them. Mathematical dissertations are of no value to the engineer. Many complicated formulae and deductions only serve to demonstrate the inability of the author to think simply and clearly.

I would like to take this opportunity to also point out that we could not afford to build a high-speed wind tunnel if from the outset we could not use it for a considerable part of the year because of atmospheric conditions. We are compelled to design that sort of expensive installation so that we are independent of the weather.

I make the following proposals for the solution of the problems described and for the concentration of effort:

1. The industry forms a central research committee on which all the companies are represented.

2. The research institutes form a corresponding committee which plans and defines in conjunction with the industrial committee all of the research projects and systematic programmes.
   I must point out from the beginning that it is necessary to keep the committees very small so that they are really efficient.

3. A central assessment institute must be founded which evaluates and publishes all the presently available test results as well as those to be made in the future.

Finally, I would like to point out once again the necessity of a much closer contact between research and engineering. In order to really effect this, I see only one possibility, namely that of a continual interchange of personnel. It must not happen that professional staff in the research institutes have never been active in industry and, therefore, have no understanding of the requirements of industry. The prerequisite for this is, of course, that the level of payment in industry and research is the same, otherwise the good personnel will be drawn into industry, and research will be unable to carry out the necessary work with the remaining people. It must also be possible for the research institutes to adapt to the tempo of industry, with just as many hours of overtime being worked there as in our case. No bureaucratic reasons of any kind must serve to prevent this.

With my explanations I have wanted to provide the incentive to solving the problems in such a way that the existing equipment is used more intensively. I believe that it is only in this way possible to achieve the concentration of forces which is so necessary.

It is interesting that Messerschmitt had such a high regard for the research being carried out by NACA in the United States. He was obviously speaking from a close acquaintance with the results of that research as far as it was available to the world in general. His requests for increased research of a similar quality in Germany were to go unheeded. As he himself realized, even if the will had been there, there was no longer sufficient time available to obtain the required results and to make use of them.

Messerschmitt continually kept himself informed of new developments in research outside the immediate sphere of aircraft design. One such instance concerned the use of fuel derived from coal as a source of power for jet engines. Because of the continuing air raids carried out by the Royal Air Force and the American Air Force, the Luftwaffe was by 1944 suffering from a severe shortage of aircraft fuel. Germany had available a very limited supply of petroleum fuels, but had ample supplies of coal.

It was not found possible to develop a suitable anti-knock fuel from coal for use in conventional piston engines. However, although the early jet engines were far from economical in their fuel usage, as Messerschmitt points out in the letter quoted below, there was the possibility of extracting a usable fuel for them from coal. This development might go a long way towards satisfying the greedy appetites of the new Me 262 jet fighters coming into service at that time.

From the letter quoted below it would appear that Messerschmitt was giving some thought to the design of a jet-engined bomber at the time.

Work had already been carried out in Germany on producing highly inflammable liquid fuels from coal. Messerschmitt's brother-in-law, Professor Georg Madelung of Stuttgart University had been concerned with these developments and had indicated to the aircraft designer the possibility of using the product as a fuel for jet engines.

Messerschmitt's letter dated 25 February 1944 is addressed to an official of the coal mining organization carrying out the research:

Dear Dr Grimme,

My brother-in-law, Professor Madelung, gave me your confidential letter of 31 December 1943 regarding the supply of low boiling point, inflammable or very inflammable hydrocarbons by the Fischer-Tropsch process. If we disregard their use as incendiary bombs, which is being pursued by Professor

Madelung, these fuels are particularly interesting because of the possibility of using them for jet engines. Regarding the operation of jet engines the following can be said:

1. Jet engines need an abnormally large amount of fuel. For example, a fighter aircraft requires two tonnes for one mission. The hydrocarbon, amounting to 90,000 tonnes a year with a boiling point of up to 70°C provided by your process and which is unusable in any other way without further processing, would therefore suffice for 123 missions daily. It is very important to use up this fuel (which is useless for piston engines because of its knock rating) for jet engines and so to actually extend our fuel base.

2. In a jet engine the combustion is continuous so it is not important that the fuel is anti-knock.

3. Naturally what is important is the high thermal value of 11,500 kcal per kilogram.

The use of jet engines in an aircraft is tied to two prerequisites of a fundamental nature as far as the fuel is concerned:

a. The combustion must proceed without interruption, particularly for high altitude operation of jet fighters at very low temperatures and pressures relative to the piston engine. Under these circumstances and with a high velocity flow through the combustion chamber, it must not break down. High inflammability and short burning times, i.e. rapid reaction, are essential since otherwise, in some circumstances owing to the high altitude operation, the jet engines must be made larger (not just somewhat larger but unacceptably larger) relative to present practice in the longitudinal measurements of the combustion chambers.

b. The operation of jet bomber aircraft requires a volumetric thermal value as large as possible, i.e. in general high specific gravities. The density quoted by you at the moment of 0.66 tonnes per cubic metre on the average can be catered for from the start, and the required larger fuselage can be built with, for example, three cubic metres of space for fuel with no difficulty. The same aircraft with the same thermal value would have a correspondingly greater range with a relatively denser fuel.

In the ideal case, both these prerequisites should be satisfied by one fuel. However, I can envisage that, with the abnormally high consumption, two fuels are provided of which one, apparently the one supplied by you at the moment, is especially suitable for high altitude operation, whereas the other satisfies the requirements of extreme ranges at lower altitudes if necessary.

Independently of these basic questions, it appears to me at the moment that the most important thing is to check the possibility of using in jet engines the fuels already available from you. I am asking you, therefore, to let me know as quickly as possible whether such tests are already in progress. If not, I would be very pleased to be made use of to ensure that they are got under way with no delay.

Yours sincerely,

Mtt

Nothing further resulted from this approach. Aircraft powered by coal-based fuels were not to appear. It was proposed to power a version of the Me 264 with steam turbines using a mixture of petrol and powdered coal as the fuel. Nothing came of this outlandish suggestion either.

CHAPTER 19

Public relations

Throughout his life, Messerschmitt, like many famous people, received numerous requests for photographs of himself, preferably with a signature appended. He distributed these to Luftwaffe pilots, members of the general public and in one instance to the commandant of Dachau concentration camp (see his letter quoted in Chapter 15).

Presentation models of his aircraft, usually the Me 109, were given to outstanding fighter aces of the Luftwaffe. In one case, a silver model despatched to an Me 109 squadron went astray en route to its recipients and had to be replaced urgently.

In return, he received numerous gifts from well-wishers and industrial magnates, such as Professor Porsche, designer of the Volkswagen. There was also a continual exchange of birthday greetings between Messerschmitt and his political masters, Hitler and Goering. Occasionally, there would be the grant of a national decoration for services to the country.

The communications with Hitler and Goering were on a very formal basis. Messerschmitt expressed himself with careful deference to his masters and in return received equally formal acknowledgements from them.

A typical example is a telegram sent by Hitler:

Professor Willy Messerschmitt
Führer's Headquarters   20 April 1942

I express to you my sincere thanks for the good wishes which you kindly conveyed to me on my birthday.

Adolf Hitler

Messerschmitt's communications with Goering were equally formal:

Telegram   12.1.45
Reichsmarschall Hermann Goering , Berlin

On the occasion of your birthday today, I am taking the liberty of sending to you, esteemed Herr Reichsmarschall, my sincerest good wishes.

Messerschmitt

Signed photographs of Messerschmitt appear to have been distributed in large quantities. When Frau Kaltenhäuser wrote to the designer to express her birthday wishes, she received the following letter in reply:

Dear Frau Kaltenhäuser,

Thank you very much for your good wishes for my birthday. I hope to give your young son a pleasant surprise with the enclosed picture.

Yours sincerely,
Messerschmitt

Despite his urgent involvement in the design of a new jet fighter in the autumn of 1944, Messerschmitt was sufficiently touched by the receipt of the following letter from a young admirer that he immediately instructed his secretary to comply with the request contained in it.

13 November 1944

Dear Aircraft Designer Messerschmitt,

In the last bombing raid on Cologne our house was demolished by high-explosive bombs. A picture I had of you was destroyed as well. I have tried everywhere to get a new picture of you but without success. If, Herr Messerschmitt, you should still have such a picture in your possession, might I ask you most politely to make me a present of one with your signature?

Karl-Heinz Vogel

Karl-Heinz did not have to wait long for an answer:

Oberammergau
28 November 1944

Dear Karl-Heinz Vogel,

At the request of Professor Messerschmitt, I am sending you enclosed his picture with his signature.
    You can imagine that many people come and ask for his picture, but he is unable to give one to everyone. You have been lucky, therefore.
    I hope that it will give you pleasure. With all best wishes for the future.

Professor Messerschmitt's Secretary

Like most large companies, the Messerschmitt concern made a habit of distributing gifts to promote its image. It appears to have been particularly active in this respect during the war, when it was involved in the distribution of what we would today call 'freebies' to the armed services.

The Board minutes of 9 May 1943 include a self-congratulatory item on the subject:

Item 12. Appreciation of our propaganda.

Herr Kokothaki read out letters of appreciation from the Welfare Office in the High Command of the Armed Forces written by Oberst von Völkersam in which he says that he does not know of any firm which performs such effective and relevant welfare work for the Luftwaffe as Messerschmitt.

A further letter of appreciation from a lady officer in the German Red Cross was read out which praised the exemplary welfare work in hospitals by the Messerschmitt company.

Herr Kokothaki gave a summary of the promotional gifts distributed, including 13,000 calendars, 12,000 pictures and many thousands of other gifts among which playing cards and dice shakers are particularly popular at the front. He added that he had arranged for the printing in Hungary of a Messerschmitt calender for 1944.

General agreement. The organization of the Publicity Department is under Graf Thun. It consists entirely of girls since the male staff employed earlier had shown themselves not to be reliable.

It is not revealed in what way the male staff were unreliable but no doubt there were endless opportunities for the 'freebies' to be diverted into unauthorized channels.

Messerschmitt carried out an extensive correspondence with the Luftwaffe pilots of his aircraft. He took a great interest in their activities and was always pleased to receive news of their successes. He often sent letters of condolence to the families of pilots killed on active service in his aircraft.

In one particular instance the pilot involved was the son of the Air Attache at the German Embassy in Madrid. Messerschmitt received the following letter from the bereaved parent:

6 February 1942

Air Attache
German Embassy
Madrid

Dear Professor,

I have received the delightful model of the Me 109 sent to me by the intermediary of Fräulein Renz. I can assure you that it occupies a particular place of honour in my house as a memento of our dear only son who encountered a hero's death as a fighter pilot over the Channel. I thank you also on behalf of my wife for your kindness.

H. von Bülow

Messerschmitt was always quick to congratulate Luftwaffe pilots who achieved outstanding successes in his aircraft. A typical letter is the one which he sent to the leading Luftwaffe fighter ace, Erich Hartmann, who was at the time resting in the pilots' convalescent home at Wiessee, on the occasion of his 300th victory in an Me 109.

12 September 1944

Dear Oberleutnant Hartmann,

With the Me 109 you have shot down more than 300 aircraft and so put yourself at the head of all the successful German fighter pilots.

I congratulate you on this splendid achievement and on the award of the highest German decoration for bravery, the diamonds for the Knight's Cross of the Iron Cross with oak leaves and swords. Your great success means for me also the pleasure that our design has been proved and the certainty that air supremacy over our homeland can be re-established.

I wish you many further victorious air battles, and in the first place a successful rest period in Wiessee. I would be pleased if you would visit me at some time in Oberammergau; I would like to show you our most recent work on improving the Me 109 and on providing new more efficient fighter aircraft.

Messerschmitt

Messerschmitt was also the recipient of gifts. His benefactors appear to have been aware of his particular likes, and to have taken steps to satisfy them. For instance, he received a letter early in 1942 in anticipation of the first visit to him of the Managing Director of Alfa Romeo, who had obviously learned of Messerschmitt's appreciation of fine wines acquired from his upbringing in Bamberg.

Milan, 21 January 1942

I know that you are an admirer of the wines of Valpolicella and, as I am from Venice, I particularly share your opinion, for which reason I have allowed myself to order for you a sample selection of such wines in order that you might let me know which is the type that most meets with your approval.

It will be a pleasure for me on the occasion of our first meeting to present you with some.

With best wishes,
The Managing Director, Alfa Romeo

An even more generous offer arrived late in 1943. The letter from the office of Dr Ferdinand Porsche announcing the gift is dated 3 November 1943. The arrangements appear to have gone astray somewhere along the line with the result that Messerschmitt did not receive the gift until a few months later than intended, as the letter from an employee at Volkswagen makes clear:

The Volkswagen Company decided on 11 August 1943 to present to Professor Messerschmitt a limousine, Type 60, as a gift from the Volkswagen Company. This vehicle was in due course transferred to me so that I could tune it and then hand it over. As a result of a change of staff the paperwork for the vehicle did not reach my hands. Consequently, after I had tuned the vehicle, it remained here somewhat longer than usual. Now I have got everything together and I would like to take the liberty of asking you where and when I can deliver the vehicle.

May I suggest that Professor Messerschmitt's driver comes here for a day to the Porsche works in Zuffenhausen, makes himself familiar with the car and perhaps himself takes charge of his master's vehicle. I can also gladly deliver the car to you wherever you wish.

Messerschmitt drove the car assiduously in the next few weeks as he reported to Dr Porsche. His comments on the relative merits of the Volkswagen and his Mercedes must surely be explained as an excess of politeness to his benefactor.

10 December 1943

Dear Herr Porsche,

Through your kind intervention, the Volkswagen Werk GmbH has let me have a car as a gift. I would like today to express my sincerest thanks to you for this with the request that you pass them on to the other members of the management. At the same time I would like to say that the car completely meets all the demands arising from business travel. The little car, in which I have already covered several thousand kilometres, satisfies all my requirements as regards performance and economy as well as comfort, so that I do not for an instant miss my 2.3 litre Mercedes and appreciate the 40 miles to the gallon as a pleasant bonus.

The Volkswagen is really a unique achievement on which I congratulate you most cordially, Herr Porsche.

Yours sincerely,
Messerschmitt

At the foot of the letter there is a hand-written note:

I would be delighted if I could show you my latest aircraft some time.

Messerschmitt's enthusiasm about the Volkswagen must have become somewhat diluted a few weeks later when he again wrote to Porsche, whom he now addresses as 'Professor' Porsche:

On my Volkswagen the front axle suspension has repeatedly seized up so that the springing temporarily ceased to work. Any attempts to cure the problem in my factory have so far failed. I assume that this happens from time to time on Volkswagens and ask for immediate instructions on what I am to do.

A repair workshop is available here.

Messerschmitt

Professor Porsche must have been particularly impressed by the suggestion that such faults were a common occurrence on his cars. There are no further references to the Volkswagen in Messerschmitt's correspondence. Perhaps he reverted to his Mercedes despite its higher fuel consumption.

Messerschmitt's transport problems were alleviated in a different way in April 1944. The chief engineer of the Phaenomen Works, a bicycle factory in Zittau near the Polish border, presented Messerschmitt with an experimental bicycle as a gift.

In return he received a letter from Messerschmitt:

Dear Herr Albert,

By sending me an experimental bicycle you have given me particularly great pleasure and a great surprise. I thank you most sincerely for this kindness. As soon as the weather allows, I will vigorously make use of the bicycle.

Yours sincerely,
Messerschmitt

As a birthday present in the same year he received a dog from a friend in Allach, a suburb of Munich. The feeding and training of the dog seem to have provided some problems for Messerschmitt as can be deduced from the letter of thanks which he sent:

Dear Herr Stegmueller,

Many thanks for your kind letter of 24 June 1944 and the birthday wishes as well as the enclosed instructions regarding the handling and care of the little schnauzer.

This birthday present, I can assure you, has given me a great deal of pleasure.

I would be grateful to you if you could let me know what quantity of food, in terms of weight, the terrier should get to eat each day. I have the feeling that he is very hungry.

The only thing that is not yet working is cleanliness. There can be no talk of 'house-trained' as yet, but that can still be introduced, given time.

The image of the famous aircraft designer worrying about how much food to give to a terrier and cleaning up the messes left by it on the floor of Hochried, or even taking it for walks along the shores of the Staffelsee, conflicts sharply with one's preconceived notions of the intense creative thinker continually engaged in producing weapons of war.

Messerschmitt was inevitably caught up in the propaganda machine of Hitler's Germany. He was personified as the aircraft designer par excellence to a much greater degree than any of his contemporaries. As a result it was necessary to enhance his image as much as possible in order to impress Germany's enemies with the superiority of the Luftwaffe.

His photograph appeared regularly in reports on meetings of aeronautical bodies such as the Lilienthal Society. Messerschmitt is often shown in conversation with dignitaries including foreign diplomats.

Correspondence concerned with such propaganda exercises is to be found among Messerschmitt's personal mail. For example, his career was to be portrayed in a film, the intention apparently being to revise the film regularly as more achievements became worthy of record:

14 February 1942

From: The Secretary of State
National Ministry for Public Information and Propaganda

To: Herr Prof. W. Messerschmitt
Augsburg

Dear Professor,

The Film Archive of Personalities, which forms part of the National Ministry for Public Information and Propaganda, would like to record a picture of you for the future in a sound film. The film, which it is intended to update and extend at appropriate times, is meant to give to future generations a living representation of you as the great aircraft designer.

I am asking you, therefore, to make yourself available for the making of the film. The Head of the Film Archive of Personalities, Dr Jeschke, will take the liberty of asking you when his visit to discuss the details is convenient for you.

It would be interesting to know whether the film was ever made and, if so, whether any copies survive today.

Messerschmitt was also to be immortalized in a book which summarized the careers of leading personalities in the armaments industry. It appears to have been intended as an up-market product of the publishing trade, since all the illustrations were to be derived from works of art and not just portrait photographs of the selected participants.

Messerschmitt received the following letter:

Feldafing, 8 February 1944

Dear Professor,

Your picture is intended to appear in a book *The German Man* under the subsection 'Work Pioneers'. Since, in the proposed book which is being published by the People's Press in Munich, only reproductions of works of art are to be used, I am asking you to kindly inform me where portraits of yourself, whether as a drawing, oil painting or sculpture, are to be found and which photographer if necessary could take photographs of them.

It would be the simplest, of course, if the required photographs were taken straight away by one of your works photographers and the pictures were sent to me for a selection to be made.

Before the final publication, a proof would be sent to you, Herr Professor, for approval and a declaration of consent.

In anticipation, my most grateful thanks for your trouble,

Georg Schorer

This letter arrived at a very awkward time. The Augsburg factory had just been bombed and the main object of attention was the evacuation of the design offices and as much of production as possible to a refuge in

Oberammergau. As a result, Herr Schorer received in reply a letter which cannot have been entirely what he was hoping for:

Oberammergau, 1 May 1944

Mr Georg Schorer
Feldafing
On Starnberger Lake

Dear Mr Schorer,

At the request of Professor Messerschmitt I thank you for your letter of 8 February 1944. Because of the intervening evacuation and overloading with work of our photographic section, we are unfortunately, for the moment, no longer in a position to satisfy your requirements.

An oil painting of Professor Messerschmitt is in the conference room of the works manager, Mr Kokothaki, in the Augsburg factory. Perhaps it would be possible for you to have a photograph of it taken.

I hope to have been useful to you with this information and am sorry that because of the circumstances caused by the war it was regrettably not possible for us to comply with your wishes.

Secretary to Prof. M.

From the extracts quoted above, one can assume that despite the failure of the Me 210 and the squabbles with Erhard Milch, Messerschmitt's public image was still intact. It was certainly still useful to the Goebbels propaganda machine for outside consumption.

CHAPTER 20

Relations with Lippisch

One of the most remarkable aircraft operated by the Luftwaffe during the Second World War was the Me 163 rocket-propelled interceptor. Its familiar designation was, however, not entirely accurate.

As Mano Ziegler said in his book *Raketenjäger Me 163*, which describes his career as a test pilot on the aircraft:

> Its bourgeois name was the 'Me 163 B' and it was, so to speak, an adopted child because its father was not called Messerschmitt, as might be concluded from its name, but Lippisch from whose genius the power-egg was born. But at Messerschmitt's it went into production and sponsorship and hence, probably, the 'Me'. In any case, it is all the same. There are any number of children in this world who do not know the name of their father but bear that of their sponsor . . .

In 1936, Professor Hellmuth Walter had developed a practical rocket motor for the propulsion of aircraft. He offered his invention to the German Academy of Aviation Research who gave a contract for the design of a suitable aircraft to the DFS, the German Institute for Sailplane Research. Despite its title, the Institute carried out research into many branches of aviation. The task of designing the aircraft was given to Alexander Lippisch who had already designed a number of unconventional aircraft.

Lippisch had concerned himself for many years with improving the efficiency of aircraft by the use of swept-back wings in a tail-less layout. He had developed very fixed ideas about the advantages of swept-back wings for high-speed aircraft at a time when designers in America and the rest of the world outside Germany had hardly given any attention to the matter at all.

On being entrusted with the design of the new rocket-propelled aircraft, he immediately started to develop the idea of a swept-wing fighter using the new revolutionary power unit. His ideas were listened to with great interest in the Air Ministry. Before long, he had sufficiently gained the confidence of the leading figures in the Ministry for them to see some advantages in producing an aircraft using Lippisch's ideas. A prototype aircraft, the DFS 194 was constructed and flew successfully. However, although Lippisch had designed a number of experimental aircraft with swept back wings, he was not regarded by the Air Ministry as the man to turn their ideas for a military aircraft into a practical project which was economical to build in large quantities.

Lippisch's knowledge of aircraft design for full-scale production was limited. It was obvious, therefore, that the design of an operational aircraft for manufacture in quantity would have to be done within the confines of one of the existing established aircraft design teams in Germany. The choice, when it was finally made, fell upon Messerschmitt. Lippisch and his team of closest associates were transferred to the Messerschmitt design office as a self-contained unit known as Department L, where they sought to maintain their independence.

In the light of Messerschmitt's known intolerance of other designers and his resentment of any interference in the carrying out of his own ideas, it might have been foreseen that the combination of Lippisch and Messerschmitt would lead to personality problems. The juxtaposition of two strong characters with very definite ideas regarding their own undoubted infallibility was a recipe for disturbances. Indeed, trouble was not long in coming.

Inevitably, Messerschmitt regarded Lippisch as a fully integrated member of his design team. He, therefore, expected to have control of what Lippisch was doing and felt it to be his right to comment on the designs which Lippisch was producing. Unfortunately, Messerschmitt had never been enthusiastic about tail-less designs, possibly as a result of his own experience with the S 9 tail-less glider which he himself had designed in 1921. As we saw earlier, it had proved to be a failure.

At the beginning of September 1942, Messerschmitt had been asked to give his comments on a letter from Lippisch extolling the virtues of a tail-less bomber aircraft which he was hoping to develop under Messerschmitt's design sponsorship. The aircraft was to be powered by piston engines mounted at the rear of the wing and driving pusher propellers.

Messerschmitt's response does rather less than express his enthusiasm for the project. Reading between the lines, one can detect the antagonism which had already developed between Messerschmitt and Lippisch:

As a result of the discussion on 28 August about the tail-less projects for a high speed bomber, I have stated my opinions regarding the performance of the said projects and proposed that, to clear up once and for all the question of whether such a large aircraft would produce an advantage in performance relative to a conventional aircraft similar to the 210 or 410, wind tunnel measurements and calculations should be put in hand, to which I will come later.

From wind tunnel measurements which were carried out with models of the 163 and the 210 and 262, it can be calculated that the drag coefficient per unit area is probably smaller for the tail-less machine, but by a simple multiplication by the wing area, the drag relative to the same speed will not be smaller for the tail-less projects if account is taken of the additional drag which must necessarily occur because of:

1. perturbations which are structurally unavoidable, e.g. doors of retractable undercarriages, cabin glazing strips, etc.;

2. the necessary bulges which occur due to the engine installation;

3. the additional drag from the presence of the radiator drag and the interference drags.

I am aware that an exact comparison cannot be made on the basis of calculations since there are some unknowns present, which are not explained in any wind tunnel nor in any flight test, such as, for example, the question of the greater efficiency of a propeller situated at the back. In any case the experts here are not yet unanimous as to whether the pusher propeller really has an appreciably higher efficiency than the tractor, since the losses from the rotating slipstream from the tractor propeller are partly alleviated by the wing which acts as a flow straightener, which is not the case with a tractor airscrew lying behind the wing with no additional flow straightener; and this again would mean more drag.

Now as ever, I am of the opinion that an advance can be achieved in some circumstances with a tail-less aircraft but that it is necessary to weigh up carefully how small this tail-less aircraft can be built in order to realize the advantage of the missing tailplane and the shorter fuselage.

To clarify this point, I have proposed that, in a joint effort between the aerodynamicists of Department L' [Lippisch's own workers] and the aerodynamicists of the Project Office, the drag coefficients should be built up separately and not just on the basis of wind tunnel tests and aircraft which do not exhibit any of the perturbations of the type mentioned above. I consider this co-operative work and the accurate explanation of the individual drags, in so far as it is possible by calculation, to be absolutely necessary before the tail-less aircraft is finally built. The weights of the 210 and 410 have been clearly determined by weighing. The landing speed of the 210 is roughly achieved with the wing loading required for a high speed bomber. How important a low landing speed is has been shown by experience to date, since the Luftwaffe would rather have a higher landing speed than a lower maximum speed because the maximum speed is the 'weapon'.

If now the result of the weight estimate for the tail-less aircraft shows that its weight is so much higher than the weight of the 210, the reason certainly cannot lie in the equipment, since it is by no means more extensive than that for the 210, but only in the excessively large lay-out of the tail-less aircraft. The main thing to check here is how the weight of the airframe diminishes as it gets smaller because really the unit weight of the airframe on a tail-less machine must not be greater than that of a conventional machine with a tail unit.

Naturally, it is true of both aircraft that all the latest experience, the possibility of using jet engines, the improved installation of radiators and the reduction of interference drags, are made use of. It should be noted, however, that by a new arrangement of the whole tail unit the drag of a conventional machine with a tail can probably be reduced by 10%.

I therefore propose that Herr Lippisch declares himself ready to join in on these detailed investigations to avoid any comeback later, because the results of the investigation can in no way speak against the tail-less machine but can only serve to ensure the success of the tail-less aircraft or to make it appear as great as possible.

However, worse was to follow. On a visit to Berlin, Messerschmitt discovered that Lippisch was submitting schemes for the bomber to the Air Ministry without reference to the management of the Company. This sort of behaviour was anathema to Messerschmitt who believed in keeping a tight rein on the activities of his subordinates.

His report to the directors makes his feelings amply clear:

On 10 September 1942 I went to see Oberstleutnant Pasewaldt in Berlin.

On that occasion, Pasewaldt spoke to me about the above matter (i.e. the tail-less high-speed bomber) and explained to me that Herr Lippisch had presented to the Secretary of State some time ago a project for a high-speed 'tail-less' bomber with the engines arranged in the middle. In the meantime, Lippisch has withdrawn the project from the experts in the department as being impracticable. The Secretary of State still knows nothing of this, however. In answer to my question as to why this had not been passed on to the Secretary of State, Pasewaldt explained that this was a matter for Lippisch and our company, since Lippisch had by-passed the official channels and personally given the project to the Secretary of State. The responsibility for this was carried by the company, naturally. I took note of this and agreed that the matter will be straightened out by the company.

The new P10 projects were familiar to Pasewaldt. He stated that he and his experts had doubts about this lay-out. I then told Pasewaldt that there was a contract from the Air Ministry for the design and construction of a flying experimental aircraft, whereupon Pasewaldt explicitly stated that this contract related to the original project under the obvious condition that everything was in the open. In no way did this contract relate to further projects. These must first be examined by the department and be approved for design and construction if satisfactory. The work must, therefore, be stopped immediately in so far as it went beyond the project work and what pertained to it. Also, the demand for personnel and accommodation by Lippisch personally was inappropriate in so far as the project was not approved.

On this matter I discovered yet again that Lippisch and/or Stender are making visits to the Air Ministry without informing the Berlin Office and involving Urban. As the matter stands at the moment, I consider an immediate intervention to be necessary. Lippisch is giving project schemes with performance figures to the Ministry and the company then has to take the responsibility for them. As the responsible leader of the whole of the technical development, I must insist that this is conducted along properly controlled lines. As I have already demanded some days ago, I must have the possibility of checking all information before it is sent to the Ministry.

I propose, therefore, that the whole matter is aired at a meeting of the Board and that Lippisch gets an instruction as to how he has to fit into the company.

A few days later, Messerschmitt is writing again on the subject to the directors. Squabbles have obviously broken out between Lippisch's people and Messerschmitt's trusted collaborators, including Dr Wurster who had been the chief test pilot on the Me 109. Somebody has apparently accused Wurster of being 'amateurish'.

The letter certainly conveys the impression that Messerschmitt does not want to get too close to the project:

I have not closely studied the sketch but I propose to wait for the investigation already under way. I must only point out that a tail-less aircraft designed for the same landing speed could not be faster than a conventional aircraft for the same state of the engineering art. The investigation which I have put in hand has the intention of clearing up basically whether aircraft for a specified application, if built tail-less, would be faster or more capable than aircraft with a tail and how much the higher capability amounts to.

I consider this investigation to be absolutely necessary so that a picture is obtained of how big the tail-less aircraft can be designed with capabilities considerably higher than those of the developed 210 (410). In this respect, care must essentially be taken to ensure that the landing speed of the 210 is not exceeded. If the investigation should show that the tail-less aircraft is a good bit faster than the developed 210 (410) but the landing speed is lower than that of the 210, that would be a further gain and an advantage for the tail-less machine.

By this investigation I only want to prevent an aircraft being built whose most important performance figure, namely speed, is no higher than that of the developed 210 (410), since otherwise the problem would not be properly solved.

I would like to avoid going in detail into the comparison of Herr Stender, since the investigation already set up will clarify all these questions.

Nevertheless, I consider it important that these reciprocal reproaches between Lippisch, Stender and Dr Wurster be eliminated, particularly as they are not well founded. The proposal from Dr Wurster is certainly not amateurish but has a number of advantages relative to the other proposal which are undeniable. I am certainly capable of forming an opinion on the basis of my many years of practical experience.

The personal differences with Dr Lippisch did not prevent Messerschmitt from suggesting possible lines of development to his colleague. At the beginning of 1943, Messerschmitt was considering the design of another high-speed aircraft to be known as the Me 329. He obviously had firm ideas about swept-back wings and butterfly tail units which he needed to discuss with other experts.

On 8 January 1943 he sent a memo to the head of his design office with a copy to Lippisch expressing his opinions on these topics. Later in that same year he was to give a lecture to the pilots at the test establishment in Rechlin in which he proposed combining the advantages of the Me 163 and the Me 262 by fitting a rocket engine in the latter.

In the memo to Lippisch quoted below, Messerschmitt presented a wide range of ideas on the basic layout of an aircraft. Many of these were to be put into practice later by other designers.

Introduction of Swept-back Wings

I

The swept-back wing will undoubtedly be necessary for high speed aircraft. When designing swept-back wings it will be advantageous to make the wing extremely stable in all cases. With engines in the central or almost central position, it will then be possible to get away with a short fuselage like the one that Herr Lippisch uses.

That leaves the question to be decided of whether the following benefits relative to the tail-less layout can be obtained by splitting the fin into two surfaces in the form of a V-tail:

1. With the conventional layout the aileron is pulled up during banking and when landing. This reduces the lift on the whole wing exactly when I want to have it as big as possible. When using the V-tail it is possible that, if the aircraft is stable as required about the transverse axis as on its own account even without tail surfaces, the pitch control could be effected not with the ailerons but by moving both the control surfaces on the V-tail in the same direction.

2. The use of the V-form split tail unit would have the advantage that this tail unit permits a larger centre of gravity range than until now, i.e. that part of the trimming can be done with this tail unit, the remainder with the flaps.

3. The use of this V-tail unit would have the advantage that a more effective flap could be used over a part of the span or possibly over the whole span, in order to increase the lift coefficient. It will be convenient to use an asymmetric airfoil section for the tail unit to increase the negative lift coefficient, or in some circumstances, in fact, to use a fixed or extendable slat on the V-tail so as to be able to balance out the nose-down moments from the flaps with the minimum weight of the tail unit.

4. It needs to be checked whether there is the possibility of using a control surface without a fixed tailplane as was once tried on the M 29, but it might meet up with difficulties because of the change of the position of the centre of pressure at extremely high speeds.

II

Because of the new attack tactics of fighters, where the bombers are basically attacked first from the front, and because of the development of better gun-sights, it is questionable whether the full view cockpit will be retained in the long term and whether it would not be better for safety reasons to put the crew behind the engine. In this way, the aircraft with a central engine position again increases its importance as a bomber. We should investigate the question of whether we put two engines one behind the other with a tractor propeller and a pusher. In this arrangement, depending on the centre of gravity, the two engines can be arranged one behind the other with the following possibilities:

a. The forward engine with a tractor propeller in front of the crew, the rear engine with a pusher propeller behind the crew.

b. Both engines one behind the other in front of the crew, where the engine directly in front of the crew drives the pusher propeller (will probably produce an excessively long nose or bad vision for the crew).

c. Both engines, one behind the other, in front of the crew, perhaps somewhat staggered, so that the shaft running aft has to have a universal joint for the aft airscrew to prevent the airscrew from pushing at an angle if we will not or cannot accept the asymmetric effects on the aircraft.

d. There is a further possibility: to use engines of different powers if the second engine is to be used as a stand-by when the main engine fails. A very small engine with a tractor airscrew is installed at the front. Its maximum continuous power output is just enough to allow the aircraft to fly with a climb performance of about two to three metres per second. The pusher airscrew is driven by the main engine.

I regard it as useful for us to discuss all these points and, as far as possible, when modifying the 163 for the piston engine, to make use of the possibility of variants, particularly the proposals for the tail unit.

Mtt

Despite these technical exchanges of opinion, it soon became obvious that relations between Messerschmitt and Lippisch were beyond repair. The affair soon reached such proportions that it became intolerable to the Ministry also. Because of the conflicting messages that they were receiving from the two sources, the Ministry officials insisted that the work of Lippisch's department be more closely integrated into the activities of the overall design procedures of the Messerschmitt company.

On 26 March 1943 a meeting was held at which Lippisch and the Managing Director of the company, Seiler, were present, but not Messerschmitt. The official minutes of the meeting read as follows:

Herr Seiler informed Herr Lippisch of the order of Oberst Pasewaldt dated 20 March in accordance with which Department 'L' is to be entirely incorporated into the overall organization of Messerschmitt AG. Herr Lippisch stated that he was in agreement with this action. As a result Herr Seiler informed Oberst Pasewaldt that this order had been carried out.

It is now agreed that Herr Lippisch will give up his position as an employee of the Messerschmitt company and take up a professorship in Vienna. In accordance with a proposal of the Messerschmitt company, Herr Lippisch will conclude a consultancy agreement with the Messerschmitt company. The draft of such an agreement submitted to the Secretary of State was presented to Herr Lippisch and received his basic approval. As far as it concerns the ownership of the patents which are taken out because of the collaboration of Herr Lippisch within the framework of this agreement, Herr Lippisch proposed that all these patents, even if they were attributable to his own inventions, should belong to Messerschmitt AG and that he himself is not interested in their industrial exploitation. Only the free right to joint use is to belong to Herr Lippisch.

Herr Lippisch was given a copy of the draft of the consultancy agreement. He will give his opinion on this, if possible before 2 April, particularly regarding the amount of the indemnification, about which he would first like to speak when he knows what income he is to expect from the Research Institute in Vienna.

Herr Seiler declared that Herr Lippisch's salary from the present contract with Messerschmitt AG would in any case continue to be paid until Herr Lippisch was enjoying the salary from the Research Institute.

Herr Seiler asked Herr Lippisch explicitly about the wishes that Herr Lippisch might have in connection with the termination of the present contractual conditions with Messerschmitt AG. He emphasized in this respect that Professor Messerschmitt recognized the services of Herr Lippisch in the field of aeronautical research and estimated highly the value of his work. He placed great importance on the need to completely reconcile the differences with Professor Messerschmitt evoked by Herr Lippisch's letter and insisted that the departure of Herr Lippisch from the Messerschmitt company should take place in a friendly spirit. The financial demands of Herr Lippisch had been treated by Messerschmitt AG in such a way that they would in no way become an impediment to a complete agreement.

Herr Lippisch only made the request that five of his closest colleagues, whose names he has already given to Herr Bley, should be allocated to him for his future work. Herr Seiler stated his agreement to this. As far as the financial requirements are concerned, Herr Lippisch will make his views known after discussion with the Research Institute.

On receiving his copy of the minutes of this meeting Messerschmitt may have believed that his troubles were over. Unfortunately, that does not appear to have been the case. Even as a consultant, Lippisch continued to have dealings directly with the Ministry without reference to Messerschmitt, as is evinced by a very sharply worded memo from Messerschmitt to Lippisch on 10 November 1943:

As I am continually hearing that you are conducting project negotiations with the Ministry on your own initiative, I must earnestly demand, yet again, that you cease doing this in the future, and that you discuss in detail with me in advance all the projects which you wish to present at the Ministry. I can no longer tolerate that you, as a member of the Messerschmitt Company, undertake steps which have not been defined in detail in advance by the management. Moreover, under all circumstances you, like anyone else, must take with you a man from the Berlin Office to discussions at the Ministry.

The reference by Messerschmitt to Lippisch still being 'a member of the Messerschmitt Company' does not appear to tie up with the account of the meeting reported above. It seems that Messerschmitt still regarded consultants as members of the Company.

The complaint about the unacceptability of not taking a representative of the Berlin Office to meetings at the Ministry is rather ironic. Messerschmitt himself had earlier been rebuked by the head of his Berlin Office for doing exactly the same thing.

Berlin, 15 January 1942
Dear Professor Messerschmitt,

I would like to approach you on a matter which I regard as extremely important with regard to the policy of the Messerschmitt Company relative to the Technical Office (of the Air Ministry).

Some time ago, on the occasion of your visit to Berlin, you established personal relations with Oberst Vorwaldt and since then you have been in close contact with the new Head of the Technical Office. In particular, in the interest of getting a quick decision, you have gone over to settling questions directly with Oberst Vorwaldt.

But it is only in the most rare cases that the Head of the Technical Office reaches a decision without consulting his responsible section heads and group leaders. On the other hand, most of the questions from the Office to the Messerschmitt Company are sent not from Oberst Vorwaldt but from the relevant departments. In one instance, for example, following a question on your part, Oberst Vorwaldt would ask for an explanation from General Reidenbach, Oberst Hertel, Eisenlohr or Christensen etc. without these gentlemen having the opportunity beforehand to acquaint themselves in any way with the matter in hand. In other cases, these gentlemen would learn the answers of the Messerschmitt Company to their own questions from the lips of their boss whom they should have informed on the matter, possibly in conjunction with other questions.

As an example, let us take the announcement of the deadline for the Me 210s which was proposed by Reidenbach by way of the Technical Office for 5 January, but which was put off on your suggestion until the 10 January. This announcement was urgently awaited on 10 January by Reidenhall, Hertel and Christensen so that it could be conveyed to Oberst Vorwaldt after preliminary discussions. However, it went directly to the Head of the Office as a telegram.

The fact is that the departments mentioned above are extremely annoyed about the way in which the Messerschmitt Company deals directly with the Head of the Office. Apart from the purely factual reasons, a contributing factor may be that these people feel that they have been passed over.

I do not believe that this was or is intended. We may have a particular attitude to the behaviour towards us of some individuals among these people. I consider it essential, however, in the interests of the Company, to retain their good opinion of the Messerschmitt Company. In any case, the Company itself can achieve more in many cases in this way than if some of these people, who are listened to in the Office when decisions are made, are irritated by trifles.

I would like to request you most sincerely, therefore, in future to send letters and telegrams to Oberst Vorwaldt where possible by way of the Berlin Office which will ensure both that Oberst Vorwaldt is immediately in possession of the information and that the technical departments interested in the relevant questions are informed where necessary. In this way it will be simultaneously achieved that the Berlin Office also is informed about current questions and does not have to hear the attitude of its own firm for the first time from the lips of a Ministry official. Also, in this way, you will quite considerably reduce the work of the Berlin Office and provide the Technical Office at the same time with the opportunity of taking in hand any doubtful questions on the spot and hence of coming to the most rapid decision in co-operation with the different departments of the Air Ministry.

Perhaps there will be an opportunity of discussing these questions again with you personally on my next visit to Augsburg.

Meanwhile, I remain,
Yours faithfully, V. Urban

Although the collaboration between Lippisch and Messerschmitt resulted in the production of the Me 163, it does not appear to have been a happy experience for either of them. Messerschmitt at least had the satisfaction of seeing his name permanently associated with the project.

CHAPTER 21

Messerschmitt the inventor

From his earliest childhood Messerschmitt's active mind had attracted the attention of his teachers and family. Early in his life he developed the gift of refusing to accept conventional solutions to problems, and he became adept at devising original ideas of his own. Evidence of this approach can be seen in many of his early aircraft. He was not content to adopt the ideas of other designers, but tried out — not always successfully — novel solutions of his own devising. As recounted in earlier chapters, he conducted many experiments with wing warping as a means of flight control on his gliders, including the design with a separate control column for each wing. Even when his novel ideas failed to succeed he learnt from his mistakes. He at least had proved that he had been exploring a dead end, which spared him more wasted effort from then on. He profited from the experience that he had gained and produced a developed version for use at a later stage.

In addition to novel concepts such as the wing control system, he also paid careful attention to even the smallest details of design, looking for new ways to facilitate production, to reduce overall weight or to improve the flying characteristics of his aircraft.

Many of his inventions were patented in Germany and in many foreign countries, including Great Britain, France, Italy and Japan. Details of all these patents are listed in the surviving Messerschmitt company documents.

The earliest patent bearing Messerschmitt's name was registered on 16 May 1928 and covers what was Messerschmitt's most strongly held belief in the field of wing design, the single-spar wing. It is entitled 'Single spar aircraft wing with a torsionally stiff box using load-carrying external skin'. This was a structural arrangement which Messerschmitt used throughout his career. In this design, the bending strength of the wing was provided by one spar only, situated at about 35 per cent of the chord. Depending on whether the wing was of wooden or metal construction, the whole of the wing forward of the spar was covered in plywood or light alloy sheet to form a tube capable of withstanding the twisting forces trying to distort the wing. Behind the spar, the wing was covered in fabric on the earlier aircraft. Later the whole of the wing had a light alloy skin back to the aileron hinge line.

During a car journey from London Airport to Hatfield, accompanied by the author, the sight of the Handley Page aerodrome at Radlett was sufficient to cause Messerschmitt to reminisce about his relationship with Frederick Handley Page, whom he evidently regarded with a great deal of respect and affection. He recounted how he had given the English designer the free use of his patent on the single-spar wing in exchange for the free use of the Handley Page slot. 'And we sealed the bargain with a litre of good German beer in a beer garden in Frankfurt,' he added.

It was not a surprise, therefore, to find in the records that the English agent named in the British patent for the Messerschmitt single-spar wing was Frederick Handley Page. Messerschmitt made extensive use of the Handley Page slot on all his aircraft up to and including the Me 262.

Messerschmitt inventions, which were the subject of patents, followed thick and fast from that beginning. In 1931 there was a patent for 'Airbrakes for aircraft'.

In 1932 patents were taken out on a number of inventions including 'Retractable undercarriage for aircraft', 'Cantilever undercarriage for aircraft' and 'Device for securing actuators for wing flaps'. The cantilever undercarriage made its first appearance on the M 29 sporting aircraft in the same year.

By the next year, Messerschmitt's thoughts were obviously turning to means of reducing aircraft drag by retracting the undercarriage in flight. In 1933, two more patents were registered covering 'Retractable tailskid' and 'Retractable aircraft undercarriage'. Some of these concepts were to be developed in further patents taken out to cover improvements on the original ideas.

The areas involved in the patents extend over many unconnected topics. For instance, in 1934 they included 'Aileron (spoiler) for aircraft', 'Metal aircraft fuselage', 'Retraction device for aircraft undercarriages' and, once again, 'Cantilever undercarriage for aircraft'.

1935 resulted in two new patents entitled 'Airbrake installation for aircraft' and 'Aircraft control system'.

1936 was a very productive year in which patents were registered for a surprising range of different ideas. Messerschmitt's growing interest in variable pitch propellers is evinced by one patent — 'Drive gear for altering the pitch of propellers'. A patent which appears to be somewhat ahead of its time is a 'Device for influencing the movement of wing flaps depending on the static pressure'.

Later in that same year there appeared patents for 'Signalling and communication device on aircraft' and 'Mass balancing, particularly for aircraft control surfaces'. A growing interest in military aircraft was the incentive to register two patents on aircraft armament: 'Arrangement of weapons, particularly on aircraft', and 'Ammunition feed for machine guns, particularly on aircraft'.

The variety of the inventions listed above is convincing evidence of the wide range of Messerschmitt's interests in aircraft design. He had new ideas in the field of structural design, aerodynamics, aircraft control systems and armaments.

One invention — if one can call it that — which is not listed above was the Göttingen 535 airfoil section. Messerschmitt had had so much trouble with his early aircraft from shifting of the wing centre of pressure, that he decided to produce a new airfoil section whose centre of pressure had a more permanent position at all stages of flight. This section was used in many of his early aircraft and was eventually adopted into the Göttingen series of airfoils as Section No. 535.

As the Messerschmitt companies underwent transformations over the years, Messerschmitt was concerned about his rights with regard to his many registered patents. There seemed to be doubt at times as to whether he had ceded his rights to the company and as to the amount of payment he should receive in recompense.

This question was to lead to endless discussions at Board meetings as to the exact position regarding the use of Messerschmitt's patents. In 1936, at the time when BFW AG first received a firm order for production of the Bf 109, the increasing awareness of the number of aircraft likely to built again brought to the surface Messerschmitt's own financial reward for the use of his patents in large-scale production.

A Board meeting held on 18 February 1936 was devoted almost entirely to that question. The Board were on the verge of signing a contract with the Air Ministry for the manufacture of the 'Null-Serie' or pre-production run of the new fighter. Messerschmitt refused to append his signature to the agreement until his own position regarding the use of his patents was clarified. It is clear from the minutes of the meeting that he was adopting a very firm position:

> Messerschmitt explained that he not only had an interest as a director of BFW AG in being Chief Designer, but also in keeping a decisive influence within the AG and, moreover, in not entirely losing to the AG his rights as holder of the Messerschmitt patents. He explained, therefore, that it must be a pre-condition to his signing the agreement that his position as Chief Designer must maintain his existing rights. Regarding the formulation of this requirement, agreement was reached that now, after the initial series production order for the Bf 109 has been released, an approach will be made on the part of Herr Seiler to the Air Ministry directly after the signing of the agreement, that approach being based on the statements of the people in the Ministry that a suitable payment is given to the designer of aircraft which are put by the Ministry into initial series production.

> The position which Messerschmitt was trying to achieve was seen by Herr Seiler as:

> 1. He retains his existing position on the Board of BFW AG to its full extent, but without any fixed monthly payment.

2. He can claim the following payments for his work at BFW:

a. A payment yet to be determined for the making-over of the proprietary rights on all the earlier patents belonging exclusively to Herr Messerschmitt since the enforced settlement (i.e. following the bankruptcy proceedings) and any other copyrights on which are based the new designs of BFW. Herr Seiler proposed the sum of 100,000 Reichsmarks as an appropriate payment. Herr Seiler explained that he regarded this sum as the minimum base figure for the discussions with the Air Ministry.

b. Messerschmitt had, since the enforced settlement, been nominally in his own person the sole possessor of all the patents, but in fact the Messerschmitt GmbH has the right to the use of the patents. In accordance with this legal position, the compensatory payments for the transfer of ownership of the patents to BFW AG were being conveyed to the Messerschmitt AG.

c. For every new design which is released by the Air Ministry for initial series production, a further fixed special payment will be made to the Messerschmitt AG. For this, Herr Seiler considers an appropriate minimum amount to be a sum which is equivalent to Herr Messerschmitt's annual salary.

d. Basically, for each aircraft that is designed by Messerschmitt, whether it is built by BFW or outside aircraft manufacturers, an appropriate licensing payment will be paid to Messerschmitt AG.

Herr Messerschmitt stated that his position within BFW was the same as that which he had imagined for a designer working independently within the company and indeed was based on his work until now in his present position in BFW.

Herr Messerschmitt stated that in any circumstances, in the case of a total or partial conveyance of the ownership of the patents, he would have to retain the right to the use of them in the past and in the present. This was expressly agreed by Herr Seiler.

Herr Messerschmitt insisted on the attitude that, in the case of the granting of licences for the use of the patents still belonging to him today, half of the amount of the licensing payments is due to him and/or the GmbH.

Herr Seiler accepted Messerschmitt's position on this as being binding.

Herr Seiler explained further:

The patents developed since 1 May 1933 (since that time the payments have been made to the account of BFW AG) cannot be regarded as the sole property of Messerschmitt.

Herr Messerschmitt stated that he was demanding payment for these patents in so far as other designers as owners or directors of aircraft constructing companies have received payment for this.

Herr Seiler stated that he would support making similar payments to Messerschmitt if concrete examples of precedents of that kind were demonstrated. The above agreement on the future handling of patent rights between BFW AG and Messerschmitt AG, and/or Herr Messerschmitt, would still be valid in the case of an alteration to the patent laws, which would prescribe the registration of patents in the name of the designer, Messerschmitt, only. In other words: the usufruct of the

patents will even then be arranged in accordance with the present decisions of BFW AG and Messerschmitt GmbH.

Herr Messerschmitt stated that, through the representation of the existing guiding principles by Herr Seiler, he was giving his unreserved assent
to the signing of the agreement with the Air Ministry.

Although the agreements reached at that meeting appeared to have settled the arguments once and for all, Messerschmitt must still have been
dissatisfied with his position with regard to the use of his patents. The
topic came up again in 1939 and, in an attempt to finalize the position, it
was necessary for the Messerschmitt AG company to write to its
Managing Director, the selfsame Willy Messerschmitt.

It must be assumed that this time he found the settlement satisfactory
because no further mention of the matter ever appears in the minutes of
the Board meetings again.

13 November 1939

Your patents and designs

We acknowledge the negotiations carried on with you several times which
were concerned with the settlement of our compensatory payment for the
earlier use of your patents and the discharge of our obligations arising from
the contract of 5 April 1938.

As a result we declare ourselves ready to indemnify you for the taking
over of your patent rights and the earlier use of these patents since 1927 by a
single payment of 6 million Reichsmarks.

MESSERSCHMITT AG

As can be seen, the value of Messerschmitt's patents had risen steeply in
the intervening years since 1936 when an 'appropriate payment' of
100,000 Reichsmarks had been considered adequate. There is no doubt
that a substantial part of Messerschmitt's income throughout his life
must have come from licensing payments for the use of his patents. The
single payment in 1939 alone would have made him a wealthy man.

An invention which found very early employment in the
Messerschmitt factories was what we would today call the automatic
riveting machine.

This was a powerful aid to speeding up the manufacture of structures
formed of sheet metal, and is in widespread use world-wide today.
Despite the introduction of techniques such as integral machining and
diffusion bonding, many aircraft structures have to be assembled from
detail parts made of folded thin metal sheet material. These have to be
fastened together by riveting, a time consuming and relatively expensive
process.

Computer-controlled machines can today drill the required size of
hole in the structure at the appropriate position, insert a length of rivet
wire, close the head and tail of the rivet and, if necessary, machine off the
outside head to produce a flush surface on the skin.

The Messerschmitt production engineers were developing a machine of this type as early as 1939. In the absence of computers at that time, the concept must have been much simpler than that in use today. Even so, from the very limited information available, it is obvious that some sort of working prototype was employed on the Me 262 jet fighter more than 20 years before a similar device was first widely employed in Britain.

The annual company report of the Messerschmitt factory at Kematen in the Tyrol, issued in 1939, contains the following reference:

> In our factory, within a period of approximately eight months, a new fully- and semi-automatic riveting machine has been developed. The development of the fully-automatic riveting machine was designated by the Air Ministry as 'secret' and thus its importance in the aircraft industry was recognized.

It was probably a development of the same machine that was in use in the production of the Me 262 jet fighter at Oberammergau in 1945. When the Allies arrived to survey the plant, their findings were contained in a report published by the Combined Intelligence Objectives Sub-committee, entitled 'German Airframe Tooling and Methods — Messerschmitt Works'.

The existence of the machine does not appear to have impressed the investigator who summed up his findings as follows:

Oberammergau, 12 July 1945

A riveting machine of an experimental sort was seen there. This machine first drills a hole in sheets, inserts and cuts wire stock to proper length and finally heads (both sides of sheets) into a fairly good flush type rivet. Mr Arbogast (in charge of tooling) pointed out that the machine was capable of performing the job at the rate of 20 rivets per minute. However, the machine was one of only two ever built and had given much trouble. The writer did not consider further study worthwhile.

There is no reason to suppose that Messerschmitt himself was involved in the design of the machine. He had a very efficient tool design department at his disposal. However, he did encourage inventive thinking among his associates and created an atmosphere in which innovative ideas could flourish.

Other later applications for patents are to be found in the Messerschmitt files. One very surprising example appears at a remarkably early date. In 1941 the jet engine was still in its infancy and the first jet aircraft capable of being introduced usefully into service was still some time away. It is disconcerting at the least to discover that even then Messerschmitt was already proposing a turboprop. The proposed application for a patent is dated 14 May 1941.

Herr Eidinger, Patent Office

Secret

Please register the following patent:

Jet engine or similar device which simultaneously drives an airscrew, characterized by the fact that step-by-step, or continuously with increasing speed, less power is input to the airscrew (but it rotates slowly) and more power is transferred to the aircraft by way of the jet. This is a secret patent. The idea originates from me.

Messerschmitt

A more trivial idea concerns the installation of a searchlight in the spinner of an aircraft.

To: Herr Eidinger   26 February 1942

Patent registration

Searchlight in the spinner of an airscrew. Either rotating or (with a hollow shaft) fixed.

The inventor is Professor Messerschmitt.

His interest in structural design and ways to facilitate the assembly of aircraft structures is illustrated by another application for a patent in 1942. A reproduction of Messerschmitt's own sketch is included in the illustrations to this book:

To: H. Eidinger

Please register the following type of spar construction as a patent:

First claim:

Spar web (1), angle (2), if necessary (tapered) spar boom (3), on top a relatively wide strap (4) welded, to which only the skin is riveted. Advantage:

Everything is spot-welded or continuously welded together. The skin, which consists of different material, is riveted to the topmost strap or welded in the case of the same material.
    For the attachment of the main ribs etc., no thick sections have to be drilled, the loss of material is thus small, the drilling requires less time.

Second claim:

The spar construction as in Claim 1 is characterized by the fact that the angle and the boom are perpendicular to the spar web, i.e. there are only right angles present, and that the cover plate which is spot-welded to the spar boom or the angles, is adapted to the contour of the wing by joggling.

It is indicative of Messerschmitt's mental processes that the two last patents should have been thought out at the time when the Me 210 was at crisis point and Messerschmitt was under severe pressure from the Air Ministry to sort out the many problems associated with it. No matter what the outside pressures, his mind continued to turn over new ideas and come up with new proposals for improving the design of aircraft.

Messerschmitt did possess a remarkable ability to think about work at all times, even when he was involved in other concerns. His attitude to work and the pleasure which it gave him are well illustrated by a talk which he gave on the radio in 1943. After a series of interviews with some of his workers, he added the following postscript:

> You have just had the opportunity to cast a glance into my place of work. You have seen the shining faces of my fellow workers and gained the impression that working makes them happy. They know that I have already been working for more than two decades on the design of aircraft and they are surprised that I am, nevertheless, still so untiringly active. In reply I can only say: Work is no trouble if we have gained the right conception of it, if we perceive a goal before us that we can attain with its help. Today I could certainly no longer live without work. Here in the factory, with my colleagues in the comradeship of collaborative work, the thoughts and ideas which I or my colleagues produce are polished and put into place stone by stone to complete the building. For me, work is not forgotten when I leave my place of work. Whether I am at home, whether I am wandering in the mountains in search of a few days recuperation, work never leaves me. On the contrary, far from the noise and bustle of the factory, I come up with new ideas, form new projects and plan new tasks, overcome difficulties which not long before seemed insurmountable.
>
> Thus, work has become as indispensable to me in all life's circumstances as my daily bread. For me it is a mission to be able to contribute a significant portion to the development of aviation and in a higher sense to the greatness of our Fatherland.
>
> Indeed, we all serve a greater purpose than that which is apparent in the sphere of our work. Even if we must all think first of the demands of the moment, something higher, something stronger resonates in the rhythm of our work, the belief in Germany, in the immortal Spirit of Germany, which remains the final significance of all our work.

With that attitude to work it is not surprising that Messerschmitt was regarded as a work-fanatic whose whole energies were devoted to the task in hand.

In 1942 an article on Messerschmitt was published in *Magyar Szarnyak*, a Hungarian magazine, based on information provided by the Messerschmitt press office. It contained the following summary of his work ethic:

> He has no private life, he is a bachelor. Like the other German factory directors, he cycles to work because of the petrol shortage. A modest, upright man whose only love is aviation.

The final sentence could later have formed an appropriate epitaph of which the man himself would surely have approved.

CHAPTER 22

Evacuation to Murnau

In 1943 the Allied air raids were starting their task of destroying the German aircraft industry. The main onslaught would not be launched until 1944, but it was already obvious to the German High Command that things could only get worse. The Luftwaffe was losing the struggle to prevent the German homeland and the whole of German industry from being mortally damaged. The Messerschmitt factory in Augsburg had already suffered substantially from air attack. As a result plans were soon being prepared for the evacuation of vital production centres to safer locations.

This was to be done in part by installing production lines in existing disused underground workings, autobahn or railway tunnels. A search was organized for sites whose geology made them suitable for driving galleries into hillsides so that aircraft production could continue undisturbed by aerial bombing. This included the mountainous areas of Germany where air attack would be difficult because of the nature of the terrain. Factories at the bottom of deep valleys would obviously be more difficult to attack than those on the outskirts of cities like Augsburg or Regensburg where the main Messerschmitt production sites were situated.

Messerschmitt himself had already given serious consideration to the means of protecting his factories from destruction by air attack. A report which he had compiled on the subject was submitted to a special committee set up to address the problem. This report reveals once again Messerschmitt's grasp of strategic matters. He even sees the necessity of continually reinforcing bomb-proof structures as the power of bombs increases. He also describes measures which will need to be taken to protect the factories against airborne troop landings. His predictions of the effects of Allied bombing, if no attempt is made to check it, were to be proved true very soon after the report was written.

The Protection of Fighter and Fighter-Bomber Production against Air Attacks

I. Fundamentals

Fighter defence (day and night fighters) is the only means with which we can to some degree protect our armaments industry and our towns against a further increase in enemy air attacks. From the enemy's attacks in the last few months, which are directed systematically against our fighter factories, it can be seen that the enemy intends to destroy our fighter production to prevent reinforcements reaching our fighter squadrons. If he succeeds in doing this, he thinks that he will have an easy task to put the rest of our industry out of action without great loss to himself and thus make it impossible for the Supreme Command to provide reinforcements for the troops.

There are two measures that we can take to prevent this.

a. The decentralization of industry by dispersal into factories spread around the country.

b. Accommodation of industry in bombproof bunkers in order to make air attacks completely impossible.

The decentralization which is already in progress has the advantage that it can be carried out relatively quickly by evacuation into sites which have been closed down as not being important for the war. However, it has a series of disadvantages which in the long run make evacuation appear unproductive.

The dispersal of production makes it increasingly uneconomical. The enemy will reconnoitre the new sites of the evacuated factories and destroy them again. (e.g. Obertraubling). The upset caused by the continual bombing attacks on the mother factories and the daughter factories will lead to an increasing paralysis of production. Increasingly more valuable people will have to be taken from current production and employed for rebuilding.

There is one effective way to prevent production from being destroyed by air attack and that is accommodating it in bombproof bunkers. This also brings with it the advantage that a fragmentation of production can be avoided since the dispersal practised up till now which led to our present 'final assembly' system would be superfluous. We would have for the first time manufacturing facilities which are standardized and which are restricted to manufacturing one main aircraft component at one manufacturing site using day and night shifts. Today, because of the danger of air raids, in order to be able to keep production going to some degree, a large part of an aircraft has to be built at three or more places. In future, building will take place at one site only. The saving in valuable people for work planning, tool and jig manufacture and design liaison with the manufacturing sites, will very quickly lead to a lightening of the load on these people who are today particularly overloaded. The introduction of 'bunkering', because of its high cost, imposes on the one hand a very high utilization of the plant and also of the machine tools and fixtures located in the bunkers, and on the other hand it produces, in addition to the intended advantage of absolute safety against air attack, economical production such as we have never been accustomed to until now. This advantage will result in a considerable reduction of pressure on the labour market.

II. Method of bunkering

The bunkering will have to be carried out in a relatively short time. For this reason careful consideration must be given to how far existing installations can be converted to make them bombproof with the least possible outlay and to what extent completely new bunkers will have to be constructed.

1. Presently available convertible installations are:

a. Road or railway tunnels which can be shut down, e.g. Eschenlohe and Leonberg.
b. Mines.
c. Caves.

It is the duty of a department set up by the Speer ministry to search Germany systematically for such places and to check the possibility of using them.

2. Newly constructed bunkers

a. Free-standing concrete buildings which, because of their great cost, should only be used when other buildings cannot be set up, e.g. for the final assembly of aircraft on the airfield.
b. Partially free-standing concrete buildings suitably located relative to transport facilities and suitable quarries, disused slag-heaps from open-cast coal workings.
c. Tunnels to be newly constructed in rock which is as easy as possible to work. These installations also include galleries which are driven from existing tunnels or stone quarries into the mountains. In order to reduce the costs, construction of new tunnels must of course be undertaken in mountains which are convenient from an energy and transport point of view.

3. For equipping the bunkers, the material for electrical power lines, water piping, etc. from existing works must be transferred together with machines and fixtures. The tunnel works must be so laid out that small quickly prepared parts can be incorporated. In planning the arrangement, attention must be paid to the fact that the space is carefully utilized and that subsidiary installations such as toilets, etc. are only completed after the factory itself has started operation. Provision must be made for adequate extensions by driving lateral galleries.

III. Planning

If it is assumed that fighter protection must be maintained and continually extended as a prerequisite for the maintenance of the rest of the armaments industry, provision must be made for all factories, in so far as they are working in any way for fighter production, to be housed in bunkers; therefore, also the raw material and half-finished products industries, the works manufacturing engines and equipment and fuel refineries.

Even if the solution of this problem lies beyond the framework of our company and our F 2 Special Committee, I consider it to be the duty of the Special Committee to take the matter upon itself and to push it forward until it is sure that appropriate steps are being taken and carried out by the other parties. In the final assessment, the Special Committee must be aware that it has the responsibility for maintaining the programme placed upon it.

The Special Committee must, therefore, lead the planning of the safe-guarding of the whole of production. It is powerful enough to introduce the necessary steps beyond the confines of our company and to set into motion measures which it regards as important for the safeguarding of production.

The breakdown of the F 2 Special Committee will then look as follows:

1. Management.

2. Those responsible for supply of

a. Half-finished parts.
b. Standard parts.
c. Engines.
d. Armament.
e. Equipment.

3. Those responsible for production of

a. Type 109.
b. Type 110
c. Type 163.
d. Type 262.
e. Type 410.

Those responsible for supplies have the duty to check with the suppliers whether and to what extent security measures are necessary or have been taken and to ensure that these are being taken. They must constantly moni-tor whether deliveries are adequately secured and whether measures have been taken, if breakdowns occur, to be able to get round them as quickly as possible. It is also their responsibility, in the case of a breakdown, to inform the head of the Special Committee in detail and to permit him to assist by bringing in suitable workers from his whole sphere of influence to get round the blockage, be it by speeding up the authorization of alternative designs, introduction of substitute materials or bringing in a special squad of men from his own area to help in getting the production of the destroyed sub-contractor back into action.

Accommodation of workers

For the most important points, reference is made to the 'Nine shift system for bombproof industrial establishments' by Professor Madelung. A prelim-inary accommodation of the workforce will be possible in huts, adjacent bar-racks, villages or schools, later in so-called stand-by quarters which in the form of bombproof berths can be driven into the rock face.

Buildings provided with bombproof concrete roofs must be so designed from the outset that later reinforcement is possible as the effectiveness of bombs increases.

One particular point needs to be cleared up:

If the enemy has it in mind to destroy our fighter production despite it being made absolutely bombproof, there is the possibility that he lands with parachute troops close to or on an underground factory with the intention of destroying the factory in the bunker.

I do not know how possible it is to destroy concrete roofs which are accessible from outside in a similar way to that in which we destroyed tank factories during the French campaign. The few existing entrances to the factory must be defensible with machine guns and quick-firing artillery and indeed for a long time until troops can be brought up from neighbouring towns by an alarm. The German employees of the factory must be trained accordingly as they are today in air raid precautions. The entrances of tunnels will probably be the easiest to defend.

On 20 August 1943, Messerschmitt drafted a message to his senior management telling them of the moves then being planned:

> As a consequence of the constant threat of air attack, the Air Ministry has obliged the Messerschmitt AG to move their Engineering Departments (Design Office and Experimental Workshops) as quickly as possible. This concerns the whole of the fighter and fighter-bomber design of the Messerschmitt AG (about 1500 men). The experience from the raid on Augsburg shows that a factory lying open on an airfield, as is also the case here, can be almost completely destroyed in a few minutes. To ensure as unimpeded co-operation as possible with the parent factory, an excessively distant move should be avoided. In addition it should be possible to combine all of the design activities in one place. The Messerschmitt AG company has inspected a number of sites, and proposes in the first place that the barracks of the mountain troops in Oberammergau should be made available. This has the particular advantage that it can be very well camouflaged and, because of its situation in a mountain valley, is difficult to find. As a second suitable site the Messerschmitt AG proposes the training school at Sonthofen if this can all be made available. From a camouflage point of view it is not so suitable because of its situation on a hill near Sonthofen.
>
> Because of the urgency of the situation within the Programme for the Defence of the Reich and because, despite weeks of negotiations, it has been impossible for the Air Ministry to name a site, I request a rapid decision.

Just over a week later, Messerschmitt was in touch with one of his fellow-directors who was attending a meeting at the Air Ministry in an effort to get a decision:

SECRET

Please convey this telegram immediately to Herr Hentzen at the meeting in the Air Ministry.

Subject: Evacuation of the Design Office
Field Marshal Milch has informed me by telephone on Saturday that the Design Office must be evacuated as quickly as possible so that nothing happens to it. Here we have tried everything without success so far. Dr Ley does not want to give up the castle at Sonthofen. By way of the Gauleiter, I have tried to obtain a barracks in Oberammergau or in the Mittenwald. The corre-

sponding measures that the Gauleiter has initiated have also been without success.

The hotels which were offered in Marienbad are too small and without any heating and, therefore, completely unsuitable. Too much dispersion is out of the question as otherwise the supervision becomes impossible. More recently, the Armaments Inspectorate in Munich has offered the new school in Feldafing, which from its size should be sufficient and which comes under State Treasurer Schwarz. A discussion on my part with Herr Schwarz had no result. Herr Schwarz will not give up the school, he needs it himself.

Probably many other steps are being taken here but, as things are at the moment, it seems to me that it is hopeless unless an order is given by a higher authority. I request you following the meeting to inform Field Marshal Milch about the situation. So that you are in the picture: It is necessary to evacuate the Design Office including the Experimental Shop and Mock-ups — in all, therefore, about 1500 men.

After inspecting the sites, the most suitable seems to be the barracks in Oberammergau in which the Design Office and Experimental could be housed together.

What is surprising is that Messerschmitt had already opened negotiations on the purchase of a house in Murnau not far from Oberammergau in July 1943; that is, before the communications quoted above. It may be that he had decided to acquire the house regardless of the fact that Oberammergau might not be selected as his new place of work. In the event, he was justified in his decision since the barracks in Oberammergau were allocated to him as the new accommodation for his Design Office. The house which he was interested in buying became his permanent residence until the end of the war.

The house in question, Hochried, still stands today, transformed into a children's home, on the outskirts of Murnau on the shore of the beautiful Staffelsee in the Bavarian Alps.

Baroness Lilly von Michel-Raulino, who had supported Messerschmitt financially at the outset of his career and who had been closely associated with him in the management of his companies ever since, was intimately involved in the negotiations for the purchase of Hochried. The minutes of the Board of the Messerschmitt company on 2 July 1943 deal with the subject at some length. Both Messerschmitt and Baroness von Michel-Raulino were present at the meeting.

Investigations had revealed that the house actually belonged to a German émigré living in New York. Through the German embassy in Switzerland, it was discovered that the owner of the property was in some financial difficulty because of a lack of Swiss currency. As a result the proposal was made to the owner that the purchase price could be paid in Swiss francs. This would provide him with a much needed supply of Swiss currency, and Messerschmitt would get the house which he had set his heart on. In this way, all the parties involved could be satisfied simultaneously. There were some worries about the legality of the deal in American law but as America was at war with Germany not too much attention needed to be paid to that aspect.

At the time that the negotiations started the property was heavily mortgaged. An offer was made on the basis of a cash settlement and the taking over by the Messerschmitt company of the responsibility for repaying the outstanding loan. After protracted negotiations, the owner agreed to accept a cash sum of 150,000 Swiss francs.

The house thus passed into Messerschmitt's possession towards the end of 1943. An architect was engaged to carry out extensive alterations in accordance with the instructions of Baroness von Michel-Raulino.

By then the decision had been officially taken that the most suitable site for the evacuation of the Messerschmitt design and development activities was in fact Oberammergau. The former army barracks were converted into offices and workplaces. The construction of the prototypes was housed in underground emplacements. So successful was this exercise that the Allies appear to have been unaware of the activities being carried on in Oberammergau right up to the end of the war.

By January 1944 Messerschmitt and Baroness von Michel-Raulino had moved into Hochried where they were to remain until the end of the war.

This timing was partly dictated by the fact that in the attack on the Augsburg factory by the American Air Force, Messerschmitt's house had been severely damaged. Messerschmitt himself, along with his nephew, Gero Madelung, and Lilly von Michel-Raulino's son, Eberhard Stromeyer, had escaped uninjured. The principal directors of the company also survived the attack, but the damage to the factory was extensive.

As the air attacks on Germany increased in intensity, the demand became more urgent for safe accommodation for high-ranking persons who had been 'bombed out'.

One of these was General of the Luftwaffe, Kaupitsch. He wrote to Messerschmitt asking whether the designer could offer him accommodation in his newly acquired house in Murnau.

Messerschmitt's reply, dated 14 January 1944, explained why it was impossible to accede to the general's request:

Dear General,
I received your kind letter of the 25th ult. for which I thank you most sincerely. It was with sorrow that I learnt from it that your house in the Grunewald has suffered severely in the recent terror attacks. Your intention of leaving Berlin and moving into our Bavarian countryside is easy to understand.

To my great regret I cannot accommodate you in Hoch-Ried [sic] since its rooms are already fully disposed of. I am living there myself — since a part of the company has been evacuated to Oberammergau — and also some of my closest colleagues who are working in Oberammergau have taken up temporary residence there. In addition, the reception rooms for the Board of Directors and the management of Messerschmitt AG have been set up and furnished in Hoch-Ried so that in the worst case the command structure can rapidly function again.

With his usual attention to detail, Messerschmitt himself kept a close watch on all the arrangements concerned with the move to Hochried. Apart from consultations with the architect, he even went to the length of contacting local tradesmen with regard to the supply of provisions for the occupants of the house. The supply of fruit and vegetables was not beneath his attention. In order to ensure the continuance of the service that he had been enjoying, he felt it necessary to write the following letter to the greengrocer in a neighbouring village:

4 July 1944

Mr Johann Schneider
Market Gardener
Kalisch
Charlottenstr. 15

Dear Herr Schneider,

First I would like to express my thanks to you for the deliveries until now of fruit and vegetables for my household.
Unfortunately, getting hold of these items here is so difficult, so I would be very grateful to you for continuing deliveries to my household.

With best wishes,
Messerschmitt

During his time at Hochried, Messerschmitt's health appears to have suffered a number of minor setbacks. In his correspondence there are numerous references to illnesses and the need for medical treatment.

For instance, he received a letter dated 28 February 1944 from a colleague sympathizing with him because he was confined to house by a severe attack of rheumatism.

In June of the same year Messerschmitt appears to have been suffering from asthma. So much may be deduced from the letter which he wrote to the local hospital:

To Murnau Hospital

Murnau
10 June 1944

Dear Matron,

I would like to thank you most sincerely for the kind loan of the inhaler and I am taking the liberty of enclosing a small donation.

Yours sincerely
Mtt

At the foot of the carbon copy of the letter is a handwritten note:

Enclosed RM 100

Within two months of the previous letter Messerschmitt had a hernia operation. As part of his recovery he was hoping to spend some time in a convalescent home in the Allgäuer Alps not far from the site in Sonthofen which had been proposed as a refuge for his design office.

He was only just successful in getting a room as a result of a late cancellation:

Dr L. Saathoff's Sanatorium, Stillachhaus. Oberstdorf im Allgäu

21 August 1944

Dear Professor,

This morning we received a telephone call saying that you would like to be accepted immediately for a convalescent stay with us following a hernia operation.

We would be very pleased to be able to welcome you here. The Stillachhaus is at present fully occupied and all the rooms are booked for months ahead. However, we received in yesterday's post a cancellation for a room with bath, so we can accommodate you immediately.

Within three weeks Messerschmitt was back at work on his plans for a single-engined subsonic fighter.

CHAPTER 23

Gathering clouds

Unfortunately, despite the company of his old friend the Baroness Lilly von Michel-Raulino, Messerschmitt could not have been satisfied with life at that time. He was enough of a strategist to know that the war had been lost and that the defeat of Germany was certain. From a personal point of view he was still unable to come to terms with his lack of authority in his own company since the Me 210 disaster.

To add to his misfortunes, one of his oldest friends and supporters died suddenly. Theo Croneiss had been responsible for setting Messerschmitt on the road to his successes. He had been the very first to recognize his talents and to express confidence in his design abilities.

Messerschmitt was asked to give the funeral oration for his late friend and collaborator. On the assumption that most people praise in others the qualities which they most admire in themselves, it is interesting to see the characteristics which Messerschmitt underlined in his oration. His address also gives Messerschmitt's own account of the events associated with the establishment of his own company in the 1920s:

Dear Frau Croneiss, esteemed fellow mourners!

A relentless Fate has ended too early the life of a man whose personality and work are inseparably associated with the building up of the German Luftwaffe. With deep sorrow we take our leave of SS Brigade Leader Theo Croneiss, who left us for ever on the 7th of November.

Theo Croneiss came from a Rhine-Palatinate family. He was born on the 28th of December 1894 in Schweinfurth.

In December 1914 he enlisted in the Air Force Reserve in Darmstadt. He began his flying career as an observer, but in the spring of 1915 he enlisted for training as a fighter pilot and learnt to fly at the Fokker flying school in Schwerin. After a surprisingly short period of training he was given the task of delivering a fighter aircraft by air for the first time to Turkey.

Like many German soldiers who had defended their Fatherland with their lives in years of active service, he was unable after the collapse to come to terms with the shameful Treaty of Versailles. His whole aspiration was, therefore, devoted to the re-militarization of our Fatherland. In the Reichsflagge voluntary corps, whose third member he became, he helped to put down the Spartacus uprising. During this time his only wish was to be able to take an active part in aviation. So he founded in Nuremberg a sporting flying club in order to help to prepare for the establishment of a future German Luftwaffe by training aircraft pilots.

In 1924, on the occasion of a meeting in Bamberg — at that time my place of work — I met Croneiss for the first time.

There he learned of my work and, filled with interest for all that was being done for aviation, he made it his business to find out all about me. He recognized immediately the importance of transferring the experience in the field of gliding flight to powered flight and, from the first day of our acquaintance, he supported me with advice and practical help. Above all else, he first made possible the continuation of my work by immediately ordering and financing the aircraft shown to him under construction.

When he realized that sporting flying did not offer an adequate opportunity for the introduction of newly designed aircraft, he founded an air transport company. By transforming my small enterprise into a limited company with the participation of his own company, he produced the basis for a workplace from which came a greater number of aircraft.

In 1931, because of an accumulation of unfortunate circumstances, my company — which in the meantime had been amalgamated with the Bayerische Flugzeugwerke — got into difficulties. By his total dedication and indefatigability, through day and night negotiations, he was able to preserve this enterprise from collapse.

Therefore, it is thanks to him that in those economically critical times the Augsburg factory remained in existence so that a few years later the German fighter and destroyer aircraft could be produced. In this way, far beyond the narrow circle of our factory, his efforts laid the foundation for the creation of the new German Luftwaffe, and he has thus served our Führer and our Fatherland.

The success of these aircraft led to an enormous expansion of the factory, and to meet the increased demand Croneiss proposed the building of a subsidiary factory in Regensburg on the airfield which he had founded many years earlier for his air transport company. He built this new factory in 1936 and 1937.

For many years Croneiss was Chairman of the Board of Directors of Messerschmitt AG and Chairman of the advisory board of all the subsidiary factories. In addition, as Works Manager, he ran the Regensburg factory. A few months ago he also took over the management of the Augsburg works.

I have spoken of Croneiss the organizer, but I must also pay tribute to the man who was so close to us. I do not believe that he ever had an enemy among his colleagues. Through his straightforward, open character and his outstanding bravery, which was his most eminent quality, he won everyone over as a friend.

Despite the excessive burden of responsibilities from his work, the idea of national-socialism never left him, particularly in his attitude to social problems. The man who directed thousands of employees was not only understanding, but wholeheartedly a socialist. Without respite he strived to improve the living conditions of his fellow workers. It was not long before he created an exemplary apprentice school and catered for the well-being of his working comrades by providing modern dwellings.

Among the thousands of workers and staff responsible to him he created an exemplary national-socialist society. After only a year of its existence it found its crowning achievement in the granting of the Golden Flag.

In all this he always remained the same, a self-assured and yet modest leader and caring friend of his working fellow Germans.

It is, therefore, understandable that this man, who so much loved his employees, was attached in tender love to his wife and his sons. Every free hour led him, whenever possible, to his country estate or to his hunting where he always found renewed strength.

His family loses in him a truly caring father and companion. His factory loses the inexhaustible and exemplary principal worker. In Theo Croneiss I have lost my most faithful friend. He will remain unforgotten by us.

The period which Messerschmitt was now entering was probably the most worrying of his life. He was still deeply wounded by the decree that he was to be confined to design activities and had to leave the running of his company to others. Herr Seiler, a Munich banker, had now replaced him as head of the company. Unable to take direct action himself Messerschmitt was soon showering Seiler with letters complaining about the running of the company and criticizing the activities of his closest associates. His increasing bitterness is evident in every line.

4 February 1944

Dear Herr Seiler,

Yesterday you had the opportunity on the occasion of the meeting of the Board of Directors to cast an eye on our organization. I assume that it is now clear to you where the problems in our organization lie. It is really amazing that even such a simple thing as the management and recording of drawings is not perfectly in order, that planning only exists in fragments, and that there can be no mention of working to programme. These matters are, however, the prerequisites for an orderly progression of work. The people who are responsible for this bad organization and who, because of their failure, have damaged the reputation of the company to an exceptional degree, now consider it necessary to attack the very people to whom thanks are owed for the company's achievements — long recognized historically in aviation as outstanding accomplishments.

Herr Kokothaki with the Central Office organization has doubtless taken over responsibility for the whole control of programmes and all the dealings with the Air Ministry. Many years ago I built up this organization under the designation E.O. [Development Organization] through the present director, Herr Schmidt, whom I had personally obtained for this purpose. Under Herr Schmidt this organization worked perfectly. I am shattered, therefore, when I see the state this department has got into since it was taken out of my hands. Now, instead of the people responsible trying urgently to put matters in order, an attempt is being made to shrug off on to the Design Department things which have gone wrong through their own fault. In the attached notes you will find a striking example of these tactics.

In the first place, as in innumerable other cases, the responsible department has failed to produce a properly signed set of minutes which actually represents the basis for the performance of the work and which must be given to the Design Office before the work begins. Nevertheless, the Design Office has carried out the work in a reasonably short time on the basis of the minutes since, as always, the matter is urgent. After those responsible had got a bad conscience, an unprecedented amount of pressure was placed on the Design Office, and an attempt was made to establish that it would have been an easy matter for the Modifications Section to increase the strength of the aircraft from 4.5 to 6 g. It was known that the documentation had to be handed over complete at the end of January.

A few weeks before the delivery of the documentation, therefore, the Modifications Section was under pressure to increase the strength of the air-craft by 33%. The progress of the affair recorded in the report mentioned above under 2: 'Progress to Date' shows how an attempt is being made by personal discussions with the responsible people in the Drawing Office, whilst circumventing all the section leaders in the Modifications Section, to settle this by verbal agreement from the experts. What is grotesque is that on 14 January of this year a stress report was issued according to which the strengthening modifications had to be settled by 15 January, and a definition of the structural changes before 19 January. In this respect it is well known that the stress report is certainly not an agreement but only a preliminary piece of information for the planning of the work. Since then the engineers who have tried with the best will in the world to help, despite being over-loaded in other ways, are today being given a bad name. I only heard about the matter for the first time on 26 January and was able to involve myself in it personally.

Because of the amount of work involved, it is no use talking about a final decision before 3 February. It is a question of checking the whole of the stressing calculations of an aircraft type and producing schemes for the places found to be lacking in strength. Moreover, the planners must know in the first place that because of a lack of suitable manpower the work just cannot be carried out today.

The self-same Herr Bley who has signed this progress report, and in so doing accuses the Modifications Section of not having carried out the work at the right time, was here today to check the possibility of which work could be delayed because of the imposed surrender of manpower to Dornier. He now finds that there is too much effort on the 109, and that that also must be given up. On my remonstration that I need these people after the run-down of the 109 H in the Design Office to produce the documenta-tion for the necessary structural modifications to strengthen up this aircraft, he explains that that is not necessary, a contract is not yet in existence.

What a contradiction!

Dear Herr Seiler! I have made up my mind not to approve the new organi-zation planned by Herr Kokothaki. I am no longer in the position to accept responsibility when the conditions are not right. I also no longer have confi-dence that the matter will be straightened out under the present leadership. In the final assessment, it is not a question of things which are dependent on the unknown and require research effort, such as we engineers are used to, but of organizational matters such as are necessary in any enterprise. I con-sider it unjust to make reproaches to the Design Departments that this and that is not working properly as long as the organization is in such a botched condition.

I consider it grotesque that the same people who are not in a position to set up an effective organization and get it working, are throwing dirt at those who are doing everything to perform as best they can under these confused conditions. The real culprits should now finally be brought to account. If in the factory something is not done properly and, as a result, the aircraft are not in a condition corresponding to the present state of the art, I am naturally attacked from outside because the company and the aircraft carry my name. Unfortunately, I no longer have the authority to create order. Regrettably, nobody in the Air Ministry has thought to bring to account the organization of the company and the leader of this organization.

When, for example — as has often happened lately — the modifications for the strengthened wheel of the 109 (it is a question essentially of a bulge in the wing) were carried out in a few days in the Design Office (in this case before 22 November 1943), I have to put up with insolence from the Ministry at the beginning of February because the business has not yet been incorporated in a prototype aircraft, without even mentioning that series production is anticipated in the foreseeable future. What could I have done about it? With the wheels by this time already there in production quantities, I really had no alternative but to chase up the thing myself, but at least the whole of the 'other organization' could be better occupied on the bench in the works.

You, Herr Seiler, have taken over the responsibility for the company as far as the Air Ministry is concerned. Regrettably, I must now insist that you ensure that there is a ruthless clearing out, and that unambiguous conditions are finally created. It can be foreseen that under the present management the coming collapse cannot be long delayed. Unfortunately my hands are tied so that I cannot personally eliminate this deplorable state of affairs. You know exactly why.

Yours sincerely,
Messerschmitt

That is pretty plain speaking, but it was not the end of the affair. Two months later Messerschmitt returns to the same topic in another letter to Seiler. This time his main worries are the problems associated with moving production of the Me 262 into underground installations such as existing tunnels or in specially reinforced factories with thick concrete roofs, the so-called 'bunkers'. He still sees the greatest danger facing Germany as the introduction of jet fighters by the Allies for the protection of their bomber fleets which are still destroying German industry.

4 April 1944

Dear Herr Seiler,

A few days ago in the train we discussed the current complaints that the Air Ministry is making against us regarding the new organization. The accusations of the Air Ministry can only be refuted if one knows them in detail, and I would be grateful to you if you could have all the material sent to me. I already know about the complaint regarding the late introduction of the DB 605 radiator for the Me 109 and I am looking into the matter.

I know that unfortunately there are hardly any people in our organization who themselves have any great initiative. Unfortunately, Hentzen is not among those with sufficient personal initiative. I can say on my own behalf that I am one of the few among us who actually work with initiative and would rather take a chance occasionally than let things slide. I have also always pushed forward against great resistance whenever I have seen the possibility of success, and often with good effect too. That in the process sometimes something goes wrong (e.g. with the 210) is unavoidable in this life. Since the intervention of the Secretary of State, however, my authority is so undermined that the effect of any encouragement from me is getting increasingly blunted. It took me long enough to introduce the old enthusiasm into the circle closest to me — Design — and I still have a lot to do here before the old tempo soaks into the experimental shop. It is only too typically human for most people take the easier way out. It is always more comfortable to leave oneself time and to plan a thing so that it can be carried through in peace, than to accelerate something by pushing hard.

For the last six months I have been making efforts, right up to the highest levels, to increase fighter and fighter/bomber production. Bomber companies were brought in by the Air Ministry to this end but, contrary to my proposal, in the wrong way, so that any success was bound to come very late; and, without anyone noticing it in time, this course of action was partly discontinued and lost its sense of direction. With sufficient initiative that could have been avoided.

A typical example of an unnecessarily bungled affair is the 'bunkering' and the organization of the production facilities. I have stirred these up on many occasions and attempted to push them through. I expounded the idea of the 'bunkering' of aircraft factories back in 1935. Six months ago I took the matter up again and pointed out the suitability of available tunnels. Half a year had to go by, and we had to look on as much of our production was destroyed, before finally something happened and the tunnels were occupied. There is no excuse for that, such as, for example, we would not have got the tunnels any earlier because of the lack of a clear decision. We have neglected to force a clear decision. It would have been a matter for a responsible department to speak out on the subject. It would certainly have been possible by personal contact with the Reichsmarschall [Goering] or Speer to push the thing through very quickly. The same applies to the further tunnelling of the whole of production. On 16 February this year I made a clear proposal about 'bunkering' and demanded the preparation of an appropriate organizational plan covering 'bunkering'. My proposal gives guidelines for the associated necessary alteration in the organization. Up to today there is not, however, a space plan available for the construction of any type of aircraft, to say nothing of the whole programme. Seven weeks have gone by. There are now a mass of plans and expert opinions about the possibilities of 'bunkering' and tunnels which all show that it is not such a difficult problem. If nobody else does it, I am prepared to fight the whole 'bunkering' through with Saur and, I am convinced, successfully. But I cannot do anything until there are clear proposals available regarding the space requirements, the material requirements and the manpower requirements, with a programme of dates.

At the turn of the year we had an internal argument about the ZA organization, planning and working to programme. Despite that, nothing has happened and things are going on in the same muddle.

Several months ago I pointed out that our buying organization was in no way suitable for production and I explained that at Junkers this organization is well set up, and that it would be worthwhile studying it. But absolutely nothing has happened, not even a proposal for improvement has been prepared. Months ago (November 1943) proposals were made by myself in agreement with Herr Wagner that we should have the Opel organization examined by a mixed committee set up by ourselves and it should check how effective this Opel organization looks and what we had to learn from it. Here, too, nothing has happened.

Today it is no longer a secret that our enemies will put jet aircraft into series production this year. We are doubtless dependent on the engine. But there is not even a plan available to us on the possibility of delivering engines, and if necessary it would have to be forced out. We would then have to tailor our aircraft production closely to this plan. When will this plan be ready? We cannot tolerate any delay because we have to order quotas and materials. By extreme extraordinary measures we are now sticking roughly to the old fighter programme and can increase it and thus achieve a containment of enemy incursions. Are we to make this expected success illusory by permitting the enemy in one year's time to send in his bombers escorted by jet fighters? We have to understand that we will be to blame for such a catastrophe if we do not do everything to prevent this.

The whole of our development plan stands on very shaky legs for the future. Everybody knows that, in effect, there is no plan, but nothing is being done to shed some light on the problem. There is no time to lose, but we must first be clear in house about what we want — but we cannot even get a discussion on the subject.

If it were not so serious, our present internal reorganization could be described as farcical. Director Bauer and the experimental shop is responsible to me. According to the organization as I know it, Bauer is in charge of jig design and manufacture. Kottern, under the direction of Stehleis is, therefore, subordinate to Herr Bauer and hence to me. Nevertheless, the message coming through the grapevine is that this department has been made directly responsible to Kokothaki. How is it possible for such ill-defined circumstances to exist?

I know that Hentzen is not a strong personality. When I nevertheless defend him it is because I know that the absolutely confusing organization in the firm makes it impossible to define the limits of clear responsibilities. Whether it is right to transfer the leadership of the special committee to a man entirely unknown to us, I doubt. I believe it is better if we try to get this man, to allot him to Hentzen and bring our organization into order. It will become obvious in a short time whether the matter is going right and whether the man is suitable to lead the special committee on his own.

I have shown to you in disjointed sketches a series of deficiencies in our firm which, among others, urgently need clearing up. You must now take the time to clean up the organization. This is unfortunately not possible in a discussion of a few hours.

Yours sincerely,

Messerschmitt.

Further cares affecting both his personal and business life were soon to be added to Messerschmitt's problems. Two personal tragedies in particular must have affected him deeply.

The first concerned the lawyer, Dr Langbehn, who had acted as Messerschmitt's adviser for many years. Indeed, it was Dr Langbehn who had been entrusted with the negotiations for the purchase of Hochried and who had brought things to a successful conclusion.

So grateful was Messerschmitt to Langbehn for his assistance that the Board agreed a special payment to him for his services. Messerschmitt's appreciation was recorded in the minutes of the Board meeting of 2 July 1943:

> Professor Messerschmitt expressed his particular pleasure that it had been possible for him and Baroness von Michel-Raulino to acknowledge in the way suggested by Herr Merkel the excellent co-operation with Dr Langbehn and his outstanding services to Messerschmitt AG.
>
> He requested Dr Langbehn to consider himself as belonging to the circle of his closest colleagues and friends. He hoped that their friendly co-operation would in the future bring results just as good as those up till now.
>
> Dr Langbehn expressed his especial thanks for the acknowledgement, both spoken and in kind, of his activities. He particularly thanked Herr Messerschmitt and Baroness von Michel-Raulino for the generous settlement and for the confidence expressed in him. He was supremely pleased about his acceptance into the closest circle of their friends and colleagues and would devote his whole energies to the well-being of the Messerschmitt concerns.

Within less than four months after the happy manifestations of friendship described above, Dr Langbehn had been arrested by the Gestapo on charges of treason. He had, in fact, involved himself in a plot to overthrow Hitler. The conspirators were hoping to include Himmler in their plans, since it was known that he was favourable to the idea of a negotiated peace. Langbehn's connections with the United States by way of Switzerland had been useful to Messerschmitt in negotiating the terms for the purchase of Hochried. What Messerschmitt did not know was that Langbehn had also, through very much the same channels, contacted sources in the United States to ascertain the possibility of obtaining favourable peace terms for Germany after the deposition of Hitler. The only reply that he got from the American government was a demand that Germany had to surrender unconditionally if the war was to be stopped.

The unfortunate lawyer was arrested in September 1943. His fate was sealed from that time. After a year in prison, Langbehn was due to be tried by the Volksgericht (People's Court) presided over by the odious Roland Freisler, who delighted in shouting abuse at the defendants before sentencing them to death. There was no appeal against the verdicts which were reached in secret sessions. Messerschmitt must have regarded Dr Langbehn very highly, because he took the unusual, and potentially dangerous step for himself personally, of writing an embarrassingly grovelling letter to Hitler begging for mercy to be shown to his friend.

Oberammergau
11 October 1944

My Führer!

In a time of great trouble, I am turning to you, my Führer, with the request to be kind enough to show mercy to a man if he should come to be sentenced.

The lawyer, Dr Langbehn, has been under arrest since the 22 September 1943. As I learn from his sorrowing wife, a case against him is to be brought before the People's Court in the next few days.

I have been very friendly with Dr Langbehn for years and had engaged his services for myself as a consultant. I honestly cannot conceive that Dr Langbehn has in any way acted against you, my Führer, or against the Reich.

If, nevertheless, there should be something against Dr Langbehn, I beg you, my Führer, to let mercy prevail over justice and to preserve him at least from death.

I am enclosing with my plea the appeal for clemency from Frau Langbehn.

You know, my Führer, that I am always faithfully devoted to you.

Messerschmitt did not have to wait long for an answer, but he cannot have read it with anything other than horror, even if he had had little hope of a successful outcome to his efforts.

Military Adjutant with the Führer   Führer's Headquarters

23 October 1944

Dear Professor,

I received your letter of 11 October 1944 to the Führer with a plea for clemency for the lawyer, Dr Langbehn, on 14 October and immediately made enquiries by telephone.

As I was informed by the Security Service, at that time sentence had already been passed on Dr L. For that reason I did not present the plea to the Führer.

Heil Hitler!

Messerschmitt's plea would probably have been unsuccessful even if it had reached Hitler in time. In fact, it was already too late when he sent it. Carl Langbehn had been executed on 12 October 1944. His fate was shared by almost 200 conspirators in the 'July plot' who were done to death in conditions of inhuman brutality. Hitler disgusted the adjutants on his staff by watching with enjoyment a film of their death agonies.

The attempt to save Dr Langbehn must count as one of the most courageous actions in Messerschmitt's life. He himself had been indirectly involved in the negotiations with the United States, an enemy power, over the purchase of Hochried. It would not have been difficult for the Gestapo to attribute some of the blame for Langbehn's activities to Messerschmitt himself. In the circumstances prevailing at the time and the hysteria following the unsuccessful attempt on Hitler's life, the wisest course would have been for Messerschmitt to 'keep his head down' until the danger had passed. Instead he took the bold step of trying to contact Hitler at the risk of drawing more attention to himself.

His action testifies to Messerschmitt's great courage in standing up for his friends and is an added proof of his solicitude for his colleagues even in matters outside the immediate work environment.

Another of Messerschmitt's colleagues, this time one of the directors in charge of the Augsburg works, was to commit a different serious crime before the end of the year. The incident was reported to the management committee at its meeting in Hochried on 22 December 1944.

> Herr Kokothaki announced that yesterday information had reached the factory security officer, Captain Mühlan, that a Swiss radio station had reported that two directors of the Messerschmitt company with their wives and five children had crossed the frontier; the women and children had been interned, the men were at death's door. An enquiry by the Gestapo as to the present whereabouts of director Schmidt had shown that it could only be he. Who the second man was is not determined but it is not a Messerschmitt man. Further enquiries by Herr Mühlan revealed that Schmidt and his companion were involved in a gun battle as they crossed the frontier. It can be assumed that they have been arrested on this side of the frontier. No reason for this incident can be seen. Because of his hereditary disease it must be assumed that Schmidt undertook this crazy action in an attack of diminished mental responsibility, not forgetting his attack of nerves last September.

It is typical of the Nazi obsession with racial influences that Schmidt's attempted escape was attributed to a fault in his inherited characteristics. This time there were to be no appeals for mercy. Although Schmidt had been picked by Messerschmitt himself as the man for his job, the relations between them had cooled somewhat. Messerschmitt had, in fact, called into question at previous meetings the competence of Schmidt.

Instead it was left to Kokothaki to explain away the defection of his fellow director. A notice was circulated to all the managers in the factory:

15 January 1945

Announcement by the Managing Director

The former director of Messerschmitt AG, Augsburg, lately technical consultant in a subcontract firm,

Dipl. Ing. Eberhard Schmidt

has, because of his feeble attitude and disposition, made an attempt to leave the Reich in the direction of Switzerland. This regrettable plan was frustrated in time.

By doing this, Schmidt has put himself outside the ranks of the German people and is being delivered by the responsible authorities to the merited punishment. Rumours of any other sort have no basis in fact.

Kokothaki

Kokothaki had a more pleasant message to convey to the work-force as the war reached its final stages:

25 March 1945

Announcement by the Managing Director No. 20

The Führer has decorated the head of our company

Professor Dr Ing. e.h. Willy Messerschmitt

with the Knights' Cross of the War Service Cross with Swords in recognition of his unique achievement as the designer of the fastest aircraft in the world, and awarded the War Service Cross First Class to his colleagues,

Prof. Julius Kraus
Woldemar Voigt
Walter Rethel
Josef Fröhlich
Josef Arbogast

We are proud that the creative efforts of our Professor Messerschmitt have received this recognition and congratulate him and his colleagues most heartily on their decorations.

Kokothaki

From the names quoted it is obvious that this award applied to the work on the Me 262 jet fighter and not to the Me 163, which could rightly claim to be the 'fastest aircraft in the world'.

CHAPTER 24

Twilight of the Gods

In April 1945 the Allied forces were sweeping through Germany and her defeat was now inevitable, as must have been obvious to anyone far less intelligent than Messerschmitt. Most of the German cities were already in ruins as a result of air attacks. A few of the most beautiful of them had survived almost undamaged, and among those was the old cathedral city of Bamberg. Although Messerschmitt had not been born in Bamberg, he had always had a great affection for the city in which he had been brought up and in which he had founded his first company. The impending destruction of the city as the Allied armies advanced prompted him to send the following letter to the local Gauleiter to inform him of an approach which he had made to Hitler on the same subject.

Oberammergau
11 April 1945

Gauleiter Wächtler
Bayreuth

Dear Gauleiter,

As a son of the town of Bamberg, it is with sorrow that I have heard rumours that the intention is to defend the town.

Bamberg is devoid of any military importance. Its defence would mean the complete destruction of this unique city with its extremely German character, a destruction the responsibility for which would be placed by the cultured world not on our enemies but on ourselves. Since Bamberg so far has had relatively little to suffer from enemy attacks, it is almost the only well-preserved town. What its loss would mean for Germany, you know best, Gauleiter. When I remember that we declared cities like Florence and Rome as open cities on the basis of the same considerations, namely the preservation of irreplaceable works of art, it is obvious that a town like Bamberg should be treated in the same fashion.

I have had the same opinion conveyed to the Führer by Oberst von Below.

But I did not want to neglect to inform you also, Gauleiter Wächtler, of my attitude, the expression of which is a most sincere necessity for me as a son of the town.

With most respectful greetings,

Messerschmitt

This time Messerschmitt appears to have been successful. Whether it was because of his intervention or not, Bamberg was not defended and survived the war with very little damage. As a result it is still today one of the most attractive of German cities and retains almost all of its heritage of buildings including, in particular, its magnificent Romanesque cathedral. That must have given much satisfaction to Willy Messerschmitt.

Just before the end of the war Messerschmitt was involved in another argument with the authorities. This concerned the requirement for members of his design staff in the Research Department in Oberammergau to present themselves for training in the Volkssturm, the German equivalent of the Home Guard in Britain.

Messerschmitt was asked to nominate 81 members of his staff for training. This he refused to do on the grounds that they were doing such important work on aircraft design that they could not spare the time. In support of his refusal, he quoted a decree issued by Hitler exempting workers in essential war industries from military service. To judge from the correspondence, his attitude more than angered the local District Leader and evoked from him what must be one of the most sarcastic letters that Messerschmitt ever received.

Messerschmitt's own letter runs as follows:

To: Kreisleiter des Kreises
    Garmisch-Partenkirchen   12 April 1945
    Party Member Schiede

Nomination of 81 Members of Staff
for the German Volkssturm

According to what Herr von Plottnitz tells me, you have ordered my organization to make available from the ranks of its Volkssturm 81 men (medical category A1) firstly for a short period of rifle practice and then, if the occasion arises, for action in the locality. There is uncertainty about the length of the short period of rifle practice. Herr von Plottnitz said to me that the men are to be made available only for a short time on Sunday and will be back at work on Monday, assuming that the enemy has not overrun the area. The leader of the regiment, Herr Lechner, on the other hand, explained that the 81 men demanded must be already available on Friday according to the information he was given.

After mature consideration of the circumstances I regret that I have to inform you that I do not see myself in a position to nominate the required 81 men from my organization. I am making available the roughly 40 men of the Volkssturm picked out by the section leaders. In refusing the enlistment of the 81 men I am quoting as my authority the Führer's edict of 31 January 1945 in which it says as follows (and I quote):

'The production of those weapons, which were defined by me in the Emergency Programme, is at the moment more important than calling up men from there into the Army, the Home Guard or for other purposes.

'I order, therefore, that all skilled workers engaged in the Emergency Programme, with the exception of those of the years 1928 and younger are to be exempt from call-up in so far as they cannot be replaced completely by skilled workers from factories which have been made idle.

'Intended or planned call-ups must be made from the other armaments industries not covered by this protection.'

I quote also as my authority a personal discussion with the Führer on 23 March 1945 and an order of the Führer to General of the Waffen-SS and SS-Obergruppenführer Kammler of 27 March 1945.

As long as the Führer personally has not lifted the orders mentioned, I cannot agree to a further reduction of my workforce (who naturally, since they are all category A1, must come from the ranks of those who are my best workers).

I leave it to you, if you think it advisable, to refer to General of the Waffen-SS and SS-Obergruppenführer Kammler.

Heil Hitler!
Messerschmitt

This cool refusal to comply with his orders incited the District Leader to a state of angry frustration which could only be relieved by an unequivocal response. His intolerance of the attitude adopted by Messerschmitt was made obvious by the reply which came winging back a few days later. The designer can have received few letters in his lifetime which expressed so much contempt for the organization which he led.

The people in question were the design staff working with Messerschmitt on the design of future subsonic fighter aircraft. The research staff were known collectively as the Upper Bavarian Research Institute. The prototype of their first design, the project P 1101, was already partly completed in the underground hangar in Oberammergau.

Not only did Kreisleiter Schiede's stinging reply question the loyalty to the Reich of Messerschmitt and his staff, it also made scathing comments on their indifference to the suffering of their fellow citizens. They were demanding for their own convenience facilities which were denied to the war-torn population of Germany at large:

National Socialist German Workers' Party

Garmisch-Partenkirchen
13 April 1945

Herr Professor Willy Messerschmitt
Oberammergau

Subject: Assignment of 81 Company Members of the Upper Bavarian

Research Establishment to the Volkssturm Company of the Garmisch-Partenkirchen Region.

I am extremely surprised that you do not find yourself prepared to assign the required 81 members of the Upper Bavarian Research Institute's Volkssturm Batallion so that they can be made available, if necessary, to the Gauleiter for the defence of the frontiers of the region against enemy invaders. In this instance you wish to call upon an order from the Führer and the General of the Waffen-SS.

The first order that applies to every German today is the order of the Führer to prevent the enemy from penetrating any further into the heart of our Reich. If the Upper Bavarian Research Institute in Oberammergau wants to continue its previous work even when it is in the hands of the enemy, then of course it does not need to feel required to intervene to prevent the enemy from advancing further. If, however, the Research Institute wants to be an organization which with its staff has to be of service to the German way of life and the German struggle exclusively, then I am of the opinion that it must be realized that it cannot just look on until the enemy is in Oberammergau knocking on the doors of the Research Institute.

Herr von Plottnitz has explained to me in this connection that the operations of the Research Institute will then cease and that it is, therefore, self-evident that the required Volkssturm members from the Batallion of the Upper Bavarian Research Institute in that case will be available for active service. I can only express my amazement that you want to contradict this promise of Herr von Plottnitz.

If the work of the Upper Bavarian Research Institute were so decisive for the war effort, so decisive that in the hour of greatest need not 7% of the staff who are duty bound to the Volkssturm can be spared, it should have been a national duty for the staff in the hour of extreme effort to work, for example, over Easter and not to have given the staff, to the last man, the opportunity to go off to their families for three to four days. If not one person in the Institute can be prepared for action in the hour of extreme danger, I do not understand how members of staff today are continually being laid off or dismissed.

I know, Herr Professor, that you have earned enormous credit by your efforts. But the great regard which I have for you and your achievements is something which I really cannot give to the Research Institute. Every hour brings the enemy closer to the heartland of Germany and there are the gentlemen, Director Bartels, Director Dr von Lill, Director Koch and Herr Bergmann discussing on 23 March 1945 what furniture and fittings are necessary for the private conference room of Director Degenkolb, for the bedroom of the above-mentioned, for the public conference room, for the breakfast room, for the reception office, for the manager's office, for the Heisse bedroom, for the housekeeper.

Our doctors have no petrol to care for human beings, our tanks are standing immobilized and there are the above-mentioned gentlemen giving orders for the following transport to be arranged:

1 18 ton lorry with trailer from Augsburg to Oberammergau
1 shipment from Würzburg to Oberammergau
1 shipment from Aschaffenburg to Oberammergau for the moving of furniture

The leading authorities of the Reich have ordered that carpets and any disposable curtains must be handed over to the Volksopfer (i.e. Relief Agency). Director Bartels, whom one must assume is concerned with the production of aircraft and aircraft components, is concerned about how and by whom curtains are to be made. What other worries the gentlemen directors may also have is shown by the instruction to Director Dr von Lill to look after the provision of spirits and cigarettes for a meeting on 28 March.

Please do not take offence if I have blown my top, but I believe that I am doing you a service. The directors who want, at every suitable or unsuitable opportunity, to appeal to the Führer and the emergency programme that he has ordered, must appear significantly less appealing to the Führer in a number of ways by their manner of carrying on. I believe, however, that I am acting in the spirit of the Führer if I have asked the Upper Bavarian Research Institute to make 81 men available when necessary for the defence of the frontiers of the region. I respectfully request you to be kind enough to examine your refusal and to let me have a final decision because I do not believe that your decision of 12 April 1945 is a valid one after my explanation of the circumstances.

Schiede

This attack on the personal behaviour of respected members of Messerschmitt's staff must have been intolerable to him. However, the argument and any further bitter exchange of sentiments could not continue for long. On 29 April the American forces entered Oberammergau and proceeded to turn over the Messerschmitt works. The drawings of the secret projects prepared in the Research Institute were snatched from under the noses of the Americans by agents sympathetic to France. The half-finished prototype of the P 1101 was damaged by the American troops who did not appreciate its importance. It was only several days later that it was examined by American aviation experts, and they were very doubtful about its significance.

CIOS Report Item. No.25. FILE No. XXVIII-9 'German Aircraft Industry Friedrichshafen — Munich Area' was drawn up by a team of American aeronautical engineers. They had visited the Oberammergau plant with the intention of discovering what Messerschmitt's design team had been doing in the months immediately prior to the end of hostilities.

Their summary of the situation contains the following statement about the prototype aircraft:

Me — 1101. An experimental aircraft said to be very fast; single jet engine in fuselage; tricycle landing gear; sweep back to wings. From the construction this was very evidently only a mock-up and the jet engine was a wooden dummy. No adequate space for installation of armament was evident, yet from the fact that pilot's cockpit was provided, it was apparently not in the form of flying bomb. This team questions the seriousness of this design as an authentic project.

It was not long before a better informed expert arrived from the United States. The prototype of the P 1101 was transported to the USA, where its design formed the starting point for the American supersonic flight programme.

Messerschmitt himself was arrested and taken to London for questioning. His career as an aircraft designer was finished for the time being.

CHAPTER 25

Post-war years

Immediately after the war, teams of experts from the victorious nations were combing Germany in the search for her leading scientists and engineers. In the first place it was thought necessary to find out what had been going on in the various research establishments. If anything of military importance was to be found, it was essential that it was found by the 'right people' so that it did not fall into the hands of those who were potential enemies the next time round.

There were American teams, Russian teams, British teams and others all dredging occupied Europe to secure for their own countries the services of German experts. The Americans and Russians were particularly interested in acquiring scientists with experience of rocket design.

Among those gathered up by the British were Willy Messerschmitt and Kurt Tank, designer of the Focke-Wulf 190, along with about 40 other aeronautical experts. They were housed in a run-down hotel in London and interrogated intensively by a team of aeronautical experts. According to Messerschmitt's own account some 25 years later, he regarded his treatment as having been acceptable. Indeed, he gave the impression that he had enjoyed the experience. When the author expressed to Messerschmitt his surprise that he had been in London as early as May 1945, he replied: 'Yes, but I was catched.' He claimed that he had a charming young lady who drove him in a large car around London. This was probably an enhanced recollection of the occasion on which the German aircraft designers were driven around the capital to see for themselves the damage that their efforts had inflicted.

Their confinement was not excessively strict, but to ensure that they would entertain no thoughts of escape they were searched before each outing and prevented from carrying any money, even if it had been possible for them to obtain any.

Messerschmitt was interrogated in Maida Vale by a British team including Captain Eric Brown and Morien Morgan. Brown had been CO of the Captured Enemy Aircraft Flight at RAE Farnborough and had test-flown a wide variety of captured German aircraft during and after the war. Among these was the Me 262 jet fighter and the Me 163 rocket-powered interceptor. The latter aircraft was regarded as so dangerous that he was allowed to fly it only as a glider. Brown's account of his experiences — *Wings of the Luftwaffe* — is recommended reading for aviation enthusiasts.

Morien Morgan was at the time the Head of the Aero Department of the Royal Aircraft Establishment at Farnborough. A further member of the interrogation team, from time to time, was Handel Davies, at that time in the Ministry of Aircraft Production and later Morien Morgan's successor at the Royal Aircraft Establishment.

Captain Brown remembers the interviews as being 'surprisingly informal'. During them the interrogators took notes which were submitted to the Director of the RAE.

Brown included his recollections of the interrogations in a letter to the author in March 1992:

Messerschmitt was very forthcoming, and I remember he was very keen to have my pilot's opinion of the Me 262. My answer seemed to please him, and possibly this relaxed him for he talked very openly thereafter. Our main interest lay in his development work in transonic flight and he covered the design work on the P 1101, P 1110 and P 1111. He drew sketches of these, which were handed over to Morien Morgan for inclusion in his report.

One of the things that interested me was how little high Mach number testing had been done on the Me 262, and he blamed the Luftwaffe for interference with his test programme and for injecting inexperienced pilots into the programme when his own test pilots were cracking under the tremendous pressures of the Third Reich's terminal war efforts.

Some of the rough sketches which Messerschmitt made during his interrogation have survived and are included in the illustrations to this book.

When, in 1948, he was released from his long detention and interrogations, Messerschmitt was finally declared to be only a minor adherent of the Nazi party and subject to no further restrictions. All attempts to label him as a war criminal because of his employment of prisoners-of-war and concentration camp inmates were abandoned as it became obvious that his only interest had been to produce ever more efficient aircraft for the defence of his country.

However, his country was again banned from designing or building aircraft. He was, therefore, placed in the position of being unable to practise what was his sole interest in life. A man like Messerschmitt was unlikely to allow his creative powers to lie idle for long whilst waiting for the ban on aircraft production to be lifted. At the end of the war he was only 47 years old. He felt that he had still got plenty of energy and inventiveness which could be applied to someone's benefit.

However, his factories were in ruins and his workforce scattered and dispirited under the Allied occupation. Further involvement in aircraft design in Germany was out of the question for the moment.

Nothing daunted, as might be expected from his previous career,

Messerschmitt rose again like a phoenix from the ashes of his destroyed empire. He re-equipped the Augsburg factory for the manufacture of non-aeronautical products. He designed prefabricated houses to replace the hundreds of thousands of German homes destroyed in the air raids and land battles in Germany. A profitable business ensued. In view of his past, it is fair to assume that Messerschmitt was already building up capital for the time when it would again be possible to re-enter the world of aircraft manufacture.

Another successful enterprise was the Messerschmitt 'bubble car' which his company marketed. In a situation where petrol was in extremely short supply, a cheap economical car was an obvious winner. True, the design had a marked affinity to an aircraft fuselage and cockpit, but the car proved to be popular and found a market not only in Germany but also in other countries of Western Europe, including Great Britain.

Messerschmitt would always remain Messerschmitt, however, and his eye was continually open for the opportunity to return to aircraft design. If that was not possible in Germany, other countries might be willing to make use of his talents. Other German aircraft designers departed for South America or Asia in their quest for further employment, but Messerschmitt was looking for something nearer home.

In March 1951 he set out with his companion and future wife, the Baroness Michel-Raulino, to Spain where he was being offered a consultancy by the government of General Franco. The Spanish government had pleasant memories of their last association with Messerschmitt when his Bf 109 fighters of the Condor Legion had played a vital part in winning the Spanish Civil War.

Messerschmitt established contacts with the Spanish aircraft firm of Hispano-Aviacion early in 1951. The immediate topic of interest was the building in Spain, under licence, of the Me 109 fighter. Preliminary discussions led to a further visit in July of the same year when the Spanish Air Ministry took part in the negotiations.

In the meantime, Messerschmitt was exploring possibilities in other parts of the world. South Africa was turning its attention to the design and construction of aircraft and cars. An extract from the *Schwäbische Landeszeitung* of 27 April 1951 reports:

South African Ferment — Malan Initiates German Brain Drain
Under the leadership of Professor Messerschmitt and a staff of German colleagues, large aircraft and automobile factories are to be set up in the Union of South Africa. According to a statement from the South African Secretary of State for Trade and Industry, de Waal Meyer, the government would welcome the setting up of such an industrial enterprise. The famous German aircraft designer is at the moment on a study trip in South Africa to check the industrial and economic possibilities.

That appears to be the end of Messerschmitt's involvement in South Africa since there is no further reference to any developments.

The contacts in Spain were, however, bearing fruit. By October matters had progressed so far that a contract was signed between Messerschmitt and Hispano-Aviacion in which he was engaged as a design consultant to the company. In effect, in view of Messerschmitt's attitude to other designers, it became obvious that he was virtually the Chief Designer of the Spanish company.

Now at last it was possible for him to further the plans on which he was working in Oberammergau when Germany collapsed. Some of his previous colleagues had joined him in Seville and a design team of German and Spanish engineers was soon at work. His ambition was still to design a supersonic fighter, and Spain offered him the opportunity.

Before that could happen, however, he had to fulfil the requirement for a simple trainer for the Spanish Air Force. The aircraft was to be built in two forms, one powered by a piston engine, one by jet engines. As much as possible of the airframe was to be made common to both aircraft to reduce construction costs.

The result was the HA-100 and the HA-200 trainers. The HA-100 was fitted with a radial engine with anything between 450 hp and 800 hp. Different versions of the aircraft were equipped with Spanish engines with outputs at the bottom end of the quoted range or Wright R1300 engines of 800 hp.

In 1952 Messerschmitt at last married Lilly von Michel-Raulino whom he had known for almost 40 years. He was 54-years-old and she was 61. As a result he became the step-father of three sons from Lilly's previous marriage to one of Messerschmitt's business associates, Otto Stromeyer, which had ended in divorce in the late 1920s.

Work on the Spanish projects progressed rapidly, and the prototype HA-100 made its first flight on 10 December 1953.

The HA-200 had two Turbomeca 'Marboré 11' jet engines, each of them giving about 900 lb thrust. They were installed side-by-side in the fuselage nose and shared a common intake. The tail pipes were separate and issued near to the trailing edge of the wing.

In pursuit of the goal of commonality, the wings of the HA-100 and 200 were identical. Being of Messerschmitt design, it goes without saying that they were of single-spar construction. The rear fuselages and tail units were also common to both versions.

The HA-200 carried a military armament of two machine guns in the fuselage. Additional machine guns could be installed in the wings which also carried racks to which bombs or rockets could be attached.

With its piston engines the HA-100 had a maximum speed of 265 mph and a ceiling of 30,000 ft. The corresponding figures for the HA-200 were 500 mph and 43,000 ft approximately.

It was at about this time that Messerschmitt acquired a house in Spain which he grew increasingly fond of. He still spent considerable periods of time there until shortly before his death. He also acquired a working knowledge of Spanish to enable him to communicate with his neighbours and local residents.

Messerschmitt was still gripped by the desire to design and build a supersonic aircraft. The idea had now been in his mind for 15 years, and his investigations over that period had convinced him that he could produce an aircraft capable of supersonic performance whilst still adhering to the principles which he had laid down at the beginning of his career — minimum weight and simple construction, powered by the most powerful engine for its size.

Because of the success of the HA-100 and HA-200, Hispano-Aviacion were now looking for a supersonic fighter. The policy of the Spanish government of the day was to preserve the strict neutrality which it had maintained with success throughout the Second World War. Its intention now was to supply its own military aircraft from within its own borders. There was considerable interest, therefore, in involving Messerschmitt in the design of a small, light fighter for domestic use, with the added possibility of sales to under-developed countries.

As far as Messerschmitt was concerned, the basic scheming and research work had all taken place in 1944 and 1945 in the secret project office in Oberammergau. In the meantime, in part using the information captured from the Oberammergau office, the Americans and the British had designed and flown supersonic aircraft. Messerschmitt's ideas had been translated into reality by his former enemies. Now it was his turn to show what he could do in the same field.

The project was to be known as the HA-300 light fighter. Because of the closeness of the centre of Spain to its frontiers, there would be very little time in a war situation to intercept enemy aircraft attacking Spanish bases. Constantly patrolling fighters would be an expensive solution to the problem. What was needed was a small fighter with an extremely high rate of climb which could react quickly to ward off approaching enemy aircraft. This would inevitably mean a short duration in the combat zone, but that was accepted as a penalty worth paying.

High speed at altitude was a requirement and the Spanish Air Force were demanding a Mach number of 1.3 to 1.5.

Work on the project started in July 1952, but it soon became obvious that there was little uniformity among Messerschmitt's senior collaborators about the overall layout of the aircraft. According to instructions issued by Messerschmitt to his colleagues, the fuselage was to be designed so that it could accept a straight wing, a swept-back wing or a delta wing. It was not yet decided whether a tailplane was necessary.

In the absence of suitable wind tunnels in Spain, wind tunnel tests were contracted out to Switzerland.

The design progressed slowly. A number of possible layouts for the HA-300 were produced during 1954. The choice of engine was not yet decided and Messerschmitt was reliving one of the experiences which he had suffered so often before — the lack of a suitable engine to power his design. That problem was never satisfactorily solved for the HA-300.

The recently published book *Messerschmitt Geheimprojekte* by Radinger and Schick contains details of the numerous layouts which were considered for the aircraft. None of them was brought to a satisfactory conclusion.

In 1955 the Lockheed company in America were showing an interest in getting involved in the aircraft, but that too came to nothing. By the middle of 1955 it had been decided that the engine was to be the SNECMA 'ATAR' 101E with 7700 lb thrust. That gave a theoretical maximum speed of 870 mph, which would satisfy the specification agreed with the Spanish for the aircraft.

Messerschmitt hoped that the first flight would take place in 1957, although he could still see difficulties on the way. He expressed particular concern about the aerodynamics of the aircraft. The supersonic region was still being explored in other countries and the state of the art in designing supersonic aircraft remained at a rudimentary stage. If a mistake was made the consequences for the first flight date could be catastrophic. Unfortunately, at the same time the Spanish authorities were also beginning to have serious doubts about the viability of the project. The costs for wind tunnel testing had already grown to alarming proportions. After further discussions it was decided that what was really needed was a two-seater aircraft. This was obviously a fundamental change in the design conditions. It had also been decided that the engine for the new aircraft should be an Armstrong Siddeley 'Sapphire' 6.

Furthermore, to make confusion worse confounded, it was still not decided whether the aircraft should have a straight wing or a swept-back wing. The project was plainly far from completion.

In July 1955 Messerschmitt's old rival, Ernst Heinkel, made an appearance on the Spanish stage. He reached an agreement with the Spanish aircraft company CASA on the development of a fighter project. This was an obvious challenge to the Messerschmitt project, and the Spaniards appeared to prefer the Heinkel design. The death knell was sounding for Messerschmitt's plans in Spain.

Another factor affecting Messerschmitt's attitude to the HA-300 was the lifting by the Allies in 1955 of the ban on German aircraft design. It would now be possible for him to return to work in the more congenial surroundings of his native country.

A further setback to Messerschmitt's hopes was the decision by the German government to select as its standard trainer for the newly formed Luftwaffe the French Fouga 'Magister' instead of his HA-200. This was a bitter blow to a designer as confident as Messerschmitt of the superiority of his aircraft above all rivals.

Work on the HA-300 supersonic fighter continued, nevertheless. In its latest version, the aircraft was smaller and lighter with a delta wing and lacking a tailplane. That was again a further fundamental change to the basic design parameters.

The specification was finalized by the end of November 1955, and the main details of the intended aircraft were now as follows:

Empty weight: 2206 kg
Payload: 300 rounds: 180 kg

Fuel: 950 kg
Pilot: 85 kg
All-up weight: 3421 kg

The engine was to be a Bristol 'Orpheus' B-3 equipped with an after-burner.

In order to reduce the overall drag of the aircraft to the lowest possible level, the fuselage was designed in conjunction with the wing to satisfy the 'area rule' concept which had been pioneered at Oberammergau in the last few months before the end of the war.

Messerschmitt's attention was, however, drifting away towards other concerns. Rivalries with his Spanish collaborators were producing tense situations in the Seville design office. As has been noted on several occasions already, Messerschmitt was not one to tolerate interference from other designers in his work. He was too confident of the correctness of his own decisions to allow anyone, however talented, to question them. The alternative suggestions put forward by the Spanish designers were not welcomed, and bad feeling was an inevitable result.

Other affairs were also diverting Messerschmitt's attention away from Spanish activities. In August 1956 he finally reached an agreement with his long-standing rival, Ernst Heinkel. Together they founded Flugzeug Union Süd with the intention of building under licence the French Fouga 'Magister' as a training aircraft for the new Luftwaffe.

Later in the same year, the German government were taking advantage of the lifting of the restrictions on German aircraft design and manufacture when they issued a specification for an interceptor to be used by the Luftwaffe. Messerschmitt realized that he was involved in Spain only because at the time he had been unable to work in his own country. As the restrictions had been lifted he would obviously prefer to return to designing aircraft in and for Germany.

He began to develop a fighter design based on his work on the HA-300. Using as his basis the research work carried out in Spain, he came up with a canard design, but it attracted no interest in the German Air Ministry. At the same time the Spanish project was running into further serious difficulties. The enterprise was proving much more expensive than the Spanish government had anticipated. Construction of the prototypes was delayed.

By the middle of 1957 design staff were being withdrawn from Spain to work on projects for the German Ministry of Defence in Munich. By the end of the year there were only ten German designers still working in Seville.

Although work on the HA-300 continued despite the reduced staff involved, it was already clear that the project was doomed. The Spaniards were no longer able to finance the work, and the Messerschmitt staff were looking to opportunities back in their homeland.

Messerschmitt and Heinkel now involved another leading figure from the German aircraft industry in their plans for the future. Together with Bölkow they formed a new association of companies, the Entwicklungsring Süd, which was soon at work producing schemes for future fighters.

Following unsuccessful trials with a glider version of the HA-300 which barely survived its first and only flight, work on the aircraft in Spain was finally halted. In an effort to rescue something from the remnants of the luckless venture, the Spaniards sold the design of the HA-300 to the United Arab Republic, where Nasser was still smarting from his defeat by Israel in the Sinai Campaign. He realized that he had been overcome by the technical superiority of the Israeli military equipment. What he saw as necessary was a domestic aircraft industry capable of designing and building its own aircraft without having to rely on purchases from abroad. The HA-300 appeared to offer that hope.

South of Cairo, at Heluan, there was a large airfield built by the British which included an aircraft factory. The Egyptians had at one time intended to use the factory for the construction of a fighter-bomber aircraft designed by Ernst Heinkel. After two years' work the whole project failed to materialize, and the factory stood empty and unused in the desert. It was now decided to recruit a team of German designers to design an aircraft capable of standing up to the best that the Israelis could use in any future renewal of the conflict.

A representative of the Egyptian government, Hassan Kamil, was entrusted with the recruiting of suitable engineers. Small advertisements soon appeared in German newspapers over the name of Ferdinand Brandner, an engine designer who had worked for the Russians after the war, but who had been unsuccessful in obtaining a position in post-war Europe. While Brandner was recruiting staff from German universities and engineering firms, the Egyptians had made contact with Willy Messerschmitt. At the end of November 1959 Messerschmitt signed a contract with the Egyptian government at a reported fee of 100,000 Egyptian pounds.

Messerschmitt was soon ensconced in an office not far from Cairo surrounded by a team of German aircraft engineers, including his old colleague Fritz Hentzen. Despite the difficulties of the Egyptian economy the Germans were paid extremely high salaries, which enabled them to sustain a luxurious standard of living in the suburbs of Cairo.

Work was started immediately on the construction of a training aircraft, and the new military aircraft based on the HA-200 and HA-300 respectively. But, again, fate was not to be kind to Messerschmitt. He was soon expressing dissatisfaction with the standards operating in the factory, and demanding the dismissal of some of his colleagues who did not match up to his high requirements.

The basic problem was that, despite the excellence of the design, there was no domestic industry in Egypt capable of manufacturing components with the precision required. Importing suitable components was difficult because of financial considerations and the understandable reluctance of some European countries to be involved in the project.

There had also been difficulties in obtaining a suitable engine. In the first place it had been intended to use the Bristol 'Orpheus' but the British manufacturer had decided to stop production at just about the time that the Egyptian aircraft was being designed. As a result Brandner was given the task of designing a new engine for the aircraft. This obviously added more problems at the manufacturing stage in view of the lack of high quality precision engineering in Egypt.

However, despite all the problems, the aircraft was rolled out for the first time on 23 July 1963 on the occasion of Egypt's National Day. The first flight took place, after further modifications, on 7 March 1964. This resulted in even more modifications before the second prototype flew on 22 July 1965.

Development dragged on slowly for the next two years until events were overtaken by the Six Day War in June 1967. Two months later Messerschmitt finally severed his connections with Egypt and restricted his future activities to work in his own country.

CHAPTER 26

End of a mission

In the early 1960s the Messerschmitt company had started again to build military aircraft. This time their main products were to be the American F-104 fighter and the Fiat G 31 built under licence for operation in the re-constituted Luftwaffe. To the outside world it seemed as if Messerschmitt was interested only in continuing with the production of military aircraft. It came as a surprise, therefore, when at the Paris Airshow of 1963, the Messerschmitt company exhibited models of two civil projects.

The first was a commercial aircraft designed to carry five to six persons and equipped with two Turbomeca Marboré jet engines. It was to be a low-wing monoplane of all-metal construction with a retractable undercarriage. It was obvious from the outset that with this aircraft Messerschmitt was endeavouring to capture a similar market to that taken by the Bf 108 'Taifun' of 1934. The proposed aircraft was given the designation Me P 308 and — to make its intentions even clearer — the name 'Jet-Taifun'.

The project was never converted into reality. Probably even the genius of Willy Messerschmitt was unable to satisfy the demands of the specification which called for six people to be carried over a distance of 2000 kilometres in an aircraft with a take-off weight of only 2370 kg.

The second model portrayed a short-range feeder liner capable of transporting 40 to 58 passengers over a distance of 1000 kilometres (620 miles). This aircraft was targeted at the Lufthansa requirement for such an airliner after the retirement of its Convair Metropolitans in 1967.

The aircraft was designated the Me P 160. It was to be powered by three General Electric CF 700 engines installed in the tail fuselage. All of the flying controls were to be manually operated to avoid the extra maintenance associated with hydraulically powered systems.

The most remarkable design feature concerned the installation of the third by-pass engine in the tail fuselage. In similar situations on the De Havilland DH 121 'Trident' and the Boeing 727, the air supply to the centre engine had been provided by way of an S-bend intake duct threaded through the leading edge of the fin. On the Me P 160, the air supply to the fan was to be taken from an annular duct surrounding the rear fuselage. The air to the core engine intake was taken from a duct in the base of the T-tail similar to the De Havilland and Boeing arrangements. In view of the structural complications involved, it is not easy to see the supposed advantages in separating the two intake flows. Messerschmitt had shown a great interest in designing intake ducts for jet engines installed in fuselages since his work on the P 1101 at Oberammergau. The idea of the annular duct may, therefore, have originated in his mind at that time.

It was all a wasted effort because the aircraft never progressed past the project stage.

The last aircraft in the design of which Messerschmitt played a significant role was the Me P 141 'Bush Transporter'. This was intended for use in Third World countries and hence had to be as cheap, as simple and as maintenance-free as possible. The fuselage was a simple rectangular box which, like the 'Gigant' of 30 years earlier, could be loaded by means of hinged doors in the nose. In contrast to all his earlier designs of the previous 40 years, the wings were braced to the sides of the fuselage instead of being pure cantilever structures. The aircraft was to be powered by two turboprop engines with an output of 1000 hp each.

Again, the project did not progress beyond the preliminary design stage.

Messerschmitt must have realized that the glory was over. He was now reaching his late 60s and he had not produced an outstanding design since the Me 262. He had at least designed and built for the Egyptians a supersonic fighter which had flown successfully, but it had never achieved production in quantity.

In June 1969 he presided over the formation of the Messerschmitt-Bölköw-Blohm group. He was appointed Chairman of the supervisory board until 1973, when he became Honorary Chairman.

In the autumn of 1969 he was working together with Kurt Tank in an office in the Arabellahaus headquarters of Messerschmitt-Bölköw-Blohm in Munich. Colleagues said what a pleasure it was to see the two great designers, who had for so long been rivals, working together on future projects. If one were less romantic, the two old warriors might be more rightly regarded as having been put out to grass as a reward for their respective services to German aviation. A new generation had taken over.

The office which they occupied was furnished in a truly Bavarian style. The conference table in the centre of the floor had an oak top three centimetres thick. The chairs surrounding it were upholstered in thick brown leather.

Around the walls of the room ran a shelf on which were placed models of Messerschmitt's most outstanding designs. On the wall behind the models were photographs of incidents associated with Messerschmitt's long career. Adolf Galland appeared on one of the photographs with his Me 109 in which he scored so many victories.

Although he can hardly have failed to know that the active work of aircraft design had passed on to a younger generation of German engineers, Messerschmitt would never abandon his main interest in life. He had always lived for aviation and would continue to do so as long as he had breath in his body. His brain was still a fertile source of new ideas. He was still prepared to challenge the ideas of other designers if he regarded them as ill-founded.

This latter aspect of Messerschmitt's character came into the open on the first occasion on which I personally encountered the great man. In the autumn of 1969 the British government of the day had decided that there was no future for the European Airbus project. Luckily, Hawker Siddeley Aviation decided to stay in the project as a contractor to the French and German governments. The decision had been made that design work should proceed as quickly as possible. We in England were entrusted with the design of the wing.

Late in 1969 all of the participants in the European Airbus project — French, German and British — were asked to attend a conference in a hotel near the centre of Munich where they were to present the main features of their designs so that the whole picture would be clear to all of those involved.

A delegation of design experts from Hatfield attended the meeting. Our Chief Designer was charged to present at this international gathering the overall principles of the construction which we intended to adopt.

Accordingly, when it was the turn of the British contingent to make their contribution to the proceedings, he described in detail the aerodynamic principles involved in the wing design and the type of structure which would be employed.

At the end of his presentation an elderly gentleman rose from the German side of the house. His thinning hair made even more obvious his high intellectual forehead. Unfortunately, none of us had any idea who he was. He was obviously not very impressed with the proposed wing design and began to criticize several aspects of it. For instance, he said that he did not see the necessity of attaching the wing to the fuselage by hundreds of bolts. One bolt at the top and bottom of each of the front and rear spars — four bolts in all — would be adequate. There was no need to provide powered actuators to drive the slats in and out on the leading edge of the wing. Left to their own devices, they would open and close as the aerodynamic forces dictated.

When all the objections to our design had been aired and the speaker had sat down, our Chief Designer rose to rebut the arguments put forward and, in so doing, implied considerable doubts about the extent of our critic's acquaintance with aircraft design problems.

This caused considerable unease among our German partners, to say the very least. In fact, a distinct manifestation of unrest swept through their ranks, and we realized that something had been said that had seriously disturbed their composure. The Chief Engineer of Deutsche Airbus was busy writing on a slip of paper which, with a broad smile, he then folded and passed round the conference table to where we sat. We opened the folded slip and read:

Congratulations! You have been awarded the DFC for shooting down a Messerschmitt!

Messerschmitt pursued his misgivings about the Airbus wing to such an extent that he asked whether he and Kurt Tank could come to the factory at Hatfield for a discussion on the subject. The visit took place shortly afterwards and our distinguished German visitors were entertained in the style which has long been traditional in the international aviation industry. Long discussions of the reasons for the British design took place at great length without affecting the decisions which Hawker Siddeley had taken, but alleviating Messerschmitt's misgivings about them.

On the last evening of the visit a dinner was arranged in Hawker Siddeley's guest house at Great Nast Hyde on the outskirts of Hatfield. Senior designers from the former De Havilland company were invited to meet the German visitors. It might justifiably be regarded as an historic occasion. The designers of the Mosquito sat down to dinner with the designers of the Me 109 and the FW 190.

As usual on such occasions the conversation revolved exclusively around aircraft design problems. Messerschmitt still had difficulty in accepting the fact that the Airbus wing was attached to the fuselage by so many hundreds of bolts. It conflicted with his lifelong concept of extreme simplicity in design. He asked if we had studied the wing root attachments of his Me 109 fighter now on public display in the Deutsches Museum in Munich?

A senior member of the Hatfield structural design team tried to explain that four-bolt attachments were no longer acceptable because of fatigue problems and the necessity for fail-safe design. In his anxiety to get the point over he said: 'You must remember that we are designing an aircraft with a guaranteed service life of at least 30,000 flights. What was the average life of your Me 109, Professor Messerschmitt? About three flights, I would suppose.' For a moment the old Messerschmitt fire was visible in response to this unfortunate remark. The subject under discussion was rapidly turned to other matters and the incident passed without further damage.

The dinner was accompanied by excellent wines from the cellars of Hatfield's hospitality unit. These were clearly appreciated by a man who had been brought up in the wine trade, but the peak of the evening's enjoyment came with the brandy which accompanied the coffee. Messerschmitt expressed great appreciation of the quality of the cognac and went so far as to ask if he could have a further sample.

By then the company was becoming very relaxed under the influence of the alcoholic refreshments consumed, to the extent that the diner who replenished Messerschmitt's glass topped it up to the brim instead of pouring the usual small quantity. As the party eventually broke up shortly before midnight, after a very sociable evening, it was discovered that Professor Messerschmitt had forgotten all his German and English and could converse only in Spanish.

That was one of the many enjoyable evenings in my own personal career in aviation that I recall with the greatest pleasure. I was left with a feeling of great friendship for Willy Messerschmitt and an interest in finding out more about his earlier life. The opportunity came when I retired, and this book is the result of five years of research into the background of the man who is known only because of his aircraft. I hope that it will serve to cast more light on the life and character of one of the world's greatest aircraft designers.

Baroness Lilly von Michel-Raulino died on Christmas Day in 1973. She had supported Messerschmitt financially at the start of his long career and had advised him wisely in business matters for over half a century. As might be expected after so long an association, her death affected Messerschmitt deeply.

It was with regret that the aeronautical world heard on 15 September 1978 that Willy Messerschmitt had died at the age of 80 in a Munich hospital after a major operation.

There was no great public ceremony at his funeral. He was buried in the city which he had loved throughout his life — his childhood home, Bamberg. The Green Party on the Bamberg City Council opposed his burial in the municipal cemetery, presumably because of his long association with the former Nazi party. Nevertheless, he lies together with his wife in the family grave of the Michel-Raulino family in the Porticusgruft in the large cemetery on the northern outskirts of Bamberg.

The inscription bearing his name on the memorial tablet has been squeezed into the narrow space left below that recording the death of his wife. It includes only the simple details of the dates of his birth and death and of his academic qualifications. One could pass the grave a hundred times without noticing that one of the world's greatest aircraft designers rests there.

No public memorials have been erected to celebrate his genius. His outstanding aircraft are an adequate reminder of the talents of one of the most gifted designers of aircraft that any country, not only Germany, has produced. Circumstances decreed that he should design aircraft in the service of an evil regime, which he served well. He provided his masters with two aircraft which were in their day far in advance of anything possessed by their opponents, the Bf 109 and the Me 262. If Germany had been ruled by leaders with a more profound knowledge of aviation, Messerschmitt's jet fighter aircraft could have been produced earlier and in greater quantities. The result might easily have been catastrophic for the cause of democracy.

As it was, the development of supersonic aircraft in the United States and Britain was based to a large extent on the preliminary work that Messerschmitt and his colleagues carried out at Oberammergau towards the end of the war in 1944 and 1945. Probably, the greatest disappointment of Messerschmitt's life was the fact that he himself never managed to design and build a successful supersonic aircraft which went into series production.

Despite that, his name will be forever associated with the Bf 109 fighter and the Me 262 — the world's first jet fighter — in both of which he took an immense pride. It is in keeping with his character that he would still regret that he had not achieved even greater successes. For Willy Messerschmitt, each task successfully completed provided the incentive to achieve something even better. In a world where innate inventive genius has been replaced by computerized manipulations, we are not likely to see his like again.

Bibliography

Beaman Jr, J.R. and Campbell, J.L., *Messerschmitt Bf 109 in Action*, Pt. 1, Squadron/Signal Publications, 1980.

Beaman Jr, J.R., *Messerschmitt Bf 109 in Action*, Pt. 2, Squadron/Signal Publications, 1983.

Campbell, J.L., *Messerschmitt Bf 110 Zerstörer in Action*, Squadron/Signal Publications, 1977.

Ebert, H.J., *Messerschmitt Bölkow Blohm, 111 MBB Flugzeuge 1913-1978*, Motorbuch Verlag, Stuttgart, 1979.

Green, W., *Warplanes of the Third Reich*, Galahad Books, New York, 1990.

Heinkel, Ernst, *Stürmisches Leben*, Mundus Verlag.

Irving, David, *The Rise and Fall of the Luftwaffe*, Weidenfeld & Nicolson, 1973.

Kens, K. and Nowarra, H.J., *Die Deutschen Flugzeuge 1933-1945*, J.F. Lehmanns Verlag, München, 1972.

Kens, K., *Die Flugzeuge des Zweiten Weltkriegs 1939-1945*, Wilhelm Heyne Verlag, München, 1981.

Kosin, R., *The German Fighter Since 1915*, Putnam, 1988.

Messerschmitt, W., *Probleme des Schnellflugs*, Schriften der Deutschen Akademie der Luftfahrtforschung, Heft 31, 1940.

Musciano, W.A., *Messerschmitt Aces*, Airlife Publishing Ltd, 1989.

O'Donnell, J.P. *The Secret Fight that Doomed the Luftwaffe, Saturday Evening Post*, 8 April 1950.

Radinger, W. and Schick, W., *Messerschmitt Geheimprojekte*, AVIATIC Verlag, 1991.

Richard Smith, J., *Messerschmitt — An Aircraft Album*, Ian Allen.

Snyder, Dr L.L., *Encyclopaedia of the Third Reich*, Blandford, 1989.

Ziegler, Mano, *Raketenjäger Me 163*, Motorbuch Verlag, Stuttgart, 1961.

Index

Page numbers in *italics* refer to illustrations.

A.B.C. 'Scorpion' engine 29
Aer. Macchi C. 202 168
Afrika Korps 133, 140
Airbus 245
Albert, Herr 187
Alfa Romeo 185
Angermeier, Frl. 159
Arado 55, 58
Arbogast, Josef 227
Argus As 8 engine 44
Argus tube 171
Argus variable pitch airscrew 53
Armstrong Siddeley 'Genet'
   engine 43
Augsburg 58, 158, 208, 212, 226,
   236
Automatic riveting machine 204
Avro Manchester bomber 168

Bamberg 11, 25, 228, 247
Bamberg to Rome flight 1926 30
Bartels, Director 231-2
Baudach, Oberfeldwebel 91
Bauer, Hubert 223
Bayerische Flugzeugwerke (BFW)
   34-5
Below, Oberst von 148, 228
Bergmann, Herr 231

Berlin/Adlerhof 167
Bf 108 civil aircraft 47, 52, *106*, *107*,
   142
Bf 109 fighter 44, 47, 51, 54, 55, 59,
   60, 64, *107*, *108*, *109*, *127*, 147,
   211, 220, 221, 246
Bf 110 fighter-bomber 65, 74, 78,
   110, *111*, *112*, 144, 211
Bizerta 138
Bley, Herr 162, 197, 220
Bloch 175 137
BMW jet engine 88, 170
Boeing 727 243
Brandner, Ferdinand 241
Bristol 'Cherub' engine 29, 34
Bristol 'Orpheus' engine 240, 242
Broll, inspector 138
Brown, Captain Eric 234
Brunswick wind tunnel 176
Bülow, H. von 184

Cairo 241
Caroli, Gerhard 75, 159
Cejka, Herr 160
Challenge de Tourisme
   Internationale race 1934 53
Charwomen 162
Convair Metropolitane 243
Croneiss, Theo 28, 31, 34, 43, 50,
   58, 83, 136, 145, 159, 217
Curtiss-Wright Corporation 217

Dachau 151
Daimler Benz 61, 63, 68, 78, 80, 144, 146
Danzig University 51
Davies, Handel 235
Degel, Wolfgang 167
Degenkolb, Director 231
De Havilland Mosquito 71, 131, 168, 246
De Havilland Trident 243
Deutsche Airbus 246
Deutsche Versuchsanstalt für Luftfahrt 34, 44
Deutsches Museum, Munich 94, *100*
Dieterle, Hans 62
Dornier 9, 31, 46, 129, 139, 220
Dütsch, Margarethe 11

East Prussia Flight 1928 43
Echterdingen, Zeppelin crash 13
Eckener, Dr. 139
Egypt 241
Eidinger, Herr 205-6

F 104 fighter 243
Feldafing 213
Fiat G 31 fighter 243
Fieseler 52
Fieseler Fi 103 — see V 1 flying bomb
Fischer-Tropsch process 179
Focke-Wulf 55, 58
Focke-Wulf Condor 130
Focke-Wulf Fw 190 147, 246
Focke-Wulf Fw 400 131
Fouga 'Magister' 239
French prisoners of war 152
Freyburg, Baron von 21
Fröhlich, Josef 227
Frydag, Herr 93

Galland, Adolf 89, 245
General Electric CF 700 engine 243
Georgii, Professor 134
German Academy of Aviation Research 82, 87

German Aerobatic Championship 1929 43
German Workers' Front 155, 163
Glenn Martin B 26 bomber 167
Gliding Research Institute, Einring 135
Gnome-Rhone engine 137
Goebbels, Dr. Josef 164
Göring, Hermann 48, 76, 82-4, 86, 132, 145, 148, 182, 189
Göttingen 535 airfoil section 23, 202
Grimme, Dr. 179
Gutsche, Feldwebel 159

HA 100 trainer *121*, 237
HA 200 trainer *121*, *122*, 237
HA 300 fighter *122*, 238
Hackmack, Hans 23
Handley Page, Frederick 57, 201
Harth, Friedrich 14-21, 24
Hartmann, Erich 185
Hawker Siddeley Aviation 9, 245
Heidelstein 15
Heinkel, Ernst 9, 13, 31, 52, 58, 62, 87, 88, 160, 239, 240
Heinkel He 111Z 'Zwilling' 136
Heinkel He 112 58-60
Heinkel He 162 Volksjäger 170
Heinkel He 177 146
Heluan 241
Hentzen, Fritz 83, 144, 221, 241
Hernia operation 216
Hertel, Heinrich 148
Hess, Rudolf 44, 50, 51, 55, 58, 74, *112*
Hille, Fritz 41
Himmelreich, social affairs adviser 163
Hirth, Wolf 21
Hispano Aviacion 236
Hitler, Adolf 48, 61, 89, 132, 135, 148, 182, 224, 228
Hochried 213
Hummel, sports manager 163
Hurricane fighter 68

Interavia magazine 168
International Aviation Exhibition, Frankfurt, 1909 13
International European Flight 1929 43
International Flight Competition, Munich 1925 29
Irving, David 9
Italian fighters 147

Japanese wind tunnel 175
Jeschke, Dr. 188
Joukowsky airfoils 177
Junkers, Hugo 30
Junkers Ju 52 134
Junkers Ju 88 144
Junkers Ju 90 136
Junkers Jumo jet engine 88-9
Junkers Jumo piston engine 88

Kaltenhäuser, Frau 183
Kamil, Hassan 241
Kammler, General 230
Karinhall 145
Kaupitsch, General 214
Kematen 119, 152, 205
Koch, Direktor 231
Kokothaki, Rakan 48, 51, 92, 163, 184, 219, 223, 226
Koppenberg, Heinrich 144
Kosin, Rudiger 52, 59
Kötzner, Anne Marie 12
Kraus, Professor Julius 227

Landsberg 153
Langbehn, Dr. Carl 145, 223
Lange, Herr 93
Leipheim 135
Lill, Dr. von 231, 232
Linder, Karl 168
Lippisch, Dr. Alexander 190-9
Lockheed 239
Lucht, Roluf 79
Lufthansa 39,47
Lusser, Robert 52, 170, 172

M 17 light aircraft 28, 31, 74, 100

M 18 all metal aircraft 31, 35, 100, 101
M 19 light aircraft 33, 101
M 20 airliner 39, 42, 55, 102, 103
M 21 trainer 43
M 22 bomber 43
M 23 sporting aircraft 43, 57, 103, 104
M 27 sporting aircraft 46, 104
M 29 two-seater 47, 57, 104, 105
M 31 trainer 105
M 32 trainer 49
M 33 'People's Aeroplane' 49
M 35 aerobatic aircraft 51, 105, 106
M 36 transport aircraft 52
M 37 — see Bf 108
Madelung, Professor Georg 44, 179, 211
Madelung, Gero 214
Malz, Herr 143
Marienbad 213
Mauss, Major 137, 138, 140
Mayer, Friedrich 163
Me 108 civil aircraft — see Bf 108
Me 109 fighter — see Bf 109
Me 110 fighter-bomber — see Bf 110
Me 163 fighter 110, 114, 190, 227, 235
Me 209 record breaking aircraft 62, 109
Me 209 fighter 71, 127, 147, 148
Me 210 fighter-bomber 78, 83, 112, 113, 145, 152, 192
Me 262 jet fighter 57, 71, 87, 115, 148, 205, 221, 227, 235
Me 264 America Bomber 96, 115-7, 131, 146-9, 181
Me 309 fighter 147, 168
Me 321 glider 24, 118, 126, 133, 136
Me 323 transport aircraft 118, 119, 127, 133, 137-47
Me 328 fighter 128, 171
Me 329 project 194
Me 410 fighter-bomber 86, 113, 120, 147, 192

Me P 141 – 'Bush Transporter' project *124*, 244
Me P 160 project *124*, *125*, 243
Me P 308 'Jet-Taifun' *124*, *125*, 243
Merignac 137
Merkel, Konrad 224
Messerschmitt-Bolkow-Blohm group (MBB) 244
Messerschmitt, Heinrich 11
Messerschmitt, Johann Baptist 11
Messerschmitt, Johann Baptist Ferdinand 11-13, 15
Messerschmitt, Willy
– Birth 12
– Sees Zeppelin airship in Friedrichshafen 12
– Meeting with Harth 14
– First flight in a glider 14
– Called up for military service 16
– Student in the Technische Hochschule, Munich 16
– Report for 'Flugsport' on 21-minute flight 17
– Sets up gliding school on the Wasserkuppe 21
– Founds his first company 25
– Meets Theo Croneiss 31
– Agreement with BFW 35
– Lectureship at Technische Hochschule, Munich 46
– Designs Bf 109 55
– Gains world speed record 61
– Hess flight to Scotland 74
– Problems with Me 210 86
– Me 262 jet fighter 87
– Me 264 America bomber 96
– Proposals for military transport aircraft 133
– Meeting with Goering at Karinhall 145
– Meeting with Hitler 148
– Employment of prisoners 151
– Association with Lippisch 190
– Move to Oberammergau 214
– Funeral oration for Theo Croneiss 217

– Association with Dr. Langbehn 224
– Appeal for Bamberg 228
– Arrested by Allies 232
– Interrogation 234
– Post-war commercial enterprises 235
– Designs for Spain 236
– Working in Egypt 241
– Death in Munich 247
Michel-Raulino, Baroness Lilly von 40, 42, 213, 217, 224, 236, 237, 247
Milch, Erhard 9, 41, 47, 55, 58, 86, 89, 92, 94, 145, 148, 149, 161, 166, 212, 213, 222
Mitteldeutsch Motoren Werke 134
MK 108 cannon 149
Morgan, Morien 234
Morzik, Fritz 43, 44
Mühlan, Captain 226
Murnau 208
Murnau hospital 215

NACA reports 177
NACA test centre 175
Nallinger, Fr. 70
Nazi party 47, 48
Neuburg a/Donau 94
Nordbayerische Verkehrsflug 31, *100*
Nordhausen 154

Oberammergau 155, 156, 212, 214
Oberfrankenflug 1925 29
Obersalzberg 148
Obertraubling 135, 138, 209
Ohain, Hans von 87
Olympic Games Berlin 1936 60
Opel 223
Oranienburg 155-6

P 1101 project *120*, *127*, 230, 231, 235, 244
P 1110 project 235
P 1111 project 235
Paris Air Show 1963 243

Paris Salon 1928 43
Pasewaldt, Oberstleutnant 193
Patents 200
Peenemunde 149, 173
Phänomen cycle 187
Ploch, Generalmajor 136, 159
Plottnitz, Herr von 156, 229, 231
Poll Giant Triplane 130
Porsche, Dr. Ferdinand 49, 186
Prisoners, employment in factories
    152
Propaganda film 188

Ratier airscrews 138
Rechlin 58, 85, 149, 194
Regensburg 154
Reidenbach, General 198
Research 174
Research Department 229
Rethel, Walter 227
Rhön 14
Rhön Competition 1922 21
Rhön Competition 1923 23
Rhön Competition 1924 25
Rolls-Royce Kestrel engine 59
Rolls-Royce Merlin engine 68
Round Europe Flight 1930 44
Round Europe Flight 1932 47
Rowehl, Oberst 149
Russian aircraft industry 169
Russian prisoners of war 152

S 4 glider 15
S 5 glider 15, 97
S 6 glider 16, 97
S 7 glider 16
S 8 glider 17, 98
S 9 tail-less glider 20, 98, 191
S 10 glider 21, 99
S 11 glider 22
S 12 glider 22
S 13 glider 23
S 14 glider 23, 99
S 15 powered glider 25, 100
S 16a 'Bubi' 27
S 16b 'Betti' 27
Saathoff, Dr. L. 216

Sachsenflug 1927 33
Saur, Herr 93
Schaller, Anna Maria 11
Schaller, Johann 12
Schiede, Kreisleiter 229-32
Schmidt, Eberhard 144, 219, 226
Schnauzer terrier 187
Schneider, Johann 215
Schorer, Georg 188
Schwarz, State Treasurer 213
Sdzuy, Alois 159, 160
Seiler, Friedrich W. 90, 152, 196,
    202-4, 219
Seywald, Heinz 25, 27
Short Stirling bomber 146
Siemens-Halke Sh 11 engine 33
Siemens Sh 14a engine 44, 51, 53
SNECMA 'ATAR' engine 239
Sonthofen 212
Speer, Albert 93, 148, 172
Spitfire 65, 68, 70, 71, 145
Stegmueller, Herr 187
Stender, Herr 139, 193, 194
Stör, Willi 43, 51
Stromeyer, Eberhard 214
Stromeyer, Otto 40, 41, 237

Tank, Kurt 148, 177, 234, 244, 246
Thun, Graf 184
Tränkle, Augsburg test pilot 94
Troika-Schlepp 136
Tschersich, Herr 144
Turbomeca 'Marboré 11' engine
    237, 243
Turboprop proposal 205

Udet, Ernst 48, 58, 61, 62, 66, 76,
    80, 133, 136, 144, 160, 166, 167,
    176
United States 96, 169, 174
Urban, Herr 193, 198
Ursinus, Oskar 17

V 1 flying bomb 52, 149, 170
V 2 rocket 154, 173
Vogel, Karl-Heinz 183
Valpolicella 185

Voigt, Woldemar 168, 172, 227
Völkersam, Oberst von 184
Volkswagen 185
Vorwaldt, Oberst 198

Wächtler, Gauleiter 228
Wagner, canteen manager 163
Wahl, Gauleiter 148
Walter, Professor Hellmuth 190
Wasserkuppe 21
Weil, Emma 11
Weiss, Sturmbannführer 151
Wendel, Fritz 62, 89, *109*, 159, 160

Weser Flugzeugbau 144
Woltmann 159
Wright Field, wind tunnel 175
Wright T.P. 176
Wright R1300 engine 237
Wurster, Dr. Hermann 61, 194

Zapfendorf 11
Zeppelin 12, 139
Ziegler, Dipl. Ing. 159
Ziegler, Mano 190
Zugspitze Trophy 51
Zürich-Dubendorf 1937 60